PATHWAYS TO STUDENT SUCCESS

Case Studies From The College and Career Transitions Initiative

Edited by Laurance J. Warford

League for Innovation in the Community College

With Support From PLATO Learning

The League for Innovation in the Community College is an international organization dedicated to catalyzing the community college movement. The League hosts conferences and institutes, develops web resources, conducts research, produces publications, provides services, and leads projects and initiatives with more than 750 member colleges, 100 corporate partners, and a host of other government and nonprofit agencies in a continuing effort to make a positive difference for students and communities. Information about the League and its activities is available at www.league.org.

The opinions expressed in this book are those of the authors and do not necessarily reflect the views of the League for Innovation in the Community College or the U.S. Department of Education, Office of Vocational and Adult Education.

Requests for permission should be sent to
League for Innovation in the Community College
4505 E. Chandler Boulevard, Suite 250
Phoenix, AZ 85048
Email: publications@league.org
Fax: (480) 705-8201

Copies of this publication are available through the League website at www.league.org, or by calling (480) 705-8200.

Printed in the United States of America

ISBN 1-931300-46-1

Table of Contents

FOREWORD . . . 1
Scott Hess

COLLEGE AND CAREER TRANSITIONS INITIATIVE: RESPONDING TO A QUIET CRISIS . . . 3
Laurance J. Warford

A NEW DIRECTION FOR CAREER AND TECHNICAL EDUCATION . . . 15
Scott Hess

EDUCATION AND TRAINING . . . 25
Debra D. Bragg
- Anne Arundel Community College . . . 26
- Lorain County Community College . . . 41
- Maricopa Community Colleges . . . 56

INFORMATION TECHNOLOGY . . . 67
Terry O'Banion
- Central Piedmont Community College . . . 68
- Corning Community College . . . 85
- Southwestern Oregon Community College . . . 100

LAW, PUBLIC SAFETY, AND SECURITY . . . 119
Terry O'Banion
- Fox Valley Technical College . . . 120
- Prince George's Community College . . . 135
- San Diego Miramar College . . . 147

SCIENCE, TECHNOLOGY, ENGINEERING, AND MATHEMATICS . . . 159
Elisabeth Barnett
- Lehigh Carbon Community College . . . 160
- Sinclair Community College . . . 170
- St. Louis Community College . . . 181

HEALTH SCIENCE . . . 191
Elisabeth Barnett
- Ivy Tech Community College of Indiana . . . 192
- Miami Dade College . . . 202
- Northern Virginia Community College . . . 212

APPENDICES . . . 223
- APPENDIX A . . . 225
- APPENDIX B . . . 235

ACKNOWLEDGMENTS . . . 241

ABOUT THE AUTHORS . . . 242

ABOUT PLATO LEARNING, INC. . . . 243

Foreword

It has been very obvious for those of us in the Career and Technical Education (CTE) arena that CTE has, over the past several decades, evolved into something much different from what the creators of the Smith-Hughes Act of 1917 had envisioned. Although the original "vocational education," or, as it was previously called, "manual education" served its purpose for over 70 years, the changing demands of the workplace are now requiring a significant system overhaul for us to meet employer needs by successfully transitioning students to college and careers. This redesign of CTE has been difficult for teachers and administrators, and for some, it still is, not just because things are being done differently, but because it's hard to forget how successful many traditional programs were, and there is a fear that the benefits afforded to students in the past may not be available to students in the future.

The career pathway model created through OVAE's College and Career Transitions Initiative (CCTI) is the essential component of a new CTE system designed to meet the needs of both students and employers. A major change from the old system is the realization that all students can benefit from participating in career pathways, and that the opportunities once available to only a few students should now be available for every student, regardless of career goals or interests. Expanding the scope of CTE opportunities within our high schools will result in make-sense options for all students, and students who, in the past, used their senior year as idle time will now enroll in challenging courses relevant to their future goals.

I have been convinced of an *if you build it, they will come* student response. As I first started my career as a nonvocational health educator with a background in health care, I was asked to develop a high school health occupations program. The only guidance I received was to develop a program to prepare students for careers in health care. Not knowing where to start, and with no one to ask, I met with various department heads at the local hospital and with allied health and nursing faculty members from the neighboring college. In response to this informal advisory group, I created a curriculum based on their input, using the same medical anatomy and physiology textbook used at the college. This curriculum, combined with opportunities for students to shadow in many areas at the hospital, became the first health science program in the state. Despite the rigor of the curriculum, one class quickly grew to a full-time program that eventually spread throughout the district and eventually across the state. Interestingly enough, after the second year of the program, the district vocational director called me into his office and informed me that my class was "too difficult" to be considered vocational education. Things have really changed since then.

That career pathway I developed years ago really stretched the definition of vocational education for that time, but today it is commonplace. The Office of Vocational and Adult Education (OVAE), within the U.S. Department of Education, funded the League for Innovation in the Community College through CCTI to demonstrate whether career pathways organized around the 16 career clusters (the new CTE) created through partnerships with employers and educators were effective. Effectiveness was based on the following five anticipated outcomes. These outcomes certainly support the tenets of the No Child Left Behind Act and align with the anticipated new Perkins legislation.

1. Decreased need for remediation at the postsecondary level
2. Increased enrollment and persistence in postsecondary education
3. Increased academic and skill achievement at secondary and postsecondary levels
4. Increased attainment of postsecondary degrees, certificates, or other recognized credentials
5. Increased entry into employment or further education

One needs only to review the Case Studies of the 15 CCTI exemplars in the coming chapters to allay any fears concerning the direction community colleges, high schools, and employer partnerships are headed as they implement career pathways and redefine CTE.

I would encourage community colleges from around the country to form partnerships and take advantage of the lessons learned from these model sites as they organize their own career pathways.

Scott Hess
January 2006

College and Career Transitions Initiative
Responding to a Quiet Crisis

Laurance J. Warford

"The sky is not falling, nothing horrible is going to happen today. The U.S. is still the leading engine for innovation in the world....but there is a quiet crisis in the U.S. ... that we have to wake up to." These are words of Ann Jackson, the 2004 President of the American Association for the Advancement of Science and President of Rensselaer Polytechnic Institute, as quoted by Thomas Friedman in his most recent book, *The World is Flat*. Jackson goes on to say, "The U.S. is in a truly global environment, and those competitor countries are not only wide awake, they are running a marathon while we are running sprints. If left unchecked, this could challenge our pre-eminence and capacity to innovate" (Friedman, 2005).

We are truly in a global economy brought about in large part by the 10 forces that flatten the world, according to Friedman. The initial flattening force was the Berlin Wall coming down in 1989, an event that "unlocked enormous pent-up energies for hundreds of millions of people in places like India, Brazil, China, and the former Soviet Empire and helped us think of the world as a single market, economy, and community"(Friedman, 2005). Other forces that flatten the world, according to Friedman, are the many developments in technology, including the internet and advancement of the use of personal computers. Little wonder that the world playing field has been leveled. Jobs normally held by Americans are now being outsourced to other developing countries at not only less cost, but higher production. In fact, Friedman states, "Several prominent American CEOs told me: When they send jobs abroad, they not only save 75 percent on wages, they get a 100 percent increase in productivity" (Friedman, 2005).

How the United States compares to other industrialized nations matters, because, according to Sandra Ruppert, program director with Education Commission of the States, "in today's highly competitive global marketplace, human capital is the coin of the realm. Educational attainment, measured in terms of the highest level of schooling attained by the adult population, is the international currency used to assess the strength of a country's economy and its standard of living" (Ruppert, 2003). This message is similar to Richard Florida's in his recent book, *The Flight of the Creative Class*. He states, "The United Sates today faces its greatest competitive challenge of the past century.... The reason is basic: The key factor of the global economy is no longer goods, services, or flows of capital, but the competition for people...and that field is leveling every day" (p. 16).

While it is not the purpose here to exhaustively weigh and discuss the international economic condition, it is a starting point for the discussion of the importance – the critical nature – of the work we do in education in this country

■ **CCTI is the most significant national laboratory in the country for creating models of successful student transitions from secondary schools to community colleges, four-year colleges, and the workplace. Early data from our case studies indicate numerous examples of creative and powerful strategies that will become the standards for all secondary and postsecondary institutions committed to this very important enterprise.**

Terry O'Banion, President Emeritus and Senior League Fellow, CCTI Research Team and Advisory Working Group Member

and the need to provide resources to compete globally through education. In this context, education has to be considered as a total entity: lifelong, through all the systems of education, and carefully orchestrated instead of disjointed and ineffective.

A Nation With Work To Do

Twenty-two years ago, *A Nation at Risk* reported on this nation's "mediocre education performance" and the threat it posed to U.S. economic competitiveness. What was true in 1983 is still true today as we move well into the 21st century. There is a major difference, however: "The bar for what passes as an acceptable level of educational attainment has been raised. Twenty years ago, a high school diploma was all that was needed to secure a spot in the middle class; today, a postsecondary education is mandatory. The majority of new jobs created since 1983 that pay a livable wage now require some form of education and training beyond high school"(Ruppert, 2003).

Have we improved in our educational endeavors in this country over the past 22 years? How do we stack up against other countries in terms of our investment in educating youths and adults alike? What is the prospect for the American workforce? Who will be in the workforce? Do we have a crisis, and, if we do, what are we doing about it? These are a just a few of the questions that legislators, governors, educators, and business representatives have been asking. The answers do not come easily, and the numbers are not encouraging, but one thing is certain: This quiet crisis has our attention.

Addressing the nation's governors, Secretary of Education Margaret Spellings emphasized that reforming high schools is a national priority. She said:

> Getting every child to graduate high school with a meaningful diploma in their hands is one of the biggest challenges our country faces. Today, only 69 out of 100 entering ninth graders will graduate from high school on schedule. Fewer than 20 will graduate on time from college. Meanwhile, 80 percent of the fastest growing jobs will require some postsecondary education. (Spellings, 2005)

One can readily see the challenge, and it would appear that it is more than a high school reform challenge; it's really an education reform challenge.

■ There is general agreement today that, for most Americans, education through and beyond high school is now a necessary condition – not just the most advantageous or desirable route – for developing skills required by most well-paying jobs.

Transitions: A Critical Aspect of Reform

There is general agreement today that, for most Americans, education through and beyond high school is now a necessary condition – not just the most advantageous or desirable route – for developing skills required by most well-paying jobs. How well are we doing in moving people through our systems of education?

"An astounding number of students fail to complete high school," says Richard Kazis (2003), Senior Vice President of Jobs for the Future. He presents the following statistics:

- As many as 30 percent of entering high school freshmen leave school without a regular high school diploma. In some of the largest urban districts, as many as 60 percent of ninth graders drop out before earning a diploma.
- Progress in expanding educational attainment has hit a plateau. The high school graduation rate has dropped since its 1970 high of 77 percent and has not improved over the past two decades. This is due primarily to rapid growth among groups of students that the education system serves less well: immigrants, Latinos, African Americans, the disabled, and young people from low-income families. (p. 4)

The statistics don't get better in terms of preparation for college work:

- Large numbers of high school graduates are unprepared for college work. About one of every three entering college freshmen takes at least one remedial course in math, reading, or writing; in urban community colleges, it can be as great as three out of every four new students.
- Minorities are prepared less well in high school than their White peers. Only 47 percent of African-American and 53 percent of Latino high school graduates were academically qualified for college, compared with 68 percent of White students. (Kazis, 2003, p. 4)

College success is also a major concern:

- Nearly half of all students who enter two-year institutions and more than one-fourth of students who enter four-year colleges do not return for their second year.
- Gaps in percentage of college entry between high-income and low-income students have not narrowed in three decades. (Kazis, 2003, p. 4)

Kazis reports that, in view of demographic trends, the situation is likely to grow worse if changes are not made in state policy and local practice. The fastest growing segments of most states' high school and college-age population are groups that have the greatest academic disadvantages: immigrants, minorities, and youths from low-income families.

When you look at the demographics of this country's population and what is going on with the workforce, these statistics take on real meaning. The U.S. population is aging. By 2050, persons over the age of 55 will constitute 38 percent of the population, compared with 27 percent in 2000. Minority groups are growing faster than the White majority. By 2050, Whites will constitute less than 50 percent of the U.S. population. Thus, between now and 2050, there will be a disproportionate increase of minorities in the younger cohorts. In other words, as the U.S. population ages, the younger cohorts both decline in relative size and become increasingly minority in composition. So, the people we are depending on to be our workforce in global competition are the very ones who are most challenged by our educational system.

Joint Responsibility Needed

The disconnection between our K-12 and postsecondary systems of education in this country is well documented. The final report from Stanford University's Bridge Project, *Betraying The College Dream: How Disconnected K-12 and Postsecondary Systems Undermine Student Aspirations* (2003), concludes with some interesting findings:

- America's high school students have higher educational aspirations than ever before, with 88 percent of eighth graders expecting to participate in some form of postsecondary education. Approximately 70 percent actually do go to college within two years of graduating from high school.
- However, there are barriers between high school and college, and these barriers undermine these student aspirations. (p. 6)

Among other things, here were the concerns identified by the Bridge Project:

- The current fractured systems send students, their parents, and K-12 educators conflicting and vague messages about what students need to know and be able to do to enter and succeed in college.
- High school assessments often stress different knowledge and skills than do college entrance and placement requirements.
- Coursework between high school and college is not connected; students graduate from high school under one set of standards and, three months later, are required to meet a whole new set of standards in college.
- Current data systems are not equipped to address students' needs across systems.
- And, perhaps of most concern: No one is held accountable for issues related to student transitions from high school to college and on to careers. (p. 6)

A National Project That Can Help

Perhaps there is no better segue to the body of this publication than the data presented in the Stanford Bridge Project study, which points out serious concerns that must be addressed across our educational systems. Among the many national, state, and local efforts to improve student transitions is the College and Career Transitions Initiative (CCTI), a project funded by the U.S. Department of Education's Office of Vocational and Adult Education (OVAE). The League for Innovation in the Community College was selected to administer this project in November, 2002. The League immediately established partnerships with several other organizations to take on the critical challenges.

Among the partners are

- Academy for Educational Development,
- American Association of Community Colleges,
- Center for Occupational Research and Development,
- Community College Survey of Student Engagement,
- Educational Testing Service,
- High Schools That Work,
- Maricopa Community Colleges,
- Miami Dade College, and
- Thomson Prometric.

The purpose of CCTI is to contribute to strengthening the role of the community and technical colleges throughout the United States in easing student transitions between secondary and postsecondary education as well as transitions to employment, and to improve academic performance at both the secondary and postsecondary levels.

This initiative is unique in that it is aimed directly at the community college role in helping to repair the student pipeline by providing leadership to improve student transitions and academic achievement. The proponents of CCTI stress the important role community colleges can play in linking education to careers. Community colleges, however, are not being asked to act alone. To qualify to become a site partnership for CCTI, community colleges were required to develop partnerships with secondary schools, employers, and, often, four-year colleges.

In May 2003, 15 community college-led site partnerships were selected from a large pool of applicants that applied to lead CCTI site partnerships in five high-demand occupational areas. From this selection process, programs of study were then identified at the secondary level and aligned with more advanced and technical postsecondary instruction. The alignment of courses and coordination of curriculum and training programs among local high schools and community colleges, and often four-year colleges and universities, defined new career pathways that best equip students with the skills and credentials required for success in high-growth, high-demand, high-wage career fields. The exemplar site partnerships are led by the colleges identified in the following table.

The purpose of CCTI is to contribute to strengthening the role of the community and technical colleges throughout the United States in easing student transitions between secondary and postsecondary education as well as transitions to employment, and to improve academic performance at both the secondary and postsecondary levels.

CCTI SITE PARTNERSHIPS

EDUCATION AND TRAINING
Anne Arundel Community College (MD)
Lorain County Community College (OH)
Maricopa Community Colleges (AZ)

HEALTH SCIENCE
Ivy Tech State College (IN)
Miami Dade College (FL)
Northern Virginia Community College (VA)
St. Louis Community College (MO)

INFORMATION TECHNOLOGY
Central Piedmont Community College (NC)
Corning Community College (NY)
Southwestern Oregon Community College (OR)

LAW, PUBLIC SAFETY, AND SECURITY
Fox Valley Technical College (WI)
Prince George's Community College (MD)
San Diego Community College District (CA)

SCIENCE, TECHNOLOGY, ENGINEERING, AND MATHEMATICS
Lehigh Carbon Community College (PA)
Sinclair Community College (OH)

Each site partnership is required to develop a detailed improvement plan in collaboration with its secondary and business partners that addresses these outcomes. The site partnerships are also identifying, developing, and refining practices that help students move effectively from high school to college and on to careers by better aligning curriculum between secondary and postsecondary education.

The project expectation is to develop career pathways in the selected occupational areas. Given that there are many definitions of career pathways, CCTI project management convened a significant group of representatives of secondary and postsecondary education to define career pathways for purposes of this project. A ***career pathway*** is a coherent, articulated sequence of rigorous academic and career courses, commencing in the ninth grade and leading to an associate degree, and/or an industry-recognized certificate or licensure, and/or a baccalaureate degree and beyond. A career pathway is developed, implemented, and maintained in partnership among secondary and postsecondary education, business, and employers. Career Pathways are available to all students, including adult learners, and are designed to lead to rewarding careers.

Note the keywords in this definition: *coherent*, *articulated*, and *sequence*. Rigor is called for in both academic and career courses. These pathways should begin in Grade 9 but, if done properly, should not lock students in to a career pathway choice, and they should lead to some type of degree or certification at the level a student chooses. The career pathway emphasizes the recommended process aspects of the definition. It is a collaborative process, available to all students. This suggests that we should look at all secondary students in one light: academic and career, all college bound, since most jobs will require some education and training beyond high school.

■ A career pathway is a coherent, articulated sequence of rigorous academic and career courses, commencing in the ninth grade and leading to an associate degree, and/or an industry-recognized certificate or licensure, and/or a baccalaureate degree and beyond.

The group that agreed on the definition of career pathways for purposes of this project also agreed on the essential characteristics of an ideal career pathway. The secondary pathway component

- Meets state academic standards and grade-level expectations;
- Meets high school testing and exit requirements;
- Provides additional preparation to assure college readiness;
- Meets postsecondary entry/placement requirements;
- Provides academic and career-related knowledge and skills in a chosen career cluster; and
- Provides opportunities for students to earn college credit through credit-based transition programs, *e.g.*, dual/concurrent enrollment, advanced placement, tech prep, International Baccalaureate, middle college, high schools, and articulation agreements.

The Postsecondary Pathway component provides

- Opportunities for students to earn college credit through dual/concurrent enrollment or articulation agreements;
- Alignment and articulation with baccalaureate programs;
- Industry-recognized skills and knowledge in each cluster area; and
- Employment, business, and entrepreneurial opportunities in the chosen career cluster at multiple exit points.

Pathway partners assure a culture of empirical evidence is maintained by

- Regularly collecting qualitative and quantitative data;
- Using data for planning and decision making for continuous pathway improvement; and
- Maintaining ongoing dialogue among secondary, postsecondary, and business partners.

These essential characteristics guide the development and maintenance of an effective career pathway.

Samples of career pathways that have been developed by the 15 CCTI exemplar site partnerships are provided in Appendix A.

CCTI Leadership and Products

One of the main purposes of any exemplary project is to provide leadership and experimentation that can be used broadly in the field. CCTI is certainly no exception to this. Several products are available through the CCTI website, www.league.org/ccti, and in various publications that are emerging from this work.

CCTI Virtual Reader. An impressive library of books, journal articles, and other publications on improving student transitions and the development of career pathways has been carefully selected to be included in the Virtual Reader. Selections of the literature included in the Virtual Reader were required reading for the first CCTI Seminar, held in June 2003, giving participants a common knowledge and understanding of the hallmark literature in the field.

The Virtual Reader includes 201 books and articles. In addition, 88 of the publications have been annotated and are included in a separate section of the reader. Finally, 33 websites are included for reference.

The database comprising the Virtual Reader is searchable by author or by outcome area, making it a very user-friendly document.

CCTI Toolkit. The toolkit is approximately 500 pages of online summaries and detailed documentation of the 15 CCTI partners' two-year journey. Its purpose is to share best-practice resources for institutions interested in implementing stronger high-school-to-college bridge programs. Each of the college partners has contributed a summary of collaborative work with project documents focused on a number of important areas:

- Career Pathways showing student/career/program study plans, beginning in Grade 9 through high school and community college and, if necessary, to four-year college implementation strategies that define a key objective and the college partners' planning, process, and collaborative needs toward successful outcomes
- Lessons learned from the colleges' two-year development process, sharing knowledge gained and new strategies to overcome obstacles
- Improvement plans created from analysis of implementation strategies and lessons learned to support their college's semester with defined outcomes, new strategies, and action steps toward success
- Case studies reporting history, investigative inquiry, data samples, and qualitative measures to outline and report on the colleges' workforce development experience with CCTI objectives, local needs, and community and state variables
- Contact information for college, school, and employer partners

The CCTI toolkit offers exemplary models of college strategies; shared stories of planning, implementation, adjustments, and success; and benchmarks of refinement in smoothing students' paths from career pathways to viable careers.

National Study on State Policy and Practices. In cooperation with the American Association of Community Colleges, CCTI commissioned a national study of state policies and practices that encourage or inhibit the improvement of student transitions through the development of career pathways. *Strengthening Transitions by Encouraging Career Pathways: A Look at State Policies and Practices*, by Katherine L. Hughes and Melinda Mechur Karp, was published in January 2006, and, through the sponsorship of corporate partner Educational Testing Service (ETS), was distributed to the presidents and vice presidents for instruction of community colleges in the United States.

The study includes the following points:

- Although restructuring career and technical education around career pathways is an ambitious reform, it is one that many states are beginning to undertake.
- Although no state has implemented policies addressing all pieces of career pathways, many have made strides in a number of areas.
- Perhaps the most striking issue in the study is the continued division between academic and career-technical education. This creates a problem in system structures that do not allow students the flexibility to move and transfer coursework between CTE and academic programs.
- Many problems identified in the study derive partly from the false assumption that students will pursue education and training in a linear fashion.
- Employers appear to be, for the most part, absent in policies examined in the study. Although some employers may plan a meaningful role in career pathways in practice, it was difficult to find state policies that encouraged or rewarded them for doing so.
- Whether pathways are driven by the supply side or the demand side, state policymakers have an important role to play in refining and clarifying the involvement of employers.

State Policy Forums. In addition to the national study on state policies and practices that encourage or inhibit the improvement of student transitions through the development of career pathways, CCTI engaged the collaboration of the Southern Regional Education Board's High Schools That Work Project to develop forums in several states to discuss ways to improve students' transitions from high school to postsecondary education and careers. Each forum focused on the five CCTI outcomes:

- Decreased need for remediation at the postsecondary level;
- Increased enrollment and persistence in postsecondary education;
- Increased academic and technical achievement at the secondary and postsecondary levels;
- Increased attainment of postsecondary degrees, certificates, or other recognized credentials; and
- Increased entry into employment or further education.

■ **Many problems identified in the study derive partly from the false assumption that students will pursue education and training in a linear fashion.**

State forums have been held in Kentucky, New Jersey, North Carolina, South Carolina, West Virginia, Tennessee, Nebraska, New Mexico, Louisiana, and Oklahoma, and will be held in additional states as scheduled. Despite differences in governance and state policies, the forums thus far have provided a positive common theme that there is a need to get leaders from education and business to address the development of education policies and programs that provide guidance through our education systems and on to employment. The effectiveness of getting these groups of people around a table for a day-long discussion is perhaps best summarized by the closing comments of a lifelong, respected educator about to retire. He said, "This is one of the best meetings I have ever attended, and I think it is because not only is this work critical, but we found common ground across all groups represented here."

Each state's discussion is summarized in a brief HSTW/CCTI publication, *Building Transitions From High School to College to Careers for (State) Youth*. These reports summarize the challenges that each state faces in improving transitions, and actions the discussions identified that each state can take to meet these challenges.

Career Pathway Self-Assessment. A self-assessment document for use in determining current status of the key strategies associated with a partnership's pathway program was developed by the CCTI qualitative research team. The document addresses the following major categories: Curriculum, Instructional Approaches, Support and Guidance, Articulation and Partnerships, Access, and Project Management and Evaluation.

■ ...there is a need to get leaders from education and business to address the development of education policies and programs that provide guidance through our education systems and on to employment.

Users of the assessment document can view aspects of their partnership's level of implementation by the following scale in terms of stages:

1. Planning
2. Development
3. Initial Implementation
4. Advanced Implementation
5. Institutionalization
6. Not Addressed

There are a variety of ways to use this instrument. The chief career pathway administrator could do the assessment based on close observation. The leadership advisory team for implementation of career pathways could also use the document, which would provide a group process that could be highly valuable.

A third option would be to ask each entity in the career pathway partnership to conduct its own separate assessment, using school leaders and partners, and feed this information to the central partnership to aggregate the data. In all instances, the instrument provides a graphic summary of the partnership's progress in addressing implementation strategies.

A complete copy of the Career Pathways Self-Assessment is provided in Appendix B.

CCTI Network. The large number of community colleges submitting full proposals to lead a CCTI Site Partnership project indicates that many of these institutions are developing relationships with secondary schools, businesses, and four-year colleges in an attempt to improve student readiness and success in choosing and preparing for a career while in high school and college. Community college personnel attending CCTI training sessions show a high degree of interest in becoming involved in helping to ease student transitions between education systems and the world of work.

For these reasons, CCTI leadership elected to establish a broad network of community college-led partnerships throughout the country. Community colleges have been invited to join the CCTI Network, an organization designed to help community colleges share information in their successes as well as their challenges in leading the improvement of student transitions through the development of career pathways.

Among the benefits of membership in CCTI is the focus it provides to participants in helping students achieve desired results in high school so that they can be successful in college and in preparing for a career. In addition, the network provides an opportunity for technical assistance from the national project, as well as from other colleges around the country. CCTI is viewed by many as more than a project; it is seen instead as a movement led by community colleges to help reform our educational systems.

References

Friedman, Thomas L. (2005). *The World is Flat*. New York: Farrar, Straus, and Giroux.

Florida, Richard (2005). *The Flight of the Creative Class*. New York: Harper.

Kazis, Richard (2003). *Ready for Tomorrow: Helping All Students Achieve Secondary and Postsecondary Success, A Guide for Governors*. Washington, DC: National Governors Association.

Ruppert, Sandra S. (2003). *Closing the College Participation Gap: A National Summary*. Education Commission of the States. Denver: ECS.

Venezia, Andrea, Kirst, Michael W., & Antonio, Anthony L. (2003). *Betraying the College Dream: How Disconnected K-12 and Postsecondary Education Systems Undermine Student Aspirations*. Stanford, CA: Stanford Institute for Higher Education Research.

A New Direction for Career and Technical Education

Scott Hess

In recent decades, Career and Technical Education (CTE) has undergone significant change that has slowly but certainly increased the expectations and the scope of opportunities for today's high school and college students. At the same time, students are facing the realities of uncertain economies and ever-changing needs of employers that make the selection of and preparation for a future career challenging.

Recognizing the dilemma facing today's students and eventual employers, virtually every organization overseeing secondary and postsecondary education at the national, state, and local levels has initiated policies and programs to find a solution to these changing education and workforce challenges. A review of mission and vision statements found within strategic plans in organizations at the national, state, and local levels and in colleges and high schools reveals that a high priority has always been on preparing all students for their future and careers. What seems either vague or absent in many plans, especially in our high schools, is the way all students are to be provided these opportunities, and the extent to which all student career goals and interests will be aligned with program options. More than ever before in our high schools, it is vital that the career awareness and preparation opportunities that have traditionally been provided only to a small number of students for a few jobs should now be available to all students and reflect their career goals and interests.

■ More than ever before in our high schools, it is vital that the career awareness and preparation opportunities that have traditionally been provided only to a small number of students for a few jobs should now be available to all students and reflect their career goals and interests.

The recent evolution of CTE has resulted in a variety of potential solutions to overhaul the outdated vocational education programs; each, however, falls short of providing an ideal system for a new CTE. One approach has been to focus simply on strengthening the academic component of a student's educational experience, *e.g.*, math, language arts, and science. While this will better prepare students for a postsecondary academic experience, it may not assist them in making a career connection prior to leaving high school. This focus on academics is being encouraged to more effectively prepare students for their college experience, and also to reduce the high cost of remediation and developmental courses needed by our colleges to bring many high school students up to par. A source of additional costs that are difficult to calculate accrues from the extended time required by our students, not necessarily for remediation, but for finding their career connection. Student indecision and changing of degree focus could be significantly reduced if CTE opportunities, including career planning, were available during the high school experience.

Other efforts to remedy or improve CTE focus on the implementation of industry-based certification programs, which tend to be very job or industry specific. Although they do meet the needs of some students, they fall far short and leave a wide gap that limits the number of potential students who could benefit from CTE. Just as important is the limited number of options available that align with the "all students' career goals and interests" aspect in meeting student and workforce needs. Nearly every state has begun to reorganize the traditional vocational education structured around six or seven program areas to a new CTE system. These new systems use a variety of organizing terms, such as career academies, career paths, career fields, career majors, and career clusters, as a way to align program options. There is little consistency in defining CTE, which makes it difficult and confusing to collect reliable program data for accountability, create high-school-to-college articulation agreements within and between states, collaborate on efforts to define standards, and develop curriculum.

The Office of Vocational and Adult Education (OVAE), within the U.S. Department of Education, funded two major initiatives; both emphasized strong partnerships linking secondary and postsecondary education with employers and other significant organizations. The results of these two initiatives provide a needed consistency between the wide spectrum of approaches currently reshaping CTE. The combination of OVAE's two national initiatives has resulted in the completion of two critical components needed for effective change and national collaboration, as well as 10 suggested strategies learned as a result of collaboration with diverse partners.

The combination of OVAE's two national initiatives has resulted in the completion of two critical components needed for effective change and national collaboration, as well as 10 suggested strategies learned as a result of collaboration with diverse partners.

The first critical component addresses the needed common organizational structure that defines CTE as an important part of all students' educational plans. The second critical component is the creation of a common definition for a career pathway, including a model or template outlining academic and CTE course sequences connecting high school and college. This provided a format for raising the bar to ensure that what teachers teach and what students learn (both academic as well as CTE) align with a student's future needs.

A Common Organizational Structure and Definition for CTE

The first of OVAE's initiatives was originally referred to as Building Linkages, which, as the name suggests, establishes partnerships between secondary and postsecondary education and employers to create two model career clusters that could be replicated in developing other cluster areas. The first two clusters selected for development were health science and manufacturing.

The Utah State Office of Education took the lead for the health science cluster in cooperation with the National Consortium for Health Science and Technology Education, and the Indiana Department of Education was chosen to lead the manufacturing cluster in cooperation with the Vocational Technical Education Consortium of States (V-TECS). Although Utah and Indiana were lead states, many other states joined as partners in completing the initiatives.

Three years later, an additional three cluster areas were begun: Information Technology, led by the Educational Development Center; Arts, Audio Video Technology, and Communications, led by V-TECS; and Transportation, Distribution, and Logistics, led by the Illinois State Board of Education. The lessons learned through the sharing of ideas and collaboration among these first five clusters developed into a common blueprint for the remaining clusters.

In late 1999, an additional 11 clusters were defined by OVAE, completing the final set of 16 Career Clusters. In early 2001, the State of Oklahoma, in partnership with the National Association of State Directors for Career and Technical Education Consortium (NASDCTEc), was funded by OVAE to complete the development of the final 11 career clusters. The 11 clusters were organized and aligned with employers and postsecondary-validated standards. Federal funding for the cluster initiative ended in 2002, just prior to the beginning of assessment development. At that time, NASDCTEc assumed the responsibility for continued cluster development.

The Career Clusters Initiative was led by high schools through state departments of education in partnership with postsecondary education, employers, and other significant organizations. Occupation titles were aligned with each cluster area using the Department of Labor's ONET lists of occupations, ensuring the representation of all occupational titles. The alignment of occupations was based on similar educational requirements.

There could have been many more clusters, or even fewer. However, too few clusters would not provide the level of focus or the hook needed to attract and interest students or the specificity needed for secondary-to-postsecondary education articulation programs. On the other hand, too many clusters would be impossible for high schools to offer and are not necessary at the high school level to provide the depth of information needed for postsecondary preparation and articulation.

In addition to organizing all occupations into a structure of 16 career clusters, a major part of this initiative was to create two sets of standards for each cluster based on input from postsecondary education and employers. The standards were defined based on what students needed to know and do in order to make a successful transition to postsecondary education at the minimum level of an associate degree.

The first set of standards identified the knowledge and skills needed for all occupations within the entire cluster. These standards were organized around 10 categories established in agreement by all 16 cluster groups. All students in CTE programs who master the foundation standards will do so in the context of their chosen cluster area. If students change their career focus – and many will – to another cluster area, they will still have been exposed to the concepts of the 10 categories:

1. Academic Foundations
2. Communications
3. Problem Solving/Critical Thinking
4. Systems
5. Information Technology/Applications
6. Safety, Health, and Environmental
7. Leadership and Teamwork
8. Ethics and Legal Responsibilities
9. Employability and Career Development
10. Technical Skills

■ The importance of the pathway standards is that whether they are used for a specific pathway or combined with other pathways to develop curriculum, the curriculum developed will be based on standards validated by postsecondary education and employers.

The second set of standards was identified for subsets within the 16 clusters. These subsets more narrowly grouped the occupations within the clusters into pathways. Just as with the broader cluster standards, the pathway standards identified the knowledge and skills needed for each of the occupations within, in this case, the more narrowly defined pathways. Some of the clusters were subdivided into as many as seven pathways; others had as few as two. There are a total of 81 pathways within the 16 clusters (see table on page 19).

The importance of the pathway standards is that whether they are used for a specific pathway or combined with other pathways to develop curriculum, the curriculum developed will be based on standards validated by postsecondary education and employers. The cluster foundation and pathway standards eventually connect to a student's specific occupation goal, *e.g.*, Health Science Cluster → Therapeutic Pathway → Respiratory Therapy Program → employment.

Each year, new occupations are begun; old ones may change or be eliminated, and, at times, some occupations are more in demand than others, such as the Department of Labor's High Growth Job Training Initiative (HGJTI). The table on page 20 aligns the HGJTI with the 16 clusters.

CAREER CLUSTER AGRICULTURE, FOOD, AND NATURAL RESOURCES **PATHWAYS** Power, Structural, and Technical Systems National Resource Systems Agribusiness Systems Environmental Service Systems Plant Systems Animal Systems Food Products and Processing Systems	**CAREER CLUSTER** EDUCATION AND TRAINING **PATHWAYS** Teaching and Training Professional Support Services Administration and Administrative Support
CAREER CLUSTER ARCHITECTURE AND CONSTRUCTION **PATHWAYS** Design/Pre-Construction Construction Maintenance/Operations	**CAREER CLUSTER** FINANCE **PATHWAYS** Business Financial Management Banking and Related Services Financial and Investment Planning Insurance Services
CAREER CLUSTER ARTS/AV TECHNOLOGY AND COMMUNICATIONS **PATHWAYS** Visual Arts Performing Arts Journalism and Broadcasting Audio and Video Technology and Film Printing Technologies Telecommunication Technologies	**CAREER CLUSTER** GOVERNMENT AND PUBLIC ADMINISTRATION **PATHWAYS** National Security Foreign Service Planning Revenue and Taxation Regulation Public Management and Administration
CAREER CLUSTER BUSINESS MANAGEMENT AND ADMINISTRATION **PATHWAYS** Human Resources Management Business Financial Management and Accounting Marketing Administration and Information Support Business Analysis	**CAREER CLUSTER** HEALTH SCIENCE **PATHWAYS** Therapeutic Services Diagnostic Services Health Informatics Support Services Biotechnology Research and Development
CAREER CLUSTER HOSPITALITY AND TOURISM **PATHWAYS** Restaurants and Food and Beverage Service Recreation, Amusements, and Attractions Travel and Tourism Lodging	**CAREER CLUSTER** LAW, PUBLIC SAFETY, AND SECURITY **PATHWAYS** Legal Services Emergency and Fire Management Services Correction Services Law Enforcement Services Security and Protective Services
CAREER CLUSTER HUMAN SERVICES **PATHWAYS** Counseling and Mental Health Services Family and Community Services Personal Care Services Consumer Services Early Childhood Development	**CAREER CLUSTER** MANUFACTURING **PATHWAYS** Production Manufacturing Production Process Development Maintenance, Installation, and Repair Quality Assurance Logistics and Inventory Control Health Safety and Environmental Assurance
CAREER CLUSTER INFORMATION TECHNOLOGY **PATHWAYS** Network Systems Programming and Software Development Interactive Media Information Support and Services	**CAREER CLUSTER** MARKETING, SALES, AND SERVICE **PATHWAYS** Marketing Information Management and Research Marketing Communications and Promotion Professional Sales and Marketing Management and Entrepreneurship Buying and Merchandising E-Marketing Distribution and Logistics
CAREER CLUSTER SCIENCE, TECHNOLOGY, ENGINEERING, AND MATHEMATICS **PATHWAYS** Science and Math Engineering and Technology	**CAREER CLUSTER** TRANSPORTATION, DISTRIBUTION & LOGISTICS **PATHWAYS** Warehousing and Distribution Center Operations Logistics Planning and Management Services Facility and Mobile Equipment Maintenance Transportation Operations Transportation System Infrastructure Health Safety Management Sales and Services

OVAE's 16 Career Clusters	Department of Labor's High Growth Job Training Initiative
Agriculture, Food, and Natural Resources	Energy
Architecture and Construction	Construction
Arts, Audio/Video Technology, and Communications	
Business, Management, and Administration	
Education and Training	
Finance	Financial Services
Government and Public Administration	
Health Science	Health Care
Hospitality and Tourism	Hospitality
Human Services	
Information Technology	Information Technology
Law, Public Safety, Corrections, and Security	Homeland Security
Manufacturing	Advanced Manufacturing, Aerospace
Marketing Sales and Service	Retail
Science, Technology, Engineering, and Mathematics	Biotechnology, Geospatial Technology
Transportation, Distribution, and Logistics	Automotive, Transportation

The 16 cluster areas will always remain constant, yet changes in growth and relevance of occupations within the clusters will continually fluctuate as needed. Currently, 48 of the 50 states have adopted the concept of the 16 career clusters and standards. However, progressing from the traditional vocational education system to a new CTE system organized around the 16 broad career clusters, based on employer and postsecondary validated standards for all students, will require years to accomplish. The question educators must answer is, *Aren't all students' and all employers' needs better addressed through a system that provides career planning and initial career preparation, connecting our high school and college systems?*

Increasing Program Rigor and Student Expectations

While career clusters provide needed structural changes to move CTE to a more broad-based system that expands CTE program options and opens the door of opportunity to students who have not participated in CTE, the second of OVAE's major initiatives focused on creating model career pathways as a way to implement clusters. The major objective of CCTI is to ensure that students meet both academic and CTE expectations prior to entering postsecondary programs, thus eliminating the need for remediation at the college level. CCTI is a cooperative agreement funded by OVAE and led by community colleges through the League for Innovation in the Community College. Although CCTI is led by the community college, just as the high school led the career-cluster initiative, this initiative forges a strong partnership among high schools, postsecondary education, and employers.

The expected deliverables of CCTI are fairly straightforward. In essence, the cooperative agreement asks the League to select 15 local partnerships (pilot sites) led by a community college with high school and employer partners, organized around five career clusters (Health Science; Education and Training; Law, Public Safety, and Security; Information Technology; and Science, Technology, Engineering, and Mathematics); design and define a model career pathway; implement the model pathway in each of the pilot sites; and conduct research and complete case studies at each pilot site to determine the effectiveness of career pathways based on the five CCTI outcomes: (1) Increase enrollment and persistence in postsecondary education; (2) increase academic and skill achievement at secondary and postsecondary levels; (3) decrease the need for remediation at postsecondary level; (4) increase attainment of postsecondary degrees, certificates, or other recognized credentials; and (5) increase entry into employment or further education.

Implementation of the CCTI model career pathway and incorporation of each of its essential characteristics should certainly result in completion of the desired outcomes. A career pathway is a coherent, articulated sequence of rigorous academic and career courses, commencing in the 9th grade and leading to an associate degree, and/or an industry-recognized certificate or licensure, and/or a baccalaureate degree and beyond. A career pathway is developed, implemented, and maintained in partnership among secondary and postsecondary education, business, and employers. Career pathways are available to all students, including adult learners, and are designed to lead to rewarding careers.

The essential characteristics of career pathways are as follows.

Characteristics of a secondary pathway

- Meets state academic standards and grade-level expectations
- Meets high school testing and exit requirements
- Provides additional preparation to assure college readiness
- Meets postsecondary (college) entry and placement requirements
- Provides academic and career-related knowledge and skills in a chosen career cluster
- Provides opportunities for students to earn college credit through credit-based transition programs (*e.g.*, dual or concurrent enrollment, advanced placement, tech prep, International Baccalaureate, middle college high schools, articulation agreements)

Characteristics of a postsecondary pathway

- Opportunities for students to earn college credit through dual or concurrent enrollment or articulation agreements

- Alignment and articulation with baccalaureate programs
- Industry-recognized skills and knowledge in each cluster area
- Employment, business, and entrepreneurial opportunities in the chosen career cluster at multiple exit points

Characteristics of pathway partnerships

- Regularly collecting qualitative and quantitative data
- Using data for planning and decision making for continuous pathway improvement
- Maintaining ongoing dialogue among secondary, postsecondary, and employer partners

Lessons Learned

The process of planning and the experience of working in partnerships to complete the objectives of both the career clusters and CCTI has led to lessons and strategies that will facilitate implementation and dissemination of a new CTE system. The following list of lessons learned or implementation strategies is in no particular order of importance, except for the first one, which is most important and emphasizes the critical importance of strong partnerships.

Partnerships and Communication. Collaboration among secondary and postsecondary education, employers, and other significant groups organized around each of the 16 cluster areas is the driving force behind effective CTE programs. These partnerships should exist at the national, state, and local levels to provide ongoing oversight that ensures career-cluster information is current and standards are continually updated to adequately prepare students for further education or employment. An example of the importance of ongoing oversight by a cluster partnership is the work of the Law, Public Safety, and Security cluster partnership. Currently, new career opportunities and standards, as a result of the events following the attacks of September 11, are being added where appropriate to each of the 16 clusters.

Validated Employer and Postsecondary Standards. In the past, frustrated employers asked our schools to provide students who would simply show up on time. Our schools should and do expect much more of students. Curriculum, based on validated employer and postsecondary standards designed to effectively prepare students for postsecondary education or employment, must reflect the needs of each partner.

Consistency Among Programs. Using the 16 clusters as a common structure for organizing CTE programs is essential to program consistency and allows for a common set of standards. Standards identified as necessary for students by employers and postsecondary partners for a specific career cluster should not vary among schools or states. Consistency eliminates confusion, avoids duplication of effort, and saves local and state agencies millions of dollars.

Assessments and Accountability. OVAE is charged legislatively to hold states accountable for their use of Perkins funds. The ultimate goal to assure accountability as well as high-quality CTE programs should be for states to provide CTE programs that successfully prepare students for further education or employment. Assessments or other methods of demonstrating student mastery of employer- and postsecondary-validated standards should be implemented to demonstrate student competency. Consistent standards and reliable assessments are the two main ingredients that OVAE and the states should institute together as the norm for a new CTE system. Once in place, the new CTE system would allow high-school-to-college articulation agreements for students, not only within states, but also between them.

Access. The alignment of occupations within the cluster structure provides a place for every student, regardless of career goals or interests, to access CTE programs. Although offering all 16 clusters in the traditional high school would not be feasible, schools across the country have increased the number of options for student involvement in CTE by, for example, increasing the credit options available for students, using distance learning, using teachers as facilitators in technology-equipped classrooms offering multiple cluster options, and creating specialty high schools that focus on science-related or technology-related clusters. As technology changes, so will opportunities to expand options.

Relevancy and Integration. CTE and career pathway courses are typically elective; however, many schools have recognized that, given the chance, students are likely to participate in career pathways that link to their goals. This relevancy provides a major solution to the problem many schools face of students wasting their senior year. Integration of academic course concepts into CTE has always been an important component of CTE. With states' emphasis on increasing the rigor of academic courses and the challenge of high-stakes testing, some states are reversing direction and integrating CTE concepts into academic courses. This integration helps students not only in making career connections, but also in meeting academic expectations through connections of academic principles to real-world concepts.

Remediation and Enrichment Opportunities in High School. The template established as part of CCTI outlines the sequence of courses for both academic and CTE, and requires that students be assessed during the high school experience to determine postsecondary academic and CTE readiness. Conducting the assessment early permits enrichment opportunities prior to high school completion; however, the effectiveness of remediation and enrichment programs depends on collaboration between high schools and postsecondary education in articulating expectations.

Counselor and Parent Involvement. Counselors are the first line of communication with parents and students as educational plans are developed, and early planning allows students to enroll in appropriate courses that will facilitate successful transitions. Well-conceived career pathways that identify the academic sequence of courses and the CTE options should be available in various formats. Many schools provide career pathways on school websites that connect directly to postsecondary institutions. Career pathways need to be revisited and changed as needed.

Teacher Preparation. In implementing pathways within the career clusters, administrators, particularly at the high school level, face two obstacles. Making the transition from the old vocational education program areas to the broad cluster structure requires professional development for existing faculty members, since it involves, for example, helping the current drafting instructor begin teaching the foundation standards for the Architecture and Construction cluster. The standards were developed based on what most workers within the broad cluster area would need to be able to know and do, and preparation of traditional instructors should not require extensive training because of the broad nature of the foundation standards. Providing student access to all of the career opportunities within the Architecture and Construction cluster increases the number of students in CTE. Student interest may keep the drafting program on the schedule, but ideally after many more students are exposed to the large number of career options within the broader cluster. New CTE opportunities are also available in areas where traditional teacher preparation programs do not exist. In some off these clusters, such as Human Services, Art, Audio Visual Technology and Communications, Education and Training, and Finance, high schools are offering related courses (*e.g.*, psychology, sociology, child development, art, music, and business). In areas without qualified teachers, schools may be able to use postsecondary teachers to fill vacancies or implement alternative methods of teacher certification.

Data Collection. The collection of valid, reliable data to use in reporting the effects of CTE has always been hindered by the inconsistency of the content and rigor of high school programs. Knowing the number of health science students completing two health science courses within a certain state and using that data to see how effective CTE was in assisting students in progressing to college or employment are difficult if there is little or no consistency between the health science courses. Consistent program structure and standards are the beginning of a reliable collection system that will benefit employers, lawmakers, workforce agencies, and educators.

Career and Technical Education is at a critical junction. It is at the point where national collaboration could occur that unites high schools, community colleges, baccalaureate institutions, and universities with employers, workforce agencies, and other relevant groups organized around the 16 cluster areas. These partnerships would provide the forum for ongoing dialogue between education and employers, which would improve career preparation programs at all levels.

Education and Training

- Anne Arundel Community College (MD)
- Lorain County Community College (OH)
- Maricopa Community Colleges (AZ)

Through collaboration with CCTI colleges, AACC has gained a broader understanding of the challenges and barriers endemic to successful high school student transition and has begun refocusing both human and fiscal resources. Through strong support of college and county school leadership, AACC is in the process of bringing this new instructional paradigm to scale to forward the college mission as a premier learning community whose students and graduates are among the best-prepared citizens and workers of the world.

Andrew L. Meyer, Vice President for Learning, Anne Arundel Community College

Anne Arundel Community College

Debra D. Bragg

OCCUPATIONAL AREA:	Education and Training
CAREER PATHWAY:	Teaching and Training
CCTI PROJECT DIRECTORS:	Andrew Meyer, Project Coordinator
	Kathleen Beauman, Business Director Education Partnerships
SCHOOL PARTNERS:	Annapolis High School
	Arundel High School
	Chesapeake High School
	Glen Burnie High School
	Meade High School
	North County High School
	Northeast High School
	Old Mill High School
	Severna Park High School
CORPORATE PARTNERS:	Anne Arundel County Public Schools
	Daily Discoveries

The Project Partners

The College and Career Transition Initiative project at Anne Arundel Community College (AACC) has shown a strong commitment to addressing the region's teacher shortage by enhancing its teacher preparation programs, including advocating at the state and national level for expanding the Associate of Arts in Teaching (AAT). President Martha Smith, who is passionate about improving teacher education in community colleges throughout the state of Maryland, has offered advice and encouragement to other community colleges and two-year state systems in the nation. She has worked closely with AACC to enhance elements of its teacher education initiatives for several years, with the college's early activities setting the stage for the awarding of the CCTI grant.

The overarching goal of this CCTI project is to enhance student transition from high-school-to-postsecondary education in the area of teacher education, using a number of strategies. A part-time Anne Arundel County Public Schools resource teacher provides outreach to high school students enrolled in the Introduction to Teaching and Childhood Development courses to introduce students to careers in teaching to the strategies that will help them successfully progress to college. The AACC Teacher Education and Child Care (TEACH) Institute director, resource teacher-liaison, and advisement coordinator enhance communication by providing a pivotal connection among AACC and high school guidance counselors, college advisors, and education department staff at four-year colleges and universities.

AACC's TEACH Institute has established several new programs during the two-year span of 2004-2005 and 2005-2006, including the Associate of Arts in Teaching (AAT) degree in Early Childhood Education, Elementary Education, Secondary Math, Secondary Spanish, and Secondary Chemistry. The Teaching Paraprofessional Certificate and Special Education Support Certificate are provided in addition to the Associate of Applied Sciences (AAS) degree in Early Childhood Education. To facilitate student success in these programs, the CCTI project has introduced ACCUPLACER as a means of determining Introduction to Teaching students' readiness to enter AACC's teacher training programs.

Anne Arundel Community College is located in Anne Arundel County on the Chesapeake Bay between Baltimore, Maryland, and Washington, D.C. It was established on January 2, 1961, by the county board of education, opening its doors in September 1961 to 270 students in late-afternoon and evening courses in temporary quarters at Severna Park High School. In September 1967, the college moved to its current 165-acre plot, receiving full accreditation from the Middle States Commission on Higher Education in April 1968. Growth in enrollment, curriculum offerings, and facilities continued. In August 1994, President Smith became AACC's fifth chief executive officer. Smith has encouraged AACC to be a premier learning community whose students and graduates are among the most well prepared anywhere in the world.

AACC is a fully accredited public, comprehensive community college offering credit programs leading to associate degrees and certificates and a wide array of noncredit courses leading to various forms of credentialing and letters of recognition. Areas of study range from arts and sciences to engineering to web technology. Day, evening, and weekend classes meet at various locations, including the main Arnold campus and the Glen Burnie Town Center. In fall 2003, the college's newest facility opened at Arundel Mills, a large shopping complex in the western portion of Anne Arundel County. Classes are also held at 10 county middle and high schools and at nearly 100 additional locations throughout the county. In FY 2004, the college had a headcount enrollment of 20,928, which translates into 8,284 FTE, drawing over 32 percent of the Anne Arundel county public high school graduates. Noncredit FY 2004 enrollment was 32,186, or 3,408 FTE, with a total of 3,659 noncredit contract and noncredit courses offered.

The Arundel Mills facility of AACC is the headquarters for a new University Consortium, a partnership between AACC and several four-year colleges and universities. This formal consortium connects associate degree programs to related bachelor and graduate degree programs from member institutions.

Because of Maryland's funding of community college education, students attending AACC have the opportunity to enroll in a particularly extensive array of credit and noncredit courses. In addition, AACC offers a number of credit-noncredit share classes. Students have the option to take a credit class enrolled as a noncredit student. Each semester, more than 100 credit classes are cross-listed, allowing those not interested in academic credit the opportunity to enroll in credit courses typically not found in continuing education offerings. AACC has taken advantage of a decision by the State of Maryland to fund credit and eligible noncredit courses at the same rate, to create an integrated curriculum that blurs the lines between traditional college divisions. All schools in the college participate in offering credit and noncredit classes that have been well received by the community. According to AACC officials, the college's emphasis on credit-noncredit share, lifelong learning, and community education classes does not diminish the importance of the transfer curriculum. Transfer is a prominent and successful function of the college, as evidenced by AACC's transfer students' earning a higher average first-year GPA than the average Maryland community college transfer students.

The Anne Arundel County Public Schools (AACPS) are a primary partner in CCTI. The teachers, counselors, and administrators at the local high schools, with the Academy of Teaching programs, have implemented new strategies to assist their students with progressing to college. When characterizing past partnerships involving AACC and AACPS, the message from educational leaders is consistently positive – so positive, in fact, that AACPS "didn't blink an eye" about partnering in CCTI.

As the 5th largest school system in Maryland and the 41st largest school system in the nation, AACPS serves a diverse population of students that spans urban, suburban, and rural portions of the county. AACPS is the third largest employer in the county, with about 10,500 employees and approximately 5,250 teachers. More than 75,000 K-12 students are enrolled in 116 public school facilities, including 77 elementary schools, 19 middle schools, 12 high schools, 2 centers of applied technology, 3 special education centers, 1 alternative high school, 1 middle school learning center, and 1 center for emotionally impaired students. Seven elementary schools in the district have received the National Blue Ribbon Schools of Excellence designation, and 10 have received the Maryland Blue Ribbon Schools of Excellence designation, including South River High.

In 2003, AACPS graduated 4,690 students, and of these, 79 percent attended four- or two-year colleges and universities; 9 percent went into apprenticeships; 4 percent attended business, technical, and trade schools; 4 percent went into the military; and the remainder entered the workforce without pursuing postsecondary education or military service. AACPS has more than 5,000 teachers, with an average teacher salary of $48,805.

For more than 15 years, AACC and AACPS have had a strong partnership focused on career and technical education (CTE) initiatives. Leaders from each academic institution meet regularly, and ongoing communication occurs among the offices of instruction, student services, administration, and planning and research. Through the tech-prep program, more than 20 secondary CTE programs have been sequenced and articulated into a corresponding program at AACC. Teams of secondary and postsecondary educators annually update program articulation agreements, and these updated agreements are forwarded to all AACC and AACPS staff that advise and counsel students.

AACC and AACPS have partnered in a joint venture to provide professional development to the full range of AACPS staff. The Total Teacher Training (T3) Project began in 1998, and is a component of the TEACH Institute. County guidance counselors attend annual program updates at AACC, and high school students regularly visit the campus through organized outreach activities. Interestingly, Maryland guidelines do not consider the Academy of Teaching Professions curricula to count as a legitimate tech-prep curriculum, because the course sequence is not as extensive or advanced as the state requires. However, MSDE has recently developed a fast-track proposal for the Academy of Teaching that would be eligible for funding under the Perkins legislation.

AACC leaders identify tech prep as a primary stimulus to enhanced relationships with AACPS, with instructional partnerships operating since November 1991, when the local tech-prep program began. They also attribute tech prep with the successful acquisition of grants, the creation of new curriculum, an increase in CTE enrollment, and enhanced collaborations among administrators, teachers, and counselors. These accomplishments are not surprising given that a Tech Prep Local Labor Market Team has operated continuously for 13 years, meeting monthly with representatives of AACC, AACPS, and local business and industry. This team had provided a venue for new CTE initiatives, enhancing joint strategies for student success. The Tech Prep Local Labor Market Team is co-chaired by an AACC and AACPS representative, with support from the executive leadership of each institution.

■ AACC leaders... attribute tech prep with the successful acquisition of grants, the creation of new curriculum, an increase in CTE enrollment, and enhanced collaborations among administrators, teachers, and counselors.

Four high schools within AACPS were considered partners in this CCTI initiative during FY 2004: Arundel High School, Chesapeake High School, North County High School, and Northeast High School. These schools offered the core of the teacher training curriculum via the Teaching Academy, with three schools reporting active enrollments during the 2003-2004 academic year. Five high schools were added during 2005-2006.

Daily Discoveries is a locally accredited child care and kindergarten facility that is a private-sector partner for this CCTI project, in addition to AACPS, which is also considered a corporate partner. This fully accredited child care center is owned and operated by a local family in Anne Arundel County. The center is accredited by the National Association for Education of Young Children (NAEYC) and licensed by the Maryland Department of Human Resources Child Care Administration. All staff members in charge of a group of children at Daily Discoveries have participated in the Maryland Child Care Credential program. Per state guidelines, children at the center are actively involved in a minimum of 15 minutes of prereading or reading instruction, as well as numerous other learning activities.

Explaining why Daily Discoveries wanted to partner with AACC for CCTI, an administrator said, "The child care field needs a career ladder." She foresees that CCTI can help reduce staff turnover by creating opportunities for employees to pursue further education and training. She explained, "A lot of people in child care want to move into teacher education. If our staff wants to someday teach in the schools, we want to help them with that transition." For Daily Discoveries, the CCTI project provides the initial step in the creation of a much needed career ladder, a step that would be difficult without the partnership with AACC.

The Model Career Pathway

The centerpiece of the CCTI initiative is the **Academy of Teaching Professions** (Teaching Academy), which is a joint effort developed in 2000 by AACC and AACPS. The Teaching Academy is designed as an academic completer program, wherein high school coursework is aligned and sequenced with AACC's teacher education program. Using a grow-our-own philosophy, advanced high school students (juniors or seniors) are encouraged to participate in formal learning experiences that introduce them to teaching and lead them into courses for students majoring in education at AACC or elsewhere. Again, four high schools offered the Academy of Teaching Professions during FY 2004, with nine high schools signed on for 2005-2006, reflecting enrollment of 180 students.

AACPS commits tangible and intangible resources to the Academy of Teaching, including student internships, teacher salaries, classroom space, instructional materials, and technical support. In addition to the instructional component of the Teaching Academy, contributions from AACPS are administrative in-kind services, such as professional development and employer services from the assistant superintendent for instructional services, the director of career and technology education, the director of human resources, the director of the secondary schools, and numerous school principals.

■ **Using a grow-our-own philosophy, advanced high school students (juniors or seniors) are encouraged to participate in formal learning experiences that introduce them to teaching and lead them into courses for students majoring in education at AACC or elsewhere.**

AACC's commitment to the Academy of Teaching includes holding a teacher career-day program and an early childhood development career-day program, providing admissions information to high school students, presenting workshops and in-service training for teachers, hosting the Partners in Education Program, and providing further support through the tech-prep office. CCTI funds enable further personnel support for the Teaching Academy, including the employment of a part-time resource teacher, a retired teacher from the area who works with high school classroom teachers 20 hours per week. Further, enhancements are made to high school counseling services to provide students with current information about the teaching profession, and AACC academic advisors are assigned to participate in the high schools.

AACC's Education Department offers both an Associate of Arts in Teaching (AAT) degree and an Associate of Applied Sciences (AAS) degree. These degree programs are designed to ensure that graduates have a broad general education, a firm grounding in the best practices of education, and a strong competency in the area of content knowledge. The department also offers reading courses required for all pre-service and in-service teachers by the Maryland State Department of Education. All courses provided by the Child Care Training Department are closely aligned with the outcomes, indicators, and sample assessment tasks proposed and accepted by the Consortium of Maryland Early Childhood Faculty and Administration, and meet standards and regulations set forth by the Maryland State Department of Human Resources Child Care Administration for pre-service and continued training required of all Maryland providers for licensing, registration, and relicensing.

AACC's teacher preparation programs are consistent with emerging standards for early childhood professional preparation and are aligned with the NAEYC standards for early childhood professional development, the National Council for Accreditation of Teacher Education (NCATE) standards for early childhood education, and the AAT model for the State of Maryland. All classes provide the necessary documentation for providers participating in the Maryland Child Care Credential program, a voluntary program that recognizes child care providers who go beyond the requirements of state licensing and registration regulations and meet specific education and experience requirements. Participants in this program receive bonuses from the state each time they reach one of the six credential levels.

The AACC Early Childhood Education Program meets the National Standards for Early Childhood Education and Services by integrating knowledge, skills, and practices required for careers in early childhood, education, and services; providing analysis of career paths within early childhood, education, and services; and demonstrating professional practices and standards related to working with children. The program also offers students the opportunity to complete the training necessary to meet the state's requirements for a 90 clock-hour certificate for occupation in a child care center. Students must meet academic requirements of an average grade of B or better in three child development classes, and they must have excellent attendance. The child development students who are Early Childhood Completers must finish either an internship or a work experience in a child care center. In addition, paraprofessionals are being developed to meet the outcome standards legislated in No Child Left Behind (NCLB) and Maryland state-established criteria.

Special Education resource teachers from the AACPS Central Office have assisted the TEACH staff in developing a new Special Education Support certificate, which recently received Maryland Higher Education Commission approval. This certificate will assist those interested in working with one of the neediest populations in pre-K-12 find employment as a Special Education Support Technician, a new job category in AACPS that requires completion of the certificate and the equivalent of two years of college. This opportunity will be advantageous for those who need to work while pursuing their teaching degree, those who are unsure about education as a career, or those who are unable to pursue a baccalaureate program.

AACC's TEACH Institute has been enhanced by CCTI. Patterned after AACC's Hospitality, Culinary Arts, and Tourism Institute, which brings together credit and noncredit programs and services into a one-stop-shop format, the TEACH Institute has a multifaceted approach to addressing the region's teacher shortage. Degree, certificate, and letter-of-recognition programs being awarded via TEACH include the Associate of Arts in Teaching in Elementary Education, Early Childhood Education, Secondary Math, Secondary Chemistry, and Secondary Spanish; the Associate of Applied Sciences in Early Childhood Development; Teaching Paraprofessional and Special Education Support Certificates; and the Early Childhood Development Letter of Recognition. Reflecting its one-stop-shop concept, the college's brochure on the TEACH Institute specifies that "the TEACH Institute offers one place to go, one number to call for future teachers or child care professionals, or for those already in the field who would like to improve their professional skills."

Through the one-stop shop, AACC strives to assist new students in navigating their way through the complex and confusing morass of information, agencies, and organizations related to teacher preparation. Viewing all types of students as potential participants, including high schoolers, career changers, and others, the TEACH Institute has already stimulated a dramatic increase in enrollment in AACC's education-related programs and courses. According to Vice President for Learning and Co-Director of the CCTI project Andrew Meyer, AACC experienced "over a 100 percent increase in enrollment when [the college] combined credit and noncredit under one roof."

■ Viewing all types of students as potential participants, including high schoolers, career changers, and others, the TEACH Institute has already stimulated a dramatic increase in enrollment in AACC's education-related programs and courses.

The tech-prep program allocated $420 for a half-day staff development program for AACC and AACPS enrollment, advising, and guidance staff on tech-prep programs, career clusters, and program articulation. A paraprofessional cohort program was submitted and approved as a Workforce Investment Act (WIA) fundable program, and the Child Care Training Department had two programs funded by state and local government agencies that provided training for early childhood educators and caregivers at a reduced cost. The Behavioral and Emotional Support Training (BEST) program was funded by the Anne Arundel County Local Management Board to develop and offer courses pertaining to behavioral and emotional issues that affect children.

This CCTI project emphasizes professional development. Beginning in September 2003, professional development introduced AACPS's Academy of Teaching Professions to AACC's AAT program, and AACPS's Early Childhood Education teachers to AACC's Early Childhood Development and the AAT program. AACC faculty and AACPS teachers were involved in this curriculum-alignment activity. Also in September 2003, early childhood providers throughout Anne Arundel County and faculty and staff from the TEACH Institute were briefed on the CCTI initiative. Ongoing staff development is provided for existing and new AACPS Academy of Teaching Professions faculty.

Several presentations have been developed by the TEACH Institute for high schools, including Solve the Career Puzzle – Teach!, a 30-minute presentation about careers in child care, and a 30-minute presentation titled Teacher Education 101 at AACC. In addition to these, several 30- or 60-minute presentations have been developed and delivered addressing student concerns about the transition from high school to college, including presentations titled College Potpourri; Fast Forward: Earn College Credit in High School; Myths About Your Community College; A Day in the Life of a College Student; and Failing to Plan is Planning to Fail. College 101 for Parents is an after-school presentation that covers topics on teacher education, financial aid, scholarships, tech prep, and so forth. An eight-minute video was professionally produced to aid in recruiting students, particularly males, into education careers.

Curriculum and Instruction

The director of the TEACH Institute has involved educators from AACPS schools in developing a sequential curriculum that links the high school-level Academy of Teaching Professions to AACC's TEACH Institute. A clearly sequenced and articulated program of study, beginning in high school and continuing into postsecondary education, was finalized in fall 2003. This curriculum was developed by reviewing existing programs of study; aligning course outcome competencies with college entrance requirements; addressing areas of concern related to alignment; revising and identifying the need for new program articulation agreements; and communicating the newly aligned program of study to stakeholders, including high school guidance counselors, AACC advisors, students, and parents. Throughout the academic year, professional development activities were planned to enhance instructional strategies based on learning-centered innovations. These activities entailed identifying the professional development needs of AACPS teachers and AACC instructors and designing appropriate professional development to introduce a variety of learning-centered approaches. These approaches included learning communities, classroom assessment techniques, project-based learning, service learning, and problem-based learning.

The new comprehensive curriculum offers credit programs and noncredit professional development courses. Local articulation agreements associated with tech prep use a deferred-credit model wherein students do not receive college credits earned in high school tech prep-related courses until they have completed six academic credit hours at AACC with a grade of C or better. AACC leaders acknowledge the present lack of a logical flow to the education curriculum from high school to AACC to the university, and they express a desire to create a new curriculum that will show students various pathways toward completion and that rewards them with college credits during high school. Officials describe their approach to curriculum development as both measured and strategic, requiring time to build a sequential pathway from high school to the community college and university. Instruction for the various teacher education and early childhood development programs is held at the college's Arnold campus, Glen Burnie Town Center, the Arundel Mills campus, and a number of county child care centers.

In addition, the TEACH Institute has developed and offered three online courses that are designed to meet CCTI outcomes by increasing accessibility to students, particularly provisional teachers who lack certification. These were developed using the WebCT platform and are presented as hybrids to include a face-to-face component so positive teaching strategies may be modeled. Three additional education courses are being converted to a hybrid format.

To achieve another CCTI outcome, the T3 Project established a paraprofessional cohort as a pathway to the AAT to meet NCLB "highly qualified" status. To accomplish this goal, AACC (1) recruited teaching assistants who needed additional training to meet NCLB regulations, (2) completed a letter of agreement with AACPS, and (3) engaged the TEACH Institute director. The director coordinated with various department chairs to offer courses within the AAT in a nontraditional accelerated cohort format and monitored student progress.

Further, AACC leaders wanted to create nonpaid internships as an initial stage of the curriculum for high school students in the Academy of Teaching Professions. These exploratory internships involve placing 12th grade students into a semester-long elective internship course to introduce them to the education profession. A beginning goal to place approximately 100 students into AACPS elementary schools has been fulfilled.

Bridges With Four-Year Programs

To meet the instructional needs of Anne Arundel County residents, the AACC University Consortium was established in spring 2003. AACC sought out four-year colleges and universities interested in offering baccalaureate degrees that link with associate degrees as well as graduate and certification programs of study. To date, four colleges and universities have joined the University Consortium and offer programs at the Arundel Mills and Arnold college locations. Two of the AACC University Consortium partner institutions offer educational programs including baccalaureate and graduate degrees as well as certification programs.

■ It is particularly important to AACC to create a 100 percent transferable teacher education AAT degree that transfers to "every College of Education in every public and private college and university in the state."

AACC has developed a seamless program pathway from the AAT degree into a bachelor and graduate degree in education. It is particularly important to AACC to create a 100 percent transferable teacher education AAT degree that transfers to "every College of Education in every public and private college and university in the state." Activities associated with this goal include briefing University Consortium members on the CCTI initiative, establishing articulated program pathways, identifying and participating in joint outreach and marketing activities promoting education careers, and exploring the development of joint promotional print materials with University Consortium members.

In addition, AACPS is committed to partnerships with six Maryland universities to offer 33 Professional Development Schools (PDS) in elementary, middle, and high schools throughout the county. Six of the PDSs are in the beginning phases. Higher education institutions involved in the PDSs are Towson University, Goucher College, University of Maryland-Baltimore County, College of Notre Dame, Loyola University, and Salisbury University. Complementary to the CCTI initiative, the PDSs do not play a direct role in the project.

Student Support

With the support of CCTI funding, the college hired a part-time high school liaison and full-time college advisement coordinator to facilitate successful transition of high school and college learners to a number of student services and next steps. The full-time college advisement coordinator position was institutionalized in 2005. As a result of this staffing strategy, the partnership was able to connect high school and postsecondary learners interested in teacher education with numerous support services, including academic and financial aid advising, academic program planning, and parent information sessions. Student support is offered for education students, including such functions as counseling, advising and retention, financial services, testing and tutoring, and admissions. Among the counseling staff, the college is able to provide a dedicated advisement coordinator through CCTI funds to ensure that students are aware of transfer, certification, employment opportunities, and enrollment processes. The tech-prep specialist works closely with high school graduates to facilitate their transition to college and familiarize them with the articulation process.

Special Features

CCTI was built on systemic changes brought about by

- Tech prep;
- The Academy of Teaching Professions (Teaching Academy);
- The TEACH Institute;
- The associate of arts in teaching (AAT) degree in Early Childhood Education and Elementary Education and the AAT in Secondary Math, Spanish, and Chemistry, plus the Teaching Paraprofessional Certificate and Special Education Support Certificate;
- ACCUPLACER placement testing to assess college readiness while students are in high school;
- Parent Information Sessions;
- Professional development for a wide range of education professionals; and
- Alignment with the No Child Left Behind legislation's "highly qualified" status.

The Implementation Strategies

The CCTI project emphasizes the following set of implementation strategies to attain the five CCTI objectives.

Anne Arundel Community College CCTI Program

CCTI Objective	Key Strategies
Decreased need for remediation at postsecondary level	• Provide intervention with targeted high school students to ensure successful college transition by reducing the need for remediation.
Increased enrollment and persistence in postsecondary education	• Increase enrollment in Academy of Teaching Professions. • Provide academic and career-related counseling to 100 percent of high school students enrolled in Academy of Teaching Professions and Early Childhood Completer Programs.
Increased academic and skill achievement at the secondary and postsecondary levels	• Finalize clearly sequenced and articulated program of study beginning in high school and continuing into postsecondary education. • Provide professional development to enhance instructional strategies based on learning-centered innovations.
Increased attainment of postsecondary degrees, certificates, or other recognized credentials	• Develop AAT programs in early childhood education and secondary education in the content areas of physics, math, chemistry, and Spanish.
Increased entry into employment or further education	• Develop a certificate program for Special Education Support. • Develop a seamless program pathway from the AAT/AAS degree into a bachelor's and graduate degree in education. • In conjunction with AACPS, offer the two-day Partners in Education Program, an intervention strategy for first-year teachers.

Most Effective Strategies

Among the specific implementation strategies, this CCTI project has identified three that it is particularly enthusiastic about.

Joint Staff Development. Since August 2004, high school and college faculty have worked collaboratively to strengthen, expand, and better align the high school Academy of Teaching Professions class. In addition, an AACC faculty member provided a daylong program for secondary faculty teaching a business presentations course (one of the core courses in the curriculum). Also, the Maryland State Department of Education hosted a summer institute for high school faculty teaching in the academy program. AACC hosted a best-practices program for new and existing academy teachers in August 2005.

Parent Information Session. For the past two years, the college has hosted a Parent Information Session, inviting the parents and students who are enrolled in the Academy of Teaching Professions class. Following dinner and a welcome by the college president, parents are briefed on the CCTI project, provided an overview of available services, including the ACCUPLACER, and they are told about student support services, college admission, financial aid, and transfer opportunities that are available to them. Feedback from parents has been extremely positive, and has indicated that participation in the information session has provided them with more knowledge about postsecondary expectations and the next logical steps for their children to proceed in the career pathway program.

Student Assessment. During the Parent Information Session, parents are informed and their permission is requested to pretest Teaching Academy students using ACCUPLACER. Test results are shared with students and their high school guidance counselors, and the guidance counselors work with the students to schedule requisite coursework to ensure postsecondary preparation. A new role of high school counselors is to inform students about the academic requirements and rigor of the teaching profession. All students enrolled in the Academy of Teaching Professions are encouraged to take the ACCUPLACER assessment. This has been an excellent tool in providing direction and feedback to individual students and their parents concerning future college success and academic areas needing work.

Academic Preparation. AACC is attempting to address the difficult issues associated with balancing open access, the notion of admitting students regardless of background versus preparing students who are ready to take college-level courses. Coming down on the side of valuing academic preparation, AACC is incorporating into all of its messages to prospective students the importance of college preparation during high school. AACC officials are deliberately articulating the importance of rigorous academic studies to high school students, so that they understand what the transition will be like if they are prepared and if they are not.

Least Effective Strategies

Struggles with ACCUPLACER. In reviewing CCTI plans for remediation, discussions have been undertaken between AACC and AACPS on the appropriate age for students to take the ACCUPLACER and the need for strategies to provide support services.

Struggles with dual credit. Like other CCTI partnerships, AACC has had difficulty adopting dual-credit options because of concerns about funding. Articulation agreements associated with tech prep are plentiful in this consortium, so students do have the opportunity to engage in accelerated learning opportunities as long as they matriculate from the high school to AACC according to requirements of the agreements. At this point, AACC is reviewing implementing a transcripted credit process in addition to articulated tech-prep credit, as four-year colleges and universities generally require a grade for successful course transfer. AACC officials speculate that they should move to end-of-year exams or college entrance exams in particular subjects by the end of the 2005-2006 academic year.

Plans for the Future

Future plans call for the creation of professional development coursework to meet the NCLB "highly qualified" status, which entails identifying faculty to develop content-area courses for middle school teachers who are not content certified, monitoring course development, marketing new courses to teachers requiring professional development, and offering the courses.

This CCTI partnership intends to continue to expand its program to include more high schools. At present, expansion is planned by the Academy of Teaching Professions so that all 12 high schools are involved. Expansion is also planned beyond teacher education, with the development of an academy addressing finance, business, marketing, and accounting; another dealing with travel and tourism information technology; and yet another dealing with early childhood development.

The Daily Discoveries partner has been underused to date, and there is a deliberate intention to pursue more collaboration in association with implementation of the AAT in Early Childhood Education.

Finally, future plans call for continued efforts to integrate best practices by making structured visits to campuses where students and parents get information about the various CCTI-related initiatives in place and planned at AACC. Marketing efforts are also planned to approach specific parent groups, encouraging enhanced connections to parents. Day visits with students and night meetings with parents have proven to be a winning combination in terms of reaching students and their parents. AACC has found that parents are particularly attentive to the CCTI project and opportunities it provides, because the tuition rise in the past four years has made parents particularly interested in the opportunities offered by the community college.

Lessons Learned

The CCTI project has identified several lessons that may be useful to others implementing similar teacher training programs.

Use many communication and information-gathering strategies to reach all of the constituency groups that are needed for implementation. The constituency groups that are critical to the effort are secondary and postsecondary education training students, professionals of the secondary and postsecondary educational systems, and parents – particularly parents of rising 10th graders – to explain opportunities for early college enrollment and transition to college.

Recognize that large educational systems are complicated and sometimes difficult to negotiate. Identify point people to clarify the project and facilitate support when seeking services between systems. Specifically, a staffing liaison is useful at both the secondary and postsecondary levels; a student services person at the community college is useful to interact with participating high schools; and a hotline can help high school students, guidance counselors, parents, and faculty members reach people who can provide needed information about the program.

Realize that partnerships focused on systemic change take time, energy, and ongoing nurturing from change agents. These change agents can be thought of as champions, because they promote improvements in instructional and student support services, both internally and externally.

Offer career pathways along with early high school assessments to enhance advising students, parents, and school and college personnel. Electronic communication between the secondary and postsecondary levels is very important to disseminate and promote pathways that link the secondary and postsecondary levels. The pathways need to extend to the four-year college level using formal articulation agreements.

Persevere: Over time, the system will change if given enough time and attention. AACC and AACPS officials understand well the complexity in changing a large and complex system, including the postsecondary institution, as well as the K-12 county school district. System changes can be difficult to implement, and accountability for sharing information may be limited. These problems are often known, but it takes time for the data to match common knowledge, and it is when data become available and shared that action can be taken and systemic changes can take place. As the CCTI project has continued to move forward, student performance data, including program articulation, has been disaggregated by high school and program. The hiring of a part-time academic advisor by AACC has helped to inform both students and high school faculty about college expectations, services, and programs.

■ ...when data become available and shared... action can be taken and systemic changes can take place.

Strengths, Challenges, and Recommendations

AACC has made a concerted effort to communicate with a number of stakeholder audiences about the CCTI project. These include conducting the Great Minds Re-United meeting, a joint staff development program with secondary and postsecondary guidance counselors, academic advisors, career connection facilitators, and administrators; conducting ongoing briefings of the Tech Prep Local Labor Market Team comprised of secondary and postsecondary administrators, staff, faculty, and guidance counselors; holding a briefing of AACPS high school principals; conducting an Annual Parent Information Night; briefing members of the AACC University Consortium; and briefing the AACC Academic Council and Learning Response Team. Altogether, more than 1,000 high school students and teachers were reached through classroom presentations. Also, the fall 2005 college orientation focused on student transition, program pathways, and CCTI, and more than 300 full-time faculty, staff, and administrators participated.

AACC has an exceptionally strong reputation for institutional research, including being identified as a model for outcomes assessment. The institutional research office employs six staff members: two senior researchers, two research analysts, and two technicians. A senior researcher is tasked with coordinating the data requirements for the CCTI project, and he expressed confidence in the institution's ability to produce required data. Moreover, AACC and AACPS have a long history of sharing data between their institutions, including via the local tech-prep initiative.

AACC's close working relationship with the state has brought about opportunities to share what's being learned in the Annapolis area with the rest of the state. Leaders of AACC and the CCTI project are working with the Maryland State Department of Education and the University System of Maryland to develop a statewide Teaching Academy program of studies.

One challenge has to do with privacy issues and the inability of AACPS to forward AACC student names and information that would assist in the data collection. AACC has gained cooperation from AACPS officials to attempt to overcome this barrier, but the process is slow. Both AACC and AACPS have agreed to collaborate to collect data needed to advance the project, though the data collection process has been slow to evolve, partly because of the student privacy issue. Initial efforts to collect data specific to the project had proved challenging, because of the timing of the CCTI data request in late summer and early fall.

More information about Anne Arundel Community College and the CCTI Initiative can be found at http://www.league.org/league/projects/ccti/projects/summary.cfm?key=AACC.

Lorain County Community College

Debra D. Bragg

OCCUPATIONAL AREA:	Education and Training
CAREER PATHWAY:	Teaching and Training
CCTI PROJECT DIRECTORS:	Karen Wells, Project Coordinator
	Tammy Macek, Project Coordinator
SCHOOL PARTNERS:	Lorain County Joint Vocational School
CORPORATE PARTNERS:	Elyria City Schools
	Avon Local Schools
	Avon Lake City Schools

The Project Partners

The College and Career Transitions Initiative project at Lorain County Community College (LCCC) strives to provide students with the competencies and credentials required to succeed in college and employment. The program emphasizes a comprehensive set of academic, career, and support services. LCCC and the Lorain County Joint Vocational School (LCJVS) are the primary partners for this initiative. For well over a decade, these organizations have collaborated on workforce development issues in Lorain County, Ohio. To address a growing teacher shortage, LCCC, LCJVS, and three school districts have dedicated their CCTI project to the development of a teacher education pathway that begins in 12th grade and extends to the bachelor's level. LCJVS coordinates the Teacher Education Exploration (TEE) program and helps connect its students to support services at LCCC. The mission of the TEE program is to encourage interested high school seniors to enter the teaching profession by providing them with the training and support necessary for success as both students and teachers. Three school district superintendents are in the role of corporate partners, representing the perspectives of potential employers of TEE graduates. These employers support the initiative by encouraging teachers to take the time and effort to sponsor a student intern.

Lorain County Community College has engaged more than 250,000 Lorain County residents in educational programs and services since 1963. In 2001, the college received the State of Ohio's highest quality rating for educational institutions by achieving the Tier 3 Achievement of Excellence Award through the Ohio Award for Excellence. In fall 2002, LCCC reached another milestone by enrolling more than 9,000 students, marking a record number of students in 80 credit programs and technical certifications, thereby becoming Ohio's fastest growing higher education institution.

CCTI has broadened our understanding of the role of business, government, and educators in responding to workforce shortages in high-growth careers and has given us the tools to work with various constituencies to raise the performance levels of our students.

Karen A. Wells, Vice President for Learner Services and Chief Academic Officer, Lorain County Community College

The college encourages lifelong learning through accessible and affordable academic, career-oriented, and continuing education. As evidence of this fact, more than 2,000 adults attend the University Partnership program, which brings eight universities to the LCCC campus to offer more than 30 bachelor's and master's degrees that focus extensively on the education profession alone. Looking specifically at education-related careers, the partnership offers early childhood, middle childhood, early education intervention, curriculum and instruction, educational administration, sport education, school counseling, and educational technology.

LCCC has agreements and joint programs targeting the teacher workforce shortage with the Ohio Board of Regents (OBR), the Ohio Department of Education (ODE), the Northeast Ohio Consortium for Higher Education (NOCHE), the KnowledgeWorks Foundation, and the Bill and Melinda Gates Foundation. Eight teacher education strategies are currently being implemented:

- Diversifying the teacher workforce,
- Paraprofessional pathway,
- Regional collaboration,
- NOCHE best practices,
- Early College/KnowledgeWorks Foundation,
- Tech Prep education pathway,
- Teacher Preparation Exploration program, and
- Associate of Arts in Teacher Education (AAT).

Closely associated with the teacher preparation curriculum, the LCCC University Partnership Center helps students earn a bachelor's degree or graduate degree in various growing career fields, including teacher education. Begun in 1998, this innovative partnership among LCCC and eight universities enables students to seek degrees, without leaving Lorain County, from Ashland University, Bowling Green State University, Cleveland State University, Kent State University, Ohio University, The University of Akron, The University of Toledo, and Youngstown State University.

Lorain County Joint Vocational School (LCJVS) is the main secondary partner in this CCTI project. LCCC and LCJVS are both longtime contributors to regional workforce development initiatives geared to enhance economic stability and growth. LCJVS, co-located with the Adult Career Center, opened in 1971, serving an annual enrollment of more than 1,500 high school juniors and seniors in a range of career fields. LCJVS students are drawn from 13 school districts, including Amherst, Avon, Avon Lake, Clearview, Columbia, Elyria, Firelands, Keystone, Midview, North Ridgeville, Oberlin, Sheffield-Sheffield Lake, and Wellington. Students of LCJVS receive individualized hands-on learning experiences using modern equipment, with an emphasis on contextual learning. LCJVS emphasizes a well-balanced program of academics, technical experiences, and youth club activities.

The K-12 systems and LCJVS have a long-standing relationship with LCCC. This well-established relationship builds prior initiatives such as tech prep and Post Secondary Option Education (PSEO), Ohio's policy for accelerating college credit opportunities for high school students. In addition, LCCC is implementing an Early College with support from the Bill and Melinda Gates Foundation and the KnowledgeWorks Foundation. The success of these various initiatives depends on faculties of the various educational providers working together to develop curriculum, articulation agreements, and support systems for students.

Two years ago, LCJVS implemented the TEE program that is the focus of this CCTI project. In contrast to most LCJVS programs that are offered on its own site, TEE is taught on the campuses of the high schools where it is offered. As 3 of 13 school districts participating in TEE this year, Avon Local School District, Avon Lake City District, and Elyria City Schools are the key corporate secondary partners in the project.

During the life of the project, LCJVS and all 13 school districts associated with LCJVS are expected to

- Enhance and develop exemplary models of college and career transition strategies and program of study;
- Improve academic performance of students at both the secondary and postsecondary levels;
- Collect and report baseline information and outcomes assessment data about participating students; and
- Collect and report information about the site partnership's effectiveness in enhancing and developing exemplary models. To achieve anticipated outcomes, college and career transition strategies and programs of study will be identified, developed, benchmarked, and refined.

While the college's primary partner, LCJVS, includes students from 13 school districts, superintendents from 3 of these districts (Avon Local Schools, Elyria Local Schools, and Avon Lake City Schools) play a very specific role in the project. They serve as employer representatives on the Site Partnership Team and offer support by encouraging teachers to take the time and effort to sponsor a student teacher, logistically supporting their equipment and material needs (*e.g.*, copier, paper) and accommodating schedules. Employer representatives also attend CCTI Design Team meetings, advising particularly on activities related to employment and further education.

■ The success of these various initiatives depends on faculties of the various educational providers working together to develop curriculum, articulation agreements, and support systems for students.

History of the Partnership

In 1998, the Ohio Department of Education (ODE) moved from its traditional teacher certification program to a system of licensure. That change involved each four-year college and university offering programs of education to alter their existing curricula from a course-based to a competency-based one, in alignment with the National Council for the Accreditation of Teacher Education (NCATE) (see www.ncate.org).

Also in 1998-1999, the college revised its course offerings to move from a quarter to a semester course program and align them to new licensure standards of the State of Ohio, and this change took effect in the 1999-2000 academic year. Elements of the LCCC program have been modified to better articulate with four-year partners and accommodate changes from certification to licensure (see www.ode.state.oh.us/teaching-profession/teacher/certification_licensure). Germane to both LCCC and the four-year colleges are standards established by the Interstate New Teacher Assessment and Support Consortium (INTASC) (see www.ccsso.org/projects/interstate_new_teacher_assessment_and_support_consortium), and the standards adopted from these by NCATE. Additional standards that are influencing course development at LCCC are those set forth by the National Board of Professional Teaching Standards (NBPTS) (see www.nbpts.org). Alignment efforts have also been undertaken between high school coursework outcomes that match the State of Ohio Academic Standards (see www.ode.state.oh.us/academic_content)standards) and those of LCCC. These initiatives have centered on the college's involvement in the Early College program of the KnowledgeWorks Foundation (see www.kwfdn.org).

Moreover, LCCC's faculty has been involved with the Ohio Board of Regents (OBR) multilateral articulation initiative for teacher education, and in developing an associate of arts degree for paraprofessional classroom associates. To this end, LCCC has proposed a formal partnership with the University of Akron to offer a B.S. in Secondary Math Education leading to State of Ohio licensure in Grades 7 through 12 mathematics. Math and science personnel have been involved for some time with the National Science Foundation's efforts to improve the flow of candidates for the teaching field in mathematics and science. The partnership with Bowling Green State University that began in fall 2003 provides a B.S. in Biological Sciences, which students can use as a platform for additional courses in education, math, and science on a career path to licensure in Grades 7 through 12 Integrated Science. Core college faculty have been involved with ODE's process to establish new academic standards for Grades K through 12. This core includes faculty members from the math and science departments, the teacher education coordinator, the university partnership director, and the CCTI project director, who is also the chief academic officer of LCCC. However, efforts with the University of Akron have been delayed because of financial constraints on its part.

An application to the State of Ohio allowed LCCC to pursue three new teacher education pathways, substantially expanding LCCC's teacher education curriculum. One pathway leads to an Associate of Arts (AA) in Early Childhood Education that is differentiated from the existing Associate of Applied Science (AAS) degree in Early Childhood. A second pathway is for various other AA or Associate of Science (AS) teacher education programs that transfer to several regional four-year universities in the region. The third pathway is the new paraprofessional licensure area, and this one culminates in early childhood education and K-12 transfer programs.

In recent years, ODE and OBR have collaborated to create a range of opportunities for secondary schools, joint vocational schools, and community and technical colleges to enhance the state's capacity to prepare new teachers. Well positioned to deal with teacher education, LCCC is one of only three community colleges in the state that submitted a proposal to further develop its teacher education curriculum. LCCC has been successful in acquiring other state funding, such as a $50,000 grant from ODE and OBR to conduct three convening sessions with Akron University, Kent State University, and other institutions. The goal of this grant was to develop core coursework in teacher education that is transferable to regional universities, which resulted in a proposal for four courses in the professional education arena. Through this and other new initiatives and its historic commitments, LCCC demonstrates a strong commitment to teacher preparation, including creating opportunities for high school students to explore teaching careers and engage in postsecondary coursework at LCCC and partner universities that will prepare them to be K-12 teachers.

The Model Career Pathway

In 2000, well before CCTI, LCJVS, with the support of its associate K-12 school districts, approached LCCC and its Social Sciences Division with the notion of creating a high-school-to-college career exploration program in the education field. Aspiring to create an innovative learning experience for high school students, local officials adopted the idea of addressing the region's growing teacher shortage. Continuing their long history of working together on workforce development issues, a joint initiative involving LCJVS and LCCC emerged through the formation of the Lorain County Education and Training Consortium.

As a formal organization, the Education and Training Consortium has secured approximately $2.7 million in training contracts to local employers. The consortium expanded access to resources by the partner institutions, increased the level of service to employers, and created opportunities for new program development. The partnership expanded beyond providers of higher and adult education to include community organizations such as the former Ohio Bureau of Employment Services, the County Department of Human Services, and Lorain

County Employment and Training Administration. Later, LCCC and LCJVS included the Lorain County Chamber of Commerce and the Center for Leadership in Education and formed the Workforce Institute of Lorain County. The Workforce Institute is a private, nonprofit, facilitated creation of The Employment netWork, Lorain County's one-stop system. In 2001, Lorain County's Workforce Investment Board officially designated the Workforce Institute as the region's one-stop operator.

Over recent years, LCJVS and LCCC have expanded services to meet employer needs, and they have linked to other workforce and economic development initiatives in the county and the region. The current emphasis on teacher education and CCTI is a prime example of how the consortium's initiatives have grown beyond their initial workforce development goals and included K-12 in fundamental educational initiatives.

The TEE program represents the centerpiece of CCTI and is the crown jewel of the region's current workforce development initiative. The mission of TEE is "to encourage interested high school seniors to enter the teacher profession by providing them with the support and training necessary for success as both students and teachers." TEE has the following goals for students:

- Ensure readiness and exposure to college.
- Provide education related to teaching and learning.
- Provide internship experiences under the guidance of an experienced teacher.
- Promote a positive attitude toward teaching.

■ The current emphasis on teacher education and CCTI is a prime example of how the consortium's initiatives have grown beyond their initial workforce development goals and included K-12 in fundamental educational initiatives.

Students can apply to TEE if they meet attendance and academic requirements, including enrollment in the college prep curriculum, passing all proficiency tests, passing all required courses for on-time graduation, and having a minimum GPA of 2.5. Attendance requirements are missing 10 days or less in three semesters during 10th grade and the first semester of 11th grade. Students have to obtain two teacher or counselor recommendations if attendance or GPA are in question. Finally, students must be responsible for their own transportation to LCCC and internship sites.

In terms of student benefits for enrolling in TEE, students receive three high school credits for classroom work and internship experience in Grades K through 12. Upon high school graduation and matriculation to LCCC, TEE students who maintain a B average in the program can earn six college-credit semester hours toward their teaching degree through an articulation agreement: three credits for an Educational Technology course, one credit for College 101, and two credits for the Introduction to the Teaching Professions course. Students have the option of earning an additional college credit if they take the Adventure Challenge course. Further, students earn hands-on K-8 classroom experience during their internships, and they get to meet other students from the 13 Lorain County high schools. To facilitate their decisions about college, students visit area colleges, attend seminars, and hear a variety of speakers in the field of education. Opportunities for youth club participation and speaking engagements are available to students, and students enhance their computer literacy skills by participating in an online component of TEE. Finally, students complete a professional portfolio that is intended to enhance their application to college.

LCJVS transports a program to its feeder schools, where the TEE program is taught on the high school campuses. TEE students complete field experiences four days a week at a designated school within their district, including internships in K-3, middle school, and special education classrooms. Students also have one placement of their choice (*e.g.*, high school, subject specific), so while other, non-TEE students go to LCJVS for their occupational training, TEE students complete their training at feeder schools. In 2002, LCJVS received a grant for leadership training for $3,000, in support of the TEE program. The grant for leadership training was used to provide experiential leadership training to TEE students who participated in LCCC's Adventure Challenge, an educational resource that combines physical challenges via a ropes course with quantum learning techniques.

Four secondary teachers staff the TEE program through faculty appointments at LCJVS, and at least one teacher provides on-campus student support at LCCC five days a week. Office space is provided for the secondary TEE instructors at both LCJVS and LCCC. In addition to these personnel, LCCC employs one full-time advisor for the CCTI students as they transition to the associate's degree. An LCCC advisor is the contact for LCCC on the CCTI project, and time is dedicated to coordinating the project at LCCC and with LCJVS and partner schools. LCCC provides classrooms and computer laboratory facilities for TEE students and teachers to meet on site one day a week. These meetings bring students from all Lorain County school districts, including the three school districts that act as corporate partners.

Curriculum and Instruction

Classroom instruction is enhanced with distance learning technology that is used for students to communicate with their teachers; submit assignments; and receive feedback, grades, and instructions. TEE teachers participate in staff development provided by the Ohio CTE Department, with funding from LCJVS. Two meetings per year are required as part of the pilot TEE program.

Work-based learning (WBL) is a core instructional strategy associated with the TEE program, including student rotations through a variety of educational settings and facilities. Internships are conducted by the Avon Lake Schools, Avon Lake City Schools, Elyria City Schools, and other school districts in the area. These districts encourage teachers to sponsor a student teacher, supporting equipment and supply needs and accommodating schedules. LCJVS, the University Partnership, LCCC's Learning Resource Center, and Ashland University's Education Media Lab all lend support and services to TEE, encouraging the use of technology in the classroom.

Instructors from the high schools and LCCC have formed a curriculum design team to align the secondary curriculum with the postsecondary entrance requirements and to identify contextual learning activities that can serve as an intervention strategy. Professional development has been scheduled for high school and college faculty focused on curriculum development and contextual learning. Training in curriculum design, personality profiling using Myers-Briggs Types Indicator instrumentation, assessments, reflective coaching, and team-based mentoring occurred in spring 2004. In addition, leadership and team building took place in conjunction with the Early College high school initiative.

A concerted effort has been made to establish a small learning-community approach and small group supplemental instruction, including developing articulation agreements that allow students to transcript college credit after they graduate from high school and enroll at LCCC. Career development, supplemental instruction in math and writing, and general study skills are a few of the many support services and activities that are associated with articulated courses.

Strategies that have been introduced to reduce students' remediation include small group and individualized tutoring led by tutors from the LCCC Individualized Learning Center, providing students access to an online writing center coordinated by the LCCC English faculty, and offering computerized tutorials using Skills Bank 4 Software in LCCC's Individualized Learning Center.

Bridges With Four-Year Programs

Several of the degree programs use a 3+1 or 2.5+1.5 format, allowing students to do most of their coursework at LCCC's University Partnership Center, where they pay a reduced community college tuition rate. Specifically related to teacher education, students are able to obtain a bachelor's degree in teaching from Ashland University through the university partnership, and there is a proposal with the University of Akron to offer a B.S. in Secondary Math Education. Another proposal partners LCCC teacher education programs with Bowling Green State University on a B.S. in Biological Sciences.

Student Support

This CCTI partnership places a high value on student support services to enhance enrollment and persistence, including ongoing and structured academic advising and personalized support services for students in the TEE program. Services include financial aid and course registration support; ongoing college orientation activities; individual advising sessions, including tutoring, mentoring, and career development; early-alert techniques that track student performance in the classroom; and interfaces with other LCCC retention and support initiatives, including the Opening Doors project conducted by Manpower Development Research Corporation (MDRC) and Bridges to Success.

Also, high school and college faculty and counseling staff were formed into a Support Services Design Team to support the small learning community. This team also identified support services necessary to ensure student success and to design an implementation plan. To measure the effectiveness of these enrollment and persistence plans, an Institutional Planning and Research Team designed a consistent, frequent feedback process for students to provide input.

Special Features

- Teacher Education Exploration (TEE) program
- The University Partnership program, which brings eight universities to the LCCC campus
- Three new teacher education pathways: the Associate of Arts in Early Childhood Education; A.A. or Associate of Science teacher education programs that transfer to several regional four-year universities in the region; and a paraprofessional licensure area that can culminate in the early childhood education and K-12 transfer programs
- Online delivery strategies
- Internship (work-based learning) used as core instructional strategy
- Professional development opportunities associated with the CCTI project and other complimentary grants

The Implementation Strategies

The CCTI project emphasizes implementation strategies listed in the table on page 50 to attain the five CCTI objectives.

This CCTI partnership places a high value on student support services to enhance enrollment and persistence, including ongoing and structured academic advising and personalized support services for students in the TEE program.

Lorain County Community College CCTI Program

CCTI Objective	Key Strategies
Decreased need for remediation at postsecondary level	• Assess the basic skill needs of 12th grade TEE program participants using COMPASS, a computerized adaptive test that measures skills in reading, writing, and math to determine college readiness. • Coordinate professional development activities for partner high school and college faculty using Early College professional development activities and publications of the National Council on Student Development. • Use learning community approaches and small group supplemental instruction as intervention strategies for the TEE cohort. • Develop evaluative measures.
Increased enrollment and persistence in postsecondary education	• Partner with the TEE high school program to enroll and prepare education majors at LCCC. • Provide ongoing and structured academic advising, social, and personalized support services to cohort. • Articulate 4+2 program with assistance from CORD to improve cohort transitions from high school to LCCC. • Develop evaluative measures.
Increased academic and skill achievement at the secondary and postsecondary levels	• Identify the essential learning outcomes needed by TEE cohort graduates for certification and licensure in the State of Ohio, drawing on information from the National Board of Professional Teaching and Standards (NBPTS). • Identify accelerated learning opportunities, including dual credit. • Develop evaluative measures.
Increased attainment of postsecondary degrees, certificates, or other recognized credentials	• Enroll a cohort of teacher education majors from the LCJVS TEE program, drawing on NOCHE best practices; conduct site visits to institutions with demonstrated success. • Expand course and degree offerings for education majors to ensure the AAT is developed in conjunction with ODE regulations and federal No Child Left Behind legislation. • Develop evaluative measures.
Increased entry into employment or further education	• Support students to achieve Ohio licensure for Grades 4 through 9 or high school in math, science, special education, or foreign languages. • Provide cohort members with opportunities to enhance professional development, including worksite learning experiences. • Develop evaluative measures.

Most Effective Strategies

Among the specific implementation strategies, this CCTI partnership is particularly proud of the following.

COMPASS testing. Students took the COMPASS placement test the fall of their senior year. For those who needed it, remediation and tutoring in English and math were provided when the TEE students were on campus. Students retook the COMPASS in April to measure their improvement and determine their readiness for college. Fall results showed 43 percent were at college level in math, 82 percent in reading, and 73 percent in writing. After remediation, spring retest results showed improvement, with 57 percent of the students being college ready in math, 93 percent in reading, and 89 percent in writing.

***Human resource decisions tied to curriculum development*.** The CCTI project identifies master teachers who are engaged in the development of new education and training courses at LCCC. These master teachers develop innovative courses and initiatives in the education and training pathway to prepare students for greater success in careers and college.

***The Joint Center for Policy Research (JCPR) of LCCC*.** The JCPR coordinates the administration of HSSSE and CCSSE with respective partner schools, including working with LCJVS. Further, the JCPR works with partners to continuously assess local partner capacity to deliver and to ensure that intended outcomes are attained. Ultimately, the JCPR will be responsible for reporting to the League and to CCTI partners. The HSSSE was given to the 106 students in the 2003-2004 TEE cohort. The most notable result was that the cohort reported greater teacher-student interaction than the national CCTI cohort, and this result was statistically significant. Most other indicators were significantly above the national CCTI cohort. Moreover, the JCPR has been instrumental in gathering and reporting additional results, such as results of the CCTI partners' and TEE instructors' site survey. Findings from these surveys showed notable accomplishments for the 2003-2004 school year in terms of increased enrollment in the TEE program, rising from 106 to 122 students from all 13 districts in Lorain County; increased collaboration among the partners; and a strong commitment to being on task and on time with the (CCTI) project.

***Professional development*.** CCTI is collaborating with CORD to develop additional career pathways and guide the work of the master teachers. CORD's expertise includes designing curriculum, developing new learning tools, delivering professional development, creating applications of educational technology, and conducting educational research and evaluation.

Least Effective Strategies

Articulation is viewed as a vitally important strategy to increase enrollment and persistence by further aligning programs of study with postsecondary entry requirements and state academic requirements. Despite support for the idea, the CCTI project has experienced difficulties in being able to establish agreements with the K-12 districts to award dual credit. Instead, deferred credits via articulation agreements have dominated. Reasons for this approach are tied primarily to funding concerns, *i.e.*, funding follows the students, therefore K-12 schools lose funding when their students enroll in college-level courses. As a result, advanced placement courses have flourished in local high schools, even though this strategy is not thought to be as optimal as dual credit. Some attempts have been made to find funding formulas that will allow for cost sharing between the K-12 and LCCC, though these efforts are still in initial stages.

The career pathway extending from 9th grade to the community college has not been possible in this CCTI project, because the reach of LCJVS does not extend to the starting grade level of high school. CCTE Design Team members have recognized the importance of starting the career pathway course sequence as early as possible, but do not have the authority to make curriculum changes or enforce courses upon students enrolled in their home high schools. A solution that is being considered by this CCTI project is to begin offering career awareness activities, including using the Individualized Career Plan to help students plan their program of study during the early high school years.

Plans for the Future

A new organization, the National Association of Community College Teacher Education Programs, has been formed to spearhead the effort to investigate and advocate a more comprehensive role for community colleges in the area of teacher education. LCCC personnel have been engaged with this organization, and further involvement is foreseen.

Lessons Learned

This CCTI project has identified several lessons that may be useful to others implementing similar teacher training programs.

Incorporate College 101 material into students' portfolios and provide LCCC-bound students with a summer orientation in order to address remediation problems. Also, it is important to review the remediation strategy as follows:

1. Develop a matrix of assessments to track students' progress, including OGT, ACT, SAT, and COMPASS.
2. Test students early (spring of 11th grade) using the COMPASS placement test for English, reading, and math.

3. Meet with students, parents, TEE instructors, and guidance counselors regarding students who require remediation in late spring.
4. Develop individualized plans for
   - Student requests for fourth year of math;
   - Scheduling math and English remediation minisessions on days other than seminar days;
   - Assessing students more frequently to measure their progress;
   - Ending remediation when students assess as college ready; and
   - Developing remediation plans early.

Develop a professional development writing workshop for TEE instructors with LCCC English faculty regarding writing assessments and consistency in grading students' work.

Develop innovative, low-cost ways to build learning communities among former TEE students who are attending LCCC and other colleges. Form a subcommittee from the Site Partnership Team to develop ideas and plans for ways to build the on-campus learning community. Some preliminary ideas include developing consistent online communications such as email, a web page cybercafé, or weblogs, or using the Angel course management system.

To facilitate the creation of viable career pathways that start at the 9th grade, assist students in identifying teaching as a career choice as early as 8th and 9th grade. Pilot the Meta Morph online career guidance system, developed at Sinclair Community College, in some 9th grade high school English classes. Host regional career pathway institutes use the CORD framework to communicate teacher education career pathways statewide to

- Area students and parents;
- K-12 school districts, vocational schools, and community colleges in the northeast Ohio area and other regions of the state; and
- The Ohio Department of Education.

To facilitate student transition to college, introduce more articulation credit opportunities or change articulated credit to dual credit at no cost to the school districts. With dual credit, both the high school and college credits and grades appear on the transcripts. Form a subcommittee to align the TEE program curriculum with the Praxis domains and the postsecondary course outcomes.

Strengths, Challenges, and Recommendations

The major strength of this CCTI project is the TEE program. The program offers high school students an opportunity to intern in teaching experiences in K-12 settings, enabling them to prepare for the coursework they will need to take in college to become teachers, and to make informed decisions about whether

The [TEE] program offers high school students an opportunity to intern...in K-12 settings, enabling them to...make informed decisions about whether teaching will be a rewarding career for them.

teaching will be a rewarding career for them. By drawing upon the collective resources of several K-12 districts, LCJVS, and LCCC, the region is able to engage in a curricular innovation that has the potential to produce new teachers who remain connected to the area and integral to addressing the teaching shortage.

Student support services. Another strength of this particular early, accelerated teacher education model is its commitment to provide support for students in the form of a wide range of student services and activities. The student support services of highest import to students are geared toward enhancing enrollment and persistence, involving academic advising and personalized support services, including financial aid and course registration support; college orientation; individual advising sessions, including tutoring, mentoring, and career development; early alert techniques that track student performance; and interfaces with other LCCC retention and support initiatives.

Learning communities. The conceptualization of small learning communities as part of the TEE program is another strength. Student support services that are necessary to ensure student success are part of these learning communities. Evaluation is tied to them, with support for this effort coming from LCCC's Institutional Planning and Research Team and the Joint Center for Policy Research (JCPR).

Ohio Graduation Test. Because of newly implemented state standards for graduation and the high-stakes high school graduation test, the Ohio Graduation Test, students have limited time for elective courses. To meet the new graduation requirements, the state requires college prep academics in math, science, language arts, and social studies for students who enroll in a career technology block. Because of the increased Carnegie units required in academics for graduation, local officials balk at implementing plans for the initiative, including adding the junior year to this senior-year-only program. To further challenge the initiative, some of the comprehensive high schools associated with the TEE program have added more credit requirements to the new minimum requirement of 21 Carnegie units in 2003, and 22 Carnegie units in 2004. Moreover, state standards and state testing constitute a major priority for the state, acting in alignment with the NCLB legislation. As a consequence, raising student scores on the Ohio Graduation Test is a priority. In fact, the focus for most districts is to prepare students to pass the Ohio Graduation Test in 10th grade, and little room is thought to remain in students' programs of study for electives at the 9th and 10th grades, beyond the requirement that students take a technology course and a sequence of courses in foreign language. As a result, the teacher education career pathway is difficult to move back or expand into the 9th and 10th grades.

Funding structure. Another issue, mentioned previously, is that the dollars follow the students in the state of Ohio. Therefore, dual credit courses equate to a loss of revenue for the secondary schools. Funding formulas need to be created that will enable the CCTI project activities to be sustained past the life of the grant. Some of the activities that require additional long-term funding are

- Recruiting new students (high school juniors);
- Expanding recruitment and awareness into the earlier grades;
- Easing the transition from high school to college through teacher education scholarships; and
- Purchasing student assessments such as the Learning and Study Skills Inventory to measure students' readiness for college.

Indeed, local school district issues go far deeper than too-limited funding to maximize the desired outcomes for the CCTI project. Of the 13 school districts involved in the Lorain JVS TEE program, only 1 approved its school levy during the 2003-2004 academic year, with 1 local district being taken over by the state. Some school districts have threatened to cut back on the number of students they allow to participate in programs at LCJVS, because the revenue per student FTE follows the student. Clearly, any decisions to cut back on the number of TEE students would mean a corresponding cut in the number of TEE teachers. Fortunately, the CCTI partners are determined to increase the number of TEE students from their districts, since they see this as an investment in potential future employees.

More information about Lorain County Community College and the CCTI Initiative can be found at http://www.league.org/league/projects/ccti/projects/summary.cfm?key=lcc.

■ **CCTI has been the catalyst for developing a career pathway in teacher education that aligns the policy, programmatic, and curricular levels for students in the Maricopa Community Colleges and the state of Arizona. The strength of this alignment lies in the quality partnerships developed between the K-12 school districts, community colleges, and the Arizona Department of Education. The result of this pathway is a better prepared, committed student in the teacher preparation pipeline.**

Cheri St. Arnauld, Director, National Association of Community College Teacher Education Programs, Maricopa Community Colleges

Maricopa Community Colleges

Debra D. Bragg and Elisabeth Barnett

OCCUPATIONAL AREA:	Education and Training
CAREER PATHWAY:	Teaching and Training
CCTI PROJECT DIRECTORS:	Cheri St. Arnauld, Project Coordinator
SCHOOL PARTNERS:	Peoria Unified School District (Five High Schools)
	Teacher Prep Charter High School
	ACE Program (South Mountain Community College
COLLEGE PARTNERS:	Estrella Mountain Community College
	Phoenix College
	South Mountain Community College
CORPORATE PARTNERS:	Career and Technical Education Division, Arizona Department of Education
	Arizona Business and Education Coalition

The Project Partners

The Maricopa Community College District is committed to fulfilling its College and Career Transition Initiatives project to align secondary and postsecondary education to develop seamless pathways for students in the education and training career cluster area. The focus of the Maricopa Community College District's CCTI project is the development of a coherent, articulated sequence of rigorous academic and career pathway courses. The project uses the Arizona Department of Education (ADE) Career and Technical Education (CTE) Division's Education Professions program and the Maricopa Associate in Arts in Elementary Education Degree (AAEE) program as the springboard for addressing the goals of the project. Three of Maricopa's 10 colleges participate. Estrella Mountain Community College, South Mountain Community College, and Phoenix College have identified a cohort of high school students with whom they work to implement the strategies to achieve the intended outcomes of this CCTI project.

Maricopa County Community College District (Maricopa) is one of the largest education systems of its kind in the nation. The college district recently celebrated its 40th year. Originally attached to the Phoenix Union High School District, Phoenix College became a separate entity in 1963, and a cycle of rapid growth began. By 2002, the district had 10 colleges, 2 skill centers, 15 large educational centers, and more than 200 teaching sites. The curriculum offerings of the colleges in the district are vast, including seven associate degrees, 900 certificates of completion, and almost 10,000 courses. Flexible course delivery includes online, televised, traditional classroom, hybrid, mail, accelerated, evening, weekend, and open-entry open-exit choices. Transfer agreements with public and private colleges and universities enable seamless transitions to four-year institutions. Maricopa is also the home of the Center for Workforce Development, the largest provider of job training in Arizona.

Specifically addressing the education and training cluster, Maricopa provides educational and training services to more than a quarter of a million students every year. The diverse student body represents the variety of ages, interests, backgrounds, and ethnic mix of the Maricopa County population of 3,200,000 inhabitants. Of all high school graduates in Maricopa County, 45 percent attend one of the Maricopa colleges within one year of graduation. The mission of Maricopa is to create and continuously improve affordable, accessible, effective, and safe learning environments for the lifelong educational needs of the diverse communities served.

Maricopa's National Center for Teacher Education currently provides leadership on local, state, and national level for the recruitment, preparation, and retention of high-quality and diverse pre-K-12 teachers. In doing so, the colleges are well aligned with state priorities. Governor Janet Napolitano, in her State of the State address on January 13, 2004, made this declaration:

> To build the new Arizona of our highest aspirations, we must enhance our commitment to Arizona's children and their education. This is where we stake our claim. This is where we create our legacy. In the new Arizona, every Arizona child must start first grade safe, healthy, and ready to learn. As children advance through school, they must obtain the skills they will need to succeed in the 21st century. And after they graduate from high school, they must have access to technical and vocational training, to community colleges, and to universities. (Barnett, 2004)

She emphasized the importance of having highly trained, dedicated teachers in every classroom. Concurring with her vision, Maricopa's board of directors has made teacher preparation a top priority.

The three Maricopa community colleges involved in the project are Estrella Mountain Community College (EMCC), Phoenix College (PC), and South Mountain Community College (SMCC), and the emphasis of each community college partner pertains to teacher education. The selected colleges demonstrate commitment to teacher preparation, have existing relationships with high schools, and express a willingness to carry out all planned activities related to CCTI. Particularly noteworthy is that all of the colleges serve high numbers of Latino students, a group that is underrepresented in the teaching profession.

Estrella Mountain Community College (EMCC) offers a variety of teacher education programs that transfer to a four-year university, including the AAEE statewide degree that transfers to any of Arizona's public and private universities and the Associate Transfer Partnership Degree (ATP) for elementary education that offers two pathways. One transfers to Arizona State University (ASU) West campus, and the other transfers to ASU Main campus. A third option is the Associate in Arts Degree with Special Requirements (AASR), which is appropriate for students pursuing a degree in elementary education, secondary education, or special education. This degree will transfer to any Arizona university. All of these degree programs are designed for students whose goal is to become a classroom teacher or an instructional aide.

These degrees may also lead to a Bachelor of Arts Degree in Elementary Education. EMCC offers an AAS degree that transfers to a Bachelor's in Applied Science Degree (BAS) for students who want to become instructional aids or paraprofessionals who need to meet current federal regulations. The inspire.teach program is a 2+2+2 curriculum with the first 2 representing the last two years of high school, the middle 2 representing two years at EMCC, and the last 2 representing the final two years at the ASU West campus. The inspire.teach program prepares students to excel in the teaching profession, including encouraging underrepresented groups to explore teaching careers with the goal of increasing the number of diverse professionals within Arizona's education workforce. For the CCTI project, EMCC is partnered with Peoria Unified School District. The high schools include Cactus, Centennial, Ironwood, Peoria, and Sunrise Mountain.

Phoenix College directs its teacher education programs to preparing students who want to pursue a four-year degree in elementary education (K-8), early childhood (pre-K-3), special education (K-12), or secondary education (7-12). Students enroll in general studies and lower division education requirements at PC and transfer to various four-year institutions. The statewide AAEE degree is offered at PC, and all credits associated with this degree transfer to any of Arizona's public universities. The Urban Teacher Corps (UTC), a teacher development program housed at PC, supports and encourages urban classified school district employees as they matriculate from any of the 10 Maricopa Community Colleges, transfer to ASU, obtain Arizona teacher certification, and return to their school districts as teachers. The PC Future Teachers Club provides support activities for future elementary and secondary educators through service learning projects with local schools, informational meetings with university advisors, mentoring relationships with PC faculty, and contact with dynamic educational leaders in the community. For the CCTI project, PC is engaged in a partnership with the Teacher Prep Charter High School.

■ **The inspire.teach program prepares students to excel in the teaching profession, including encouraging underrepresented groups to explore teaching careers with the goal of increasing the number of diverse professionals within Arizona's education workforce.**

South Mountain Community College offers the Dynamic Learning Teacher Education Program in partnership with the College of Education at ASU. This cohort model effort involves a structured two-step bachelor's degree program for small numbers of future teachers. Students complete the two-year Dynamic

Learning Teacher Education Program at SMCC and then transfer to the Initial Teacher Certification Program at ASU. Many courses are offered at SMCC and its other locations, including courses directed at upgrading the skills of practicing teachers or fulfilling degree and certificate requirements. SMCC's ACE Program is its secondary partner.

The **secondary schools and related programs** (Peoria Unified School District five high schools, Teacher Prep Charter High School and SMCC's ACE Program) were selected by the community colleges involved with the project. Priority was given to schools with which the selected community colleges had already established joint initiatives in teacher education. Articulated programs, dual-credit courses, academic advisement, and student mentoring have been implemented by most of these schools in association with the selected community colleges. Five of the participating high schools participated in the Arizona Department of Education (ADE), Career and Technical Education (CTE) Education Professions program implemented during the 2003-2004 school year. Following the lead of several teachers who researched high school curricula related to the teacher preparation, Arizona adopted the South Carolina-based Teacher Cadet model. This curriculum prepares high school graduates to become certified as classroom paraprofessionals, and it aligns with the colleges' introductory courses in education.

The Model Career Pathway

Maricopa's National Center for Teacher Education, created in 2001, is housed in the Maricopa Community College District Office and is working to enhance the preparation of teachers at three levels: local, state, and national. The center provided leadership for the development of teacher education programs at the 10 independent Maricopa campuses, which actively articulate with several feeder high schools as well as with three campuses of Arizona State University. The AAEE statewide degree program is described by administrators as a seamless transfer model. Implemented for the first time during the 2003 fall semester, the AAEE is a key component of Maricopa's CCTI project. This degree plan is covered by a statewide articulation agreement, so all credits transfer to any college of education in the state, with students entering at the junior level.

A related initiative is the Teacher Education Partnership Commission, a joint effort of Maricopa, local K-12 school districts, the business community, and representatives of state and local government, created to provide leadership in improving teacher recruitment, retention, and quality. Three subcommittees set annual action goals related to teacher preparation, diversity, and collaboration.

Results of the CCTI project are expected to have implications for state policy on teacher education and meeting the requirements of the No Child Left Behind Act (NCLB) federal legislation. In addition to the development of the AAEE degree, the National Center for Teacher Education (NCTE), now in its third year, provides leadership for planning for the education and certification of classroom paraprofessionals. The Maricopa Community Colleges have worked with the state to select two tests, ParaPro and WorkKeys, to certify paraprofessionals, and the staff is involved in research projects to inform policy, particularly crosswalking various sets of standards, curricula, and exams. The NCTE was created to "[serve] in a leadership role for pre-K-12 teacher education initiatives, working collaboratively with community colleges, business, education, government, and community leaders to develop programs and services that support the community college role in teacher education, locally, nationally, and internationally" (NCTE mission statement).

Curriculum and Instruction

The ADE Education Professions curriculum framework is designed to prepare secondary students for employment or postsecondary opportunities in the education field. The ADE Education Professions curriculum was introduced in the 2003-2004 school year as one of the secondary CTE programs, and it emphasizes education career choices and delivers instruction in education structure and systems, theory, pedagogy, human developmental stages, learning styles, and instructional strategies. The program also provides interactive experiences with students at different age levels, in a variety of content areas in education environments. The Education Professions curriculum framework is designed to articulate with the Introduction to Education courses in Maricopa's AAEE degree program and other paraprofessional certificate and degree programs. The AAEE program currently enrolls students in the elementary education, special education, and paraprofessional options. The curriculum framework for Education Professions may be accessed at the Arizona Tech Prep website, http://www.aztechprep.org/.

Maricopa's CCTI partnership has developed the statewide Arizona P-12 Teacher Education Career Model. In developing this model, NCTE worked with Arizona's community college districts to identify education courses within the statewide AAEE program that are appropriate for dual enrollment within the Arizona P-12 Teacher Education Career Model. The AAEE courses are articulated through community college dual-enrollment agreements with secondary and postsecondary entities on a county-by-county basis. The AAEE is articulated for transfer with all of Arizona's public university B.A. in Elementary Education degree programs. Many of Arizona's private universities also enter into AAEE articulation agreements.

By the end of 2006, NCTE plans to integrate an Associate in Transfer Partnership (ATP) degree specifically for Maricopa secondary teacher education students into the Arizona P-12 Teacher Education Career Model. The ATP degree is an articulated academic program of study established among the student, public universities, and the community college the student attends. The various ATP programs provide two-year college students with additional dual-enrollment options as they pursue secondary, special education, or other specialized teaching credentials.

Several other aspects of the teacher preparation programs at Maricopa are particularly noteworthy.

Future Teacher Clubs. Maricopa works closely with future teacher clubs from partner high schools and community colleges. Future Teacher Conferences are held to provide students with career, higher education, and professional opportunities.

Early Assessment. The Arizona P-12 Teacher Education Career Model offers benchmarks for mandatory assessment, advising, and additional preparation to assure student success and persistence. Secondary students enrolled in the ADE Education Professions program are provided with early assessment for community college course placement in the 11th or 12th grade. Community college course-placement assessments are administered during the first semester of enrollment in the program. ACCUPLACER, a computer-adaptive instrument used to assess skills in reading, English, and mathematics, is used for placement. The scores are available immediately.

Individualized College and Career Plan. Information from early course-placement assessment is used by students from secondary and postsecondary institutions to develop individualized college and career plans. The plans provide a framework for meeting individual student academic needs and education career goals, and they develop a rigorous path of academic coursework. Once developed, the high school-college partnership team determines resources needed to meet the needs of and achieve the goals for each student. Resources from the student's high school, linked community college, and local or state community partners are used to meet needs and goals.

Electronic Portfolios. The Arizona P-12 Teacher Education Career Model has established concurrent secondary and postsecondary professional development opportunities for all faculty, academic advisors, and administrators. To date, faculty have received concurrent and individualized training for an e-portfolio system, which is a tool for engaging in conversations within this project. E-portfolios assist students and faculty participating in the Arizona P-12 Teacher Education Career Model implementation process. This project's secondary and postsecondary students use TaskStream to create portfolios, and faculty use portfolio templates to assess students' portfolios online. TaskStream is also used to create and share standards-based lessons and units that include assessment rubrics. The Web Folio Builder allows students to create, organize, and share electronic portfolios that demonstrate standards compliance. To eliminate or assist with transitional issues as students move through the teacher education program, the e-portfolio is aligned with project high schools, community colleges, and universities preparing future teachers in Arizona. Information about e-portfolios can be reviewed at www.taskstream.com.

Special Features

- Leadership by the National Center for Teacher Education
- High priority placed on alignment of curriculum and other supporting components:
  - o Arizona secondary standards with the ACCUPLACER test (used by the college as a placement test)
  - o The Education Professions program with the AAEE introductory course objectives
  - o The ParaPro and WorkKeys tests with the ACCUPLACER test
  - o Dual-enrollment opportunities for students in the education foundations courses and content courses at each respective high school
  - o The AAEE coursework, with the first of two tests taken by aspiring teachers in Arizona, the Arizona Educator Proficiency Assessment (AEPA)
- Crosswalk between the Education Professions curriculum and the Arizona secondary standards
- Ongoing discussions with key stakeholders to (1) close gaps between systems; and (2) inform high schools and colleges about alignment between the recommended curricula (Education Professions, AAEE) and the gate-keeping exams (ParaPro, WorkKeys, and AEPA)
- Professional development activities, including (1) 90-minute presentation on CCTI at CTE conference; (2) training on TaskStream e-portfolio software; (3) e-portfolio faculty project to build a template for teacher education faculty; and (4) the Arizona Instrument to Measure Standards (AIMS) Maricopa faculty summer project to determine assessments for incoming students and crosswalk content and course competencies with standards

Bridges With Four-Year Programs

The teacher preparation program at Maricopa is positioned to make important and lasting contributions at the local, state, and national levels, especially influencing the ways that high schools, community colleges, and university-based colleges of education work together. The groundwork laid by this program will also be of great benefit as degrees in special education and secondary education are developed in the near future. Plans include implementing the Arizona P-12 Teacher Education Career Model with all the teacher education programs in Maricopa, and sharing this continuum model with other education profession programs and community colleges from around the state. The goal is to develop a well-aligned teacher education pathway to support purposeful recruitment, persistence through the pathway, and baccalaureate completion.

The Implementation Strategies

To attain the five CCTI objectives, the CCTI project emphasizes the implementation strategies listed in the table on page 63.

Maricopa Community Colleges CCTI Program

CCTI Objective	Key Strategies
Decreased need for remediation at postsecondary level	• Test participating high school students using ASSET to assess college readiness. • Develop individual student plans for students not ready for college work, based on the recommendations of a committee of high school and college faculty and counselors, including extra coursework at the high school, remedial coursework provided by the college, tutoring, or other options. Approximately $200 to $300 is made available to support participating students.
Increased enrollment and persistence in postsecondary education	• Implement more aggressive recruitment of high school students into the AAEE program. • Give high school students, faculty, and counselors more information and training about the AAEE and other Maricopa teacher education programs; encourage increased numbers of students to take advantage of the AAEE degree option because of its rigor and easy transferability to four-year institutions. • Offer dual-enrollment options in education or other subject areas.
Increased academic and skill achievement at the secondary and postsecondary levels	• Participating high schools and colleges will receive access to TaskStream, a web-based tool that allows students to demonstrate content competencies and develop career goals, as well as allowing instructors to design lessons and units and map them to different sets of standards, develop electronic portfolios and web pages for students, and share curriculum resource collections. TaskStream portfolios are expected to transfer seamlessly to Maricopa and to ASU.
Increased attainment of postsecondary degrees, certificates, or other recognized credentials	• The goal of this effort is to develop a continuum of electronic portfolios among high schools, community colleges, and universities. This effort will allow for the progressive growth and assessment of students' knowledge and skills and become the catalyst for continued dialogue among faculty. • Develop a pre-career test at the end of high school that will allow students to be qualified as paraprofessionals. • Develop Individual Career Plans for students to support persistence through degree attainment.
Increased entry into employment or further education	• The AAEE is articulated for transfer with Arizona's public university B.A. in Elementary Education degree programs. Many of Arizona's private universities enter into AAEE articulation agreements. • Increase the number of paraprofessionals available for classroom employment.

Most Effective Strategies

Implement alignment efforts. The success of this project is the ability to be systemic in the state of Arizona. The project elements were aligned on a statewide policy level and on a college-to-college programmatic level, and among faculty within the project using e-portfolios as the vehicle to discuss competencies and assessment across the systems.

Establish key partnerships. Nothing can be done alone. Identifying common goals with groups and individuals will strengthen the project and broaden stakeholders. Partnerships have been central in moving this project forward from a high-school-to-college program into a statewide career pathway. Each partner has a genuine interest in seeing the project succeed.

Share the big picture. Everyone involved in the project needs to know what the big picture of the project is and how it pertains to each participating group. Bringing partners together to fully understand the project vision has been vital to this project's success. Each partner is an important piece of the puzzle, but they need to know how and why everything fits together. Developing one consistent message around alignment was the driver for this project.

Least Effective Strategies

Starting too big. Starting with many partners can be a problem. It is better to start with a small core group of individuals and build partnerships slowly as the program expands. Bringing on everyone at once can lead to communication problems.

Lacking clear expectations. Individuals are most concerned with their individual role within a project. From the beginning, having clear outcomes that affect the partners within the project is critical to eliminating confusion.

Lessons Learned

This CCTI project has identified several lessons that may be useful to others implementing similar teacher-training programs.

Gain buy-in from all stakeholders to align curriculum across institutions. Since these two initiatives were developed independently from one another and formal articulation was not pursued at the onset, the project has required careful attention to facilitating collaboration among different agencies and groups, including ADE, CTE Education Professions program, and the statewide AAEE program. The CCTI project has been a catalyst in aligning the two programs and ensuring that they provide a seamless pathway for the entire state.

Support services must be created for students, parents, faculty, and academic advisors to work together to develop a career pathway. Individual institutions need to identify and support career pathways encouraging student success and persistence. Once the roles are established, ongoing communication needs to be encouraged, with institutions articulating clearly how they will work together. A formal written plan needs to be prepared and shared that identifies individuals' roles and how these roles are to be integrated to support the career pathway.

Institutions must be encouraged and rewarded for sharing data across the system. Tracking students' progress and documenting their progress with data is important to determining the success of career pathways. All institutional partners, as well as individuals, need to understand the importance of data collection that illuminates student participation in the career pathways. Collaboration on data-tracking systems is far preferable to duplication or recreation.

Community colleges are uniquely positioned to take the lead in working with secondary schools and four-year colleges and universities. Because of their historic relationships with K-12 and baccalaureate institutions, community colleges can build on positive initiatives of the past to forge articulation agreements that offer dual-enrollment opportunities for CTE students.

For keepers of the big picture, strong, committed leadership is crucial at all levels, including the institutional level. Leaders need to be committed and supportive in terms of devoting needed resources. They need to be advocates for the career pathway program. They need to set a mission and vision for the pathway and integrate the goals and strategies into core practices to ensure a systematic and sustainable career pathway.

In this project, enthusiasm has been expressed regarding the progressively closer working relationships developing between the colleges and high schools, leading to opportunities to work together on a variety of fronts. Of particular value is the focus on making sure that students graduate from high school fully prepared for college. Those involved with the CCTI project also appreciate the way it supports and complements the district's goals related to teacher education. Leadership is being provided by Maricopa at the local, state, and national levels, and these efforts are being bolstered by CCTI activities. Particularly important are efforts to address curriculum and assessment alignment problems in the system. Further, the prestige associated with a national grant from the League for Innovation in the Community College is welcome and helpful in encouraging coordinated planning involving the colleges and school districts. In addition, new ideas are being tested under the auspices of the CCTI grant that have potential for statewide replication.

■ All institutional partners, as well as individuals, need to understand the importance of data collection that illuminates student participation in the career pathways.

Challenges and Recommendations

Pursuing an ambitious agenda. Maricopa's staff has ambitious goals; they are stretched by this multifaceted project. The demand on their time and expertise to establish and monitor the progress of the three high school-college partnerships is extensive, including supporting the implementation of the AAEE and Education Professions curricula by aligning different sets of standards, tests and curricula; introducing new tools and assessments like TaskStream and

ParaPro; and developing a system to recruit, test, remediate, and track student progress. Time and resources are critical to address these demands. With the cap on CCTI funds, it is crucial that the state and local entities continue to support Maricopa's noteworthy teacher education program initiatives.

Addressing NCLB. NCLB elicits a great deal of attention from high school leadership; other projects may be considered a lower priority. The new AIMS test required for high school graduation has had a similar impact. To be viable, local entities are compelled to address federal NCLB legislation and state mandates, despite the demands they place on an already overextended educational system.

Dealing with curriculum and cohorts. Many of the individual teacher education programs are set up as block programs, with students moving as a cohort through each semester of classes. This may impede early entry by high school students. The AAEE statewide degree is designed for any student who enters any community college in the state to participate in a rigorous pathway for future teachers.

Addressing the needs of underrepresented students. There are large numbers of students with multiple challenges, including students for whom English is a second language. These students require particularly careful attention and specialized services to ensure their success in the program.

Dealing with institutional autonomy. Each participating college is independent and may choose whether or not to participate in specific grant-related activities. Colleges establish their own agendas, priorities, and schedules. To align goals and efforts, the Instructional Council should continue to serve an important and unifying curriculum-coordinating function.

Addressing inadequacies in data collection. Some difficulties have arisen in the collection of data for this project. All of the programs in the CCTI project were new at the onset of the grant. The state is grappling with data collection issues among institutions. More time and concerted effort is needed to put systematic data collection and tracking mechanisms into place.

More information about Maricopa Community Colleges and the CCTI Initiative can be found at http://www.league.org/league/projects/ccti/projects/summary.cfm?key=mcc.

Information Technology

- Central Piedmont Community College (NC)
- Corning Community College (NY)
- Southwestern Oregon Community College (OR)

Central Piedmont Community College

Terry O'Banion

OCCUPATIONAL AREA:	Information Technology
CAREER PATHWAY:	Programming and Software Engineering
PROJECT DIRECTOR:	Ron Williams
PROJECT PARTNERS:	Central Piedmont Community College
	Phillip O. Berry Academy of Technology
	TechConnect, Chamber of Commerce

Having been involved from the very beginnings with CCTI, I've seen dramatic improvements in communication, career planning, and overall focus on student performance within each of the partnerships. The most remarkable changes seem to be in the area of business and community partnerships. The sites seem to have realized the power of incorporating members of the community in planning and developing strong secondary/ postsecondary transitions for students.

Sandra H. Harwell, Vice President, Professional Development Center for Occupational Research and Development (CORD), CCTI Leadership Team Member

The Project Partners

Established in 1963 with a merger of the primarily African-American Mecklenburg College and the primarily White Central Industrial Education Center, **Central Piedmont Community College** (CPCC) has been serving the Charlotte-Mecklenburg region in North Carolina for over 40 years. During this period, the college has grown from a small establishment with a dozen programs to an institution that now provides more than 100 degree, diploma, and certificate programs in credit and noncredit offerings to 70,000 students. The college has become Mecklenburg County's premier workforce development resource, and one of its mottos is, "We've got the county covered."

The student population at Central Piedmont is somewhat typical of urban community colleges across the nation.

- The average age is 34.
- Ethnic minorities comprise 42 percent of the student population.
- 5 percent are international students, representing 157 countries.
- 20 percent are in basic skills, adult high school, GED, or ESL.
- 40 percent seek one-year certificates or two-year degrees.
- 40 percent are employed workers updating their occupational skills.
- 52 percent are females.

In CPCC's 2000-2002 self-study report prepared for the Southern Association of Colleges and Schools, college leaders noted serious challenges to the institution. Central Piedmont ranks 55 of the 58 North Carolina community colleges in space per student and 58 in state funding. Last year, the college had to return 3 percent of its state and 1 percent of its county budget, and in 2003, it had to return 4 percent of its state budget. In spite of these challenges, the college continues to expand and grow through the leadership of its distinguished innovative and entrepreneurial president, P. Anthony Zeiss.

Zeiss was selected by the board of trustees in 1992 as the college's third president, and under his leadership, the college has become a multicampus institution that now includes six physical campuses. Central Piedmont also reaches thousands of students by distance learning offered through its Virtual Campus. In addition, classes are offered in more than 200 public schools, churches, YMCAs, and business and industry locations.

Central Piedmont's vision statement is bold and reflective of the special role the college plays in the Charlotte-Mecklenburg region: "Central Piedmont Community College intends to become the national leader in workforce development." The leaders of the college have a clear understanding of the ties between CPCC and the region it serves.

In 2001, the U.S. General Accounting Office selected CPCC as one of four outstanding colleges in workforce development in the United States, and a Ford Foundation study describes Central Piedmont as one of the two best colleges in workforce development in the U.S. In 2002, the North Carolina Community College System named President Zeiss the Community College President of the Year, and the Charlotte Chamber of Commerce honored him with its Excellence in Management Award. Nationally, Zeiss is recognized as one of the leading community college presidents and as the leader in workforce development. He has served as chair of the board of directors of the American Association of Community Colleges, and in 2004, served as the chairman of the board of the League for Innovation in the Community College. All these awards were capped by the announcement in 2002 that the National Alliance of Business had named Central Piedmont the Community College of the Year, the fulfillment of the college's vision.

The National Alliance of Business made this award to CPCC in recognition of its creative response to the workforce and technology needs of local employers and job seekers. The college has forged many productive and innovative partnerships with business and industry, regional government agencies, educational institutions, and community stakeholders. Examples of the college's partnerships and collaborations are many and diverse:

- The college is the central leader for the Regional Information Technology Consortium, a partnership with 10 area community colleges, University of North Carolina-Charlotte (UNCC), and K-12 school systems. The purpose of the collaboration is to increase the number of highly qualified information technology workers in the 16-county region.

- Through its JumpStart program, Central Piedmont area students move through educational programs more quickly to achieve certificates, employment, better jobs, or higher pay. The program has been so successful that it is replicated throughout the North Carolina Community College System.
- The CPCC Pathways to Employment program, designed as a response to welfare reform, partners the college with the Mecklenburg County Department of Social Services, community businesses, and other organizations to move participants from welfare to work. In February of 2002, President Bush visited Charlotte and cited this initiative as an exemplary program of welfare to work in the nation. In the aftermath of September 11, the college responded immediately and, in cooperation with the Employment Security Commission, made presentations about retraining options at CPCC to over 500 displaced workers from more than 10 companies. As a result of these efforts, the college has been selected to establish a forensics academy with a $7.2 million facility.

Through these projects and many others, Central Piedmont Community College has become one of the most innovative and entrepreneurial colleges in community college history. It is not surprising that the college's Information Technology Division (ITD) was selected by the League for Innovation as a pivotal leader in this CCTI project.

The Information Technology Division at CPCC employs 36 full-time and more than 60 part-time faculty and staff. IT classes are taught on all six campuses, and Information Technology Services maintains over 170 computer labs for the college. Innovations at the downtown campus include a 108,000-square-foot IT building designed to house 37 computerized classrooms and laboratories.

The ITD has become a regional, statewide, and national leader in train-the-trainer programs. The college has been named one of 10 regional (North Carolina and South Carolina) Working Connections IT Faculty Development Institutes, partnering with the National Workforce Center for Emerging Technologies/Educator-to-Educator Institute and the American Association of Community Colleges. Sponsors for the institute for 2004 included Microsoft, Thompson Publishing, Prentice-Hall Publishing, McGraw-Hill Publishing, and Prosoft Training. The 2005 institute was held as a joint effort of Maryland, North Carolina, and Virginia, with faculty members from all three states participating. Central Piedmont is also a major partner in the Regional Information Technology Consortium (RITC), made up of 10 community colleges in North and South Carolina and led by Central Piedmont. RITC has taken the lead in developing such innovations as the Internet Technologies curriculum and the Database Management curriculum, as well as online courses to support those curricula.

The college works with the statewide, 16-school University of North Carolina system and has specific bilateral agreements with various colleges to accept CPCC's AAS networking degree. Central Piedmont also participates in the North Carolina Community College System's Information Technology Curriculum Improvement Project to refine the IT curricula for the state and to align state standards to the National Skill Standards Board skill set.

As with other forward-looking programs in this CCTI project, Central Piedmont Community College has been particularly successful because its Information Technology Division plans for its future. The strategic plan for the ITD states,

> Effective technology plans are short term, not long term. Five-year plans are too long. Technology is changing so fast that it is almost impossible to plan what type of technology would be available for use five years from now. Even one-year plans may now be about as far ahead as effective planning for purchases of certain types of brands and equipment can take place.

In addition, the strategic plan is based on principles that reflect the values of the instructional computing community at Central Piedmont.

- We are student centered.
- We are customer-service oriented.
- We acknowledge the importance of cooperation.
- We must remain flexible.
- Communication is vital.
- We need to practice mutual respect.
- We are committed to staff development.

In the strategic plan, these values are expanded to provide direction for action by staff members. For example, for the last five years, the plan has stated that "effective technology plans are tied to staff development plans." This particular value provides the basic rationale for much of the work of the division and builds a strong base for the ITD as the premier trainer in the entire region.

This CCTI project, led by the Information Technology Division at Central Piedmont, is fortunate for its two major partners: The Phillip O. Berry Academy of Technology (BAT) and TechConnect (TC), the latter sponsored by the Charlotte Chamber of Commerce.

The **Phillip O. Berry Academy of Technology** is the newest magnet school for the Charlotte-Mecklenburg school system and opened at the beginning of this project. BAT graduated 197 students in its first class in June of 2005. Thirty-two

■ ...for the last five years, the plan has stated that "effective technology plans are tied to staff development plans."

of these students received credit through College Experience classes offered by CPCC at Berry. The school is a comprehensive, districtwide magnet offering a full academic curriculum, including advanced placement courses and more than 20 Career and Technical Education pathways that reside within five Career Academies. The Computer Science and Information Technology Career Academy will prepare graduates for continuing education or employment with organizations that use computers to process, manage, and communicate information. Students may follow a pathway in Computer Applications, Computer Programming, Computer Engineering Technology, Computer Network Administration (Microsoft), Computer Network Engineering (Cisco), or E-Commerce. The academies, housed in a new 340,000-square-foot facility located on 45 acres, reached full capacity of 1,455 students in Grades 9 through 12 in 2004-2005. During the 2005-2006 school year, the projection is for an enrollment of 1,400 students. There is a business and industry advisory council for each academic pathway, with career mentoring internship programs provided to help students meet career goals.

As BAT has emerged as a key magnet school in the region, new entrance criteria state that students must score at or above grade level (Level 3 or 4) on the 8th grade End of Grade tests in reading and mathematics, and pass the performance and written components of the Computer Competency Test. There is also a continuation standard, which states that all students currently enrolled (annually) must pass their technical pathway course(s) to remain in the school. These entrance and continuation standards are new for 2005-2006 and 2004-2005, respectively. They were implemented to ensure that the original vision for this school is attained, and that Berry attracts a higher caliber student who is more focused on learning at higher levels. The Phillip O. Berry website is www.cms.k12.nc.us/allschools/berryacadtech/.

The second partner of Central Piedmont's Division of Technology is **TechConnect**. TechConnect is a co-curricular program for Charlotte/Mecklenburg high school students sponsored and supported by Advantage Carolina in conjunction with the Charlotte Chamber of Commerce. The primary purpose of the TechConnect club-based program is to generate technology interest within the high school community including students and teachers. The primary program is offered through short courses taught by professional experts who volunteer from area business and industry and it includes hands-on experiences through internships and mentorships for students.

The program has been enormously successful; in 2002, it received the ExploreNet SmartTech Partner of the Year Award and, in 2003, the Blue Diamond Award, regional awards for excellence. Thousand-dollar scholarships have been created by local business and industry for high school students, and $7,500 scholarships have been created for students transferring to Central

Piedmont Community College. TechConnect, only established in 2000, has already expanded to 13 of the 16 Charlotte-Mecklenburg high school districts and one middle school (eighth grade) and currently includes over 350 participating students. To keep up with the demand, TechConnect has had to add a number of additional study tracks. The Chamber of Commerce is currently reviewing the TechConnect program for possible expansion in the region.

The Information Technology Division of Central Piedmont, the Berry Academy, and TechConnect are all excellent programs created in the local pro-business, can-do environment of the Charlotte-Mecklenburg region. In their individual capacity, each of these partners is a leader and a significant resource for the region. When they partner with each other in this CCTI project, they provide a formidable base for success in regional and national leadership.

The Model Career Pathway

The Career Pathway template was developed in close collaboration among the administrative staff of the Phillip O. Berry (BAT) Academy of Technology and the Information Technology Division staff at Central Piedmont Community College. Development of the pathway also involved staff at the Charlotte-Mecklenburg Schools (CMS) System, the North Carolina Department of Public Instruction (NCDPI), and the North Carolina Community College System (NCCCS). In the Computer Programming Pathway, it is possible for a high school student to earn 15 hours of college credit due to articulation agreements and College Experience coursework in the technical courses required. A high school student taking advanced placement English and math classes could also add three to nine additional hours of college credit with appropriate test scores.

■ In the Computer Programming Pathway, it is possible for a high school student to earn 15 hours of college credit due to articulation agreements and College Experience coursework in the technical courses required. A high school student taking advanced placement English and math classes could also add three to nine additional hours of college credit with appropriate test scores.

The Career Pathway template is very useful in helping many of the constituencies understand the nature of the program. Handouts are being developed to inform high school students about the possibilities available to them in selected programs using the pathways model. Staff development opportunities focused on the Career Pathway for faculty in Grades 8 through 12 are just beginning. By having a relatively easy-to-view pathway, faculty and students begin to envision the program of study and the number of course credits that can be earned at the high school level. Parents will also be targeted with the pathways information. Parental involvement at an early level seems to be a real key to success with students.

The North Carolina Department of Public Instruction is the governing body for the K-12 education systems in North Carolina, while the North Carolina Community College System is the governing body for the community colleges in the state. NCDPI and NCCCS meet on a regular basis to establish articulation agreements between the two systems. Articulated courses allow high school students to obtain credit for courses at the community college level when students petition for such credit. Credits are awarded depending on high school course grades and the appropriate state test scores.

The University of North Carolina System governs the 16 state-supported universities in North Carolina. UNCC and NCCCS meet as needed to arrange for course articulation agreements between community college and state-supported universities in North Carolina. These articulation agreements allow community college students to receive credit for designated courses at the community college that have been passed with a suitable grade. The instruction of those courses must meet the standards of the Southern Association of Colleges and Schools. Because NCCCS has no jurisdiction over the instruction of high school classes, and because the NCDPI teachers often do not meet UNC standards (*i.e.*, master's degree and 18 hours of instruction at the master's level in the course area), courses articulated between NCCCS and UNC are not eligible for articulation between NCDPI and NCCCS.

NCCCS students who take a carefully prescribed set of courses in an official transfer program may transfer to the UNC system as juniors with full credit for the first two years spent at the community college. Other than these official transfer programs, NCCCS colleges and UNC universities (with other colleges and universities as appropriate) must work out bilateral agreements for transfer of credit up to and including full credit for freshman and sophomore years taken at the community college level. In some cases, the university or college may choose to make an agreement with multiple community colleges within its service region. The Career Pathway template was developed to reflect all these various agreements among state systems at the secondary, community college, and university level.

One additional statewide factor will have considerable impact on this project. NCCCS has recently completed an IT Curriculum Improvement Project (CIP). With chief academic officers and presidents agreeing to the recommendations, implementation may begin in the spring semester of 2006. The IT CIP is likely to have significant impact on information technology instruction in North Carolina. The six primary IT curricula were grouped together for the purposes of the CIP. Normally, only one curriculum is reviewed at a time, but for the first time, all IT curricula were included in one two-year study. A complete overhaul of all IT curricula was the goal of the CIP. All IT courses within the Common Course Library (CCL) of the NCCCS system were reviewed as taught by each community college, compared with national standards using the help of the National Skill Standards Board, compared with other like-designated courses taught at other community colleges, and compared with other unlike-designated courses that had addressed a similar set of skills. This was a massive undertaking. The results of more than two years of study by representatives from each of the 58 North Carolina community colleges, an industry-business advisory council, NCDPI representatives, and the NSSB included recommendations to

- Eliminate courses no longer needed;
- Eliminate or combine courses that had separate designators but were significantly the same;
- Change course prefix designations to better reflect the type of course being taught;
- Designate 70 to 80 percent of all detailed objectives to be taught in each class to promote uniformity of each course being taught at different colleges, which facilitates articulation between community colleges and four-year colleges and universities;
- Ensure that the objectives developed for courses correspond with national- and state-validated skill standards; and
- Develop a common core of classes among the IT curricula.

Depending on the implementation timeline and whether or not all of the recommendations are implemented, current North Carolina Career Pathway templates must be altered significantly. With a clear focus on IT courses in the NCDPI and NCCCS systems, articulation among all three statewide systems should be greatly enhanced.

Curriculum and Instruction

As the template for the Career Pathway emerged, it was necessary to determine which courses could be provided by Central Piedmont Community College for Phillip O. Berry Academy of Technology. Huskins Bill classes – college-level classes created solely for high school students who want to earn college credits – have been taught for the Charlotte-Mecklenburg Schools by CPCC since 1984. Offered on high school and CPCC campuses, the classes are taught by college instructors using college-level materials. A variety of courses is offered, including vocational-technical and college transfer courses.

Huskins Bill classes – college-level classes created solely for high school students who want to earn college credits – have been taught for the Charlotte-Mecklenburg Schools by CPCC since 1984. Offered on high school and CPCC campuses, the classes are taught by college instructors using college-level materials.

The term Huskins refers to 1983 North Carolina legislation developed by the late Representative Joseph P. Huskins; it permits community colleges and technical institutes statewide to offer college-level academic, technical, and advanced vocational classes not otherwise available to students free of charge in the 9th through 12th grades at participating high schools. Students who take and pass Huskins classes receive both high school and college credit for their work.

Each year, CPCC and CMS determine which college-credit classes are to be available for the high school students. If a class is being taught at any CMS high school, then that class cannot be taught by CPCC for credit. Given such limitations and articulation agreements in place at the state level, a first class, ITN 150 Internet Protocols, served as the pilot to be taught at Berry. A number of challenges were encountered in this first class, most notably the lockdown on the CMS computer systems available to the high school students. Problems produced by the lockdown included the students' inability to right click, which severely limited students' ability to implement certain software features. Scheduling also proved to be a minor problem since the CMS and CPCC school years do not correspond exactly and the scheduling of time periods is different in the two systems.

Over a period of time, solutions for these problems have been worked out. Beginning fall term 2005, Berry students who enroll in CPCC classes will leave the high school each day shortly after noon and will become CPCC students. The CPCC CityView facility located near Berry will be outfitted for the Berry classes. College Experience classes officially approved for the school year beginning fall 2005 are CIS152 Database Concepts and Applications, CSC160 Introduction to Internet Programming, ITN140 Web Development Tools, CIS153 Database Applications, and CET125 Voice and Data Cabling. Classes run from 12:45 to 2:15 p.m. each day. Four classes (two each term) will be taught, with one scheduled on Monday through Wednesday and the other on Tuesday through Thursday. Friday will serve as a lab day. By using CPCC computer equipment, networks, and Oracle database software, the limitations of the earlier classes are eliminated.

In addition to educating CMS students, CPCC has also aided CMS with its faculty certification needs. CPCC has an extensive IT Academy that delivers instruction for certification in areas such as CISCO and Microsoft. These IT Academy classes have been made available to CMS teachers who want to become certified, to recertify, or to upgrade skills. Phillip O. Berry has used 25 seats and more in academy classes. At least one Berry teacher has certified and has received full credentials to teach at CPCC as an adjunct faculty member.

Bridges With Four-Year Programs

As previously described, statewide articulation agreements between the North Carolina Community College System and the University of North Carolina System are in place. The Comprehensive Articulation Agreement, which became effective in fall 1997, addresses the transfer of credits among institutions in the NCCCS and the UNC System. The 16 universities of the UNC System will normally accept students at the junior level for all approved transfer programs. Students in Associate in Applied Science (AAS) degree programs will find that their General Education (GE) required courses will transfer, but many of the required technical courses for their curriculum will be transferred to state universities and colleges on a case-by-case basis, as governed by the receiving institution. Bilateral agreements among community colleges and regional schools often help to bridge this gap in transferability. The college is actively seeking to develop such agreements in the information technology area of study.

One such agreement, in Networking, now exists between CPCC and East Carolina University (ESU). With a completed AAS degree from CPCC in Networking and a CISCO certification, the student will transfer into ECU as a junior. In addition, the ECU junior and senior courseload may be taken online, allowing students to continue to live in the Charlotte area and to complete the ECU undergraduate degree. A master's degree from ECU can also be completed, with most of the coursework delivered online. Additional agreements are now being explored with regional schools, such as the University of North Carolina at Charlotte. For example, a new degree program in Management Information Systems/Systems Analysis is being developed at CPCC with the encouragement and help of UNCC. Efforts continue to develop new agreements within the North Carolina and South Carolina regions.

Student Support

Students are being supported by many people, institutions, and programs. First and foremost has been the excellent support of the Phillip O. Berry Academy of Technology administrators and faculty. Through the use of a thoughtfully developed and well-executed three-phase plan, students are given the opportunity to take at least 12 hours of College Experience courses on or near the high school campus. The courses will aid students in obtaining valuable technical certifications and give them credit within a variety of IT programs, should they continue their studies at a community college.

Surveys and tests are also being used to support students. Students have been surveyed to determine their likes, dislikes, and needs via the High School Survey of Student Engagement (HSSSE), and the information gained from HSSSE is being used to enhance the student experience at Phillip O. Berry. Likewise, students at CPCC have taken the Community College Survey of Student Engagement (CCSSE), and the college is actively using the information in committees such as the Student Success Team to better support students. CPCC supports early (high school-level) administration of ACCUPLACER tests, which are a basis for student placement at the college. By giving high school students the placement tests, the college can determine much earlier where they stand in regard to future English and math course needs at the college level. Phillip O. Berry has made extensive after-school and Saturday tutoring sessions available for students who show the need for additional help in any area of study. Berry has committed its faculty and facilities to educating each student to the maximum possible extent. In addition, the CCTI project has facilitated the hiring by the college of a technical facilitator who can go to the individual high schools, work with faculty and counselors as well as students, distribute pathways literature, and mentor students as they seek to enter CPCC. This facilitator is a graduate of the IT programs at CPCC and can provide students invaluable guidance in program selection. Guidance and mentoring by the facilitator can provide a very positive experience for a student who may have otherwise been daunted by the new college experience.

■ ...the CCTI project has facilitated the hiring by the college of a technical facilitator who can go to the individual high schools, work with faculty and counselors as well as students, distribute pathways literature, and mentor students as they seek to enter CPCC.

Special Features

CPCC's business partner TechConnect has shown tremendous support for the students who participate in TechConnect clubs. TechConnect seeks to engage students in fun IT learning experiences; many of these students would not have elected an IT track without this experience. Tracks such as personal computer assembly, website design, graphics, robotics, and computer refurbishing are taught by industry and business professionals who are volunteering their time and effort to give the students meaningful experiences. Disadvantaged students and diverse students who would not normally sign up for IT coursework are encouraged to join the after-school classes and, with the very positive experiences and support provided by local business leaders, the students learn they can do the IT work and enjoy it. Local support has allowed the students in the PC assembly tracks to build their own very capable PCs for as little as $100. Students can now go home with fully capable PCs that they can proudly say they built.

TechConnect also supports the students in obtaining real-world experience by providing them with business and industry internships, most of which are paid positions. In one track, students are taught how to dress and present themselves as they submit résumés for employment. Students must apply for internships, which entail real job interviews as the students compete for the posted intern positions. Many of the students taking these internships have returned to the same company for subsequent internships, and some have had their college programs paid for by these companies.

The Implementation Strategies

Most Effective Strategies

During CCTI Summit meetings and through the CCTI website, it has become obvious that many of the partnerships in CCTI are using similar strategies. Some are tried and true; others are relatively new. By blending these strategies, CPCC believes that the project will be successful. For this partnership, measuring the successes thus far is not particularly easy, in part because the partnership has a newly opened school as the principal high school partner. The Phillip O. Berry Academy of Technology graduated its first class in May 2005. CPCC strongly believes that certain strategies are working well, but the true proof will be in enrollment and retention data for former Berry students at Central Piedmont Community College in the next few years. Some of the most effective strategies are described in the following paragraphs.

Rapport with high school counselors and faculty. Developing a strong rapport, not only with high school counselors, but especially with high school teachers, has been very important. Each year, all high school counselors are invited to meetings on campus and are oriented to the college and many of its programs. Unfortunately, this seldom permits in-depth exploration of a particular program or programs. Some counselors tend to steer their advanced students to four-year colleges regardless of the programs available at the community college level, while others never develop a real knowledge of the true scope of programs available at the local community colleges.

Lack of knowledge of the community college programs and preference for four-year college programs also exist for the teachers who are very involved with their students' day-to-day lives and who influence the decisions those students will make. The typical high school faculty member is inundated with students and administrative requirements at their own institutions, and they will seldom find even one day to visit the local community college. Developing rapport with the administration and teachers at the high school is therefore extremely important.

CPCC has used various techniques to do this. Not just the CCTI project staff, but also other instructors from the college have visited Berry to review the facilities, resources, and classes; to participate in or lead the TechConnect clubs meetings; to meet with faculty and staff to discuss College Experience classes to be offered at the school; and to help with classroom and lab setup. These instructors from the college become involved in the planning at the high school and become known to faculty and students. Some of the college instructors have become guest lecturers, willing to serve as resources for the high school faculty.

Having faculty and staff from the high school and the system office meet on the college campus also helps introduce high school personnel to the extensive resources and programs available through the college. Because CPCC opens its extensive IT Academy classes to interested high school faculty, those faculty become familiar with the college at a very intimate level: as students at the college. They develop a much greater understanding of CPCC and its offerings, usually in a very positive way. These instructors become some of the best counselors for their students. Developing these types of bonds with high school faculty and administrators can pay great dividends.

Assessment in high school for college readiness. A commonly used strategy to ensure the success of transition programs is the administration in the high school of college placement assessments. Central Piedmont uses ACCUPLACER testing to determine English, reading, and math placement. The ACCUPLACER test is currently administered in Grade 12. The Berry administration wishes to give the test at an earlier grade, but district policy currently prevents this. This early look at college placement scores often permits remedial or additional work to be done in high school prior to college enrollment. Problems include cost, scheduling, and student apathy because of the large number of standardized tests they take.

■ Because CPCC opens its extensive IT Academy classes to interested high school faculty, those faculty become familiar with the college at a very intimate level: as students at the college.

Remediation at the high school level is more cost effective and can result in a great savings of time and money to students. More important than the time and money potentially saved is the effect that early remediation may have on the long-term success of students. Studies show that students who must take more than one remedial class at the community college level will often be lost to the system prior to finishing a degree or transferring to a four-year school. The Berry administration and faculty have aggressively developed after-school and Saturday tutoring for students who need remediation.

College facilitator in the high school. Central Piedmont uses an experienced facilitator-mentor to work with high school students planning to enter the college. Providing a technical facilitator who is experienced in curricula pathways, college requirements, and registration processes at the college can contribute significantly, not only to getting new students registered, but to getting students registered in the best program for them. Duties assigned to these technical facilitators are often performed prior to the high school student's graduation and can include

- Providing information concerning college entry requirements and processes;
- Providing information about specific IT certifications, programs, and curricula;
- Providing information about the local job market and available positions;
- Supporting student visits to familiarize students with the college campus;
- Directly aiding students in registering for the college;
- Providing information for parents and high school faculty; and
- Disseminating literature including important pathways information.

TechConnect ...is a voluntary after-school club taught by volunteers from industry and business.... Having industry volunteers teach the tracks with no tests, no course books, and so forth tends to engage the students, and they feel that they can ask any question and get an answer from someone actually working in the field.

The facilitator can greatly ease students' fears and make them feel comfortable and welcome at the college. The facilitator becomes a mentor to the students, showing them the local ropes and introducing them to college faculty members. An intimate knowledge of the college, IT programs, and faculty is extremely important for the facilitator.

IT clubs in the high school. An additional important strategy has been the use of a nonthreatening, voluntary after-school club for fun activities. Such clubs can recruit students not traditionally drawn to the IT curricula, exposing them to a wide variety of IT skills and professions. The club tracks help to demystify IT skills and provide opportunities for students to interact with practicing professionals from industry and business willing to give of their time and expertise.

TechConnect is one of several innovative programs conceived and funded by an IT group associated with the Charlotte Chamber of Commerce. It is a voluntary after-school club taught by volunteers from industry and business. Different tracks exist so that the club offerings can remain fresh to students. Students are free to take one track or as many tracks as they want. Tracks are topics that have been chosen based on student interest along with input of local industry and business. Having industry volunteers teach the tracks with no tests, no course books, and so forth tends to engage the students, and they feel that they can ask any question and get an answer from someone actually working in the field.

Most of the tracks are very hands on, with the students often taking home some sort of work that they completed themselves. In one graphics track, the students complete a design of their own and then transfer the design to a t-shirt. One problem has been getting the students to take off and wash the shirts. Another track has each student actually build a PC. Depending on the economic level of the student, a minimal charge exists for the track. At the end of the track, the students have fully working PCs, which are theirs to keep. This track has been taken by a number of students who went on to successfully complete their A+ certification prior to leaving high school.

Tracks include graphics, website design, computer refurbishing, computer assembly, and robotics. TechConnect has proven to be an excellent tool in recruiting nontraditional IT students into IT coursework.

Onsite college courses at the high school. Another fairly common strategy used at Central Piedmont is to develop college courses that can be delivered onsite at the high schools to introduce students to college-level courses and instructors. Introducing high school students to college courses and instructors gives them an inkling of what college can be like. If the first course or two is completed at the high school without time and transportation problems, then the students feel more at ease and are more likely to enroll in other classes. After the first course or two, and assuming that there have been good experiences with the material and the instructor, the students are more likely to sign up for additional courses at the college and to eventually register for a program of study there.

It is crucial to choose the proper courses and instructors for these first offerings. Students need to be challenged but also excited about the course and the instructor. Six students at Berry who took the introductory ITN150 Internet Protocols course in fall 2004 became very interested in the course and have since gone on to pick up their CIW certification. The instructors chosen for these courses need to be very knowledgeable of the course materials, the IT programs, and the college in general. They must be willing to give extra time, not only to the high school students, but also to the high school faculty and staff. These instructors become goodwill ambassadors and play an important role in helping students make successful transitions.

Least Effective Strategies

Student identity and privacy. Central Piedmont would like to target potential CTP students, TechConnect students, and others for special programs. It has met with some success, but has found that identifying these students is not easy. CPCC does not have the student identification numbers, addresses, and so forth from the high school system, which must protect the security and confidentiality of its students. Matching the identification of students within the high school, the after-school clubs, and the college has been problematic. Being able to carefully track students and their career paths from K-12 to community colleges and on to work or four-year institutions would provide a great deal of important information to improve programs and student success.

Availability of internships. Another area of concern surrounds internships. CPCC has had great success with internships when these are available. However, finding enough businesses willing to support the number of students in the system has been a problem. TechConnect seeks to provide paid summer internships for its students. Phillip O. Berry seeks to place its IT students in internships during their junior year as a graduation requirement. Berry is also moving to a year-round internship in addition to the summer internships offered in its programs. Other area high schools do not have as many technology students as Berry, but a number of these high schools are Academy of Information Technology (AOIT) schools, and they are also looking for internships.

Issues such as whether a student can take a second internship have also caused disagreements among the competing agencies. Some firms, once they find an intern who performs well, seek to bring back the same intern for a second year. Everyone agrees that internships are extremely valuable for students, but finding enough quality internships and the faculty to monitor them is an increasing challenge.

Lessons Learned

Student involvement in career path. CCTI has given the partners the impetus and freedom to learn by doing and by observing each other and other CCTI partnerships. With all of the best practices tested again and again, one thing seems to be clear: Getting students involved in and committed to a career path at the earliest possible time in their educational experience will significantly increase the likelihood that they will be successful in education and in life.

■ **Getting students involved in and committed to a career path at the earliest possible time in their educational experience will significantly increase the likelihood that they will be successful in education and in life.**

Cross-institutional collaboration. The separate educational systems – K-12, community college, and four-year college and university – each with its own counseling and advising, course and class schedule, admission requirements, and teaching approaches, make it difficult for students to move efficiently from one level to another. An established Career Pathway, agreed upon by each level of education, at least provides a clear direction for all the stakeholders, and it provides a clear roadmap to help students navigate their way through the different terrain created by each entity along the way.

High school faculty involvement. One of the most important lessons is to get the high school faculty involved in the college as soon as possible. The college can often provide invaluable training and certification programs to attract the high school faculty. As a first step, develop a comprehensive list of training possibilities at the college that are available to high school faculty. Encourage the high school faculty who qualify to become adjunct instructors at the college. Once these faculty members are engaged with the college, they tend to look at the college in a different light, and this is reflected in how they talk about the college and its programs with their students.

College faculty involvement. The college faculty also benefit from working with the secondary faculty and being on campus at the high schools. In many cases, the college faculty members are seeing the K-12 system at work firsthand for the first time. College faculty can provide guest lectures and presentations for high school classes as one way of getting students involved, or they can host high school faculty and student groups on the college campus for special events. College faculty can also teach college courses on the high school campus.

Student motivation. Entice nontraditional IT students into learning IT skills by making that learning fun, nonthreatening, and exciting. TechConnect provides students with something to show for their participation, from a self-designed pattern on a t-shirt to a complete computer system to a paid internship. After-school clubs with tracks of study but no texts or tests can lure nontraditional students into IT. The students must be made to feel comfortable, assured that they can succeed at the tasks presented, and rewarded for their efforts. Industry and business involvement is crucial to these efforts. Having working business people take time from their jobs to present an interesting topic while answering questions about the real work world can be of tremendous assistance in attracting nontraditional students. Students often crave information about the jobs that do exist in industry – the real information from someone doing the work, not just a printed study of the job market or positions available.

Facilitator roles. Find an experienced facilitator who knows your programs, and get the facilitator into the high school. Facilitators need to work with counselors, faculty members, and students. Seldom will a high school counselor or faculty member really know enough about the college's programs to provide in-depth advice to students. Detailing the available pathways course by course can be just the information needed for students and parents to feel that they know enough to commit to a course of study.

Career pathway information. Develop Career Pathways that can be explained and followed easily. Different documents may need to be prepared for counselors, faculty members, and students at the high school level. The same goes for parents: They need a clear, concise document that will give them the guidance they want. Getting parents involved is critical. Prepare materials for the facilitator to distribute and try to make sure that some of those materials get into the hands of parents.

Dual enrollment and college experience. Do not be discouraged about the time and effort it takes to identify and teach classes as dual-enrollment or college experience classes. It may take as long as two years in some cases to work through the system to officially have those courses set up for registration. It is especially good to have one or two such classes taught at the high school by a carefully selected college instructor. By choosing exciting courses and having a qualified and exciting instructor teach one or two courses at the high school, both students and faculty are introduced to a good college experience.

Student assessment. Early assessment of students is critical. High school students who will most likely need remediation to succeed in college need to be identified as soon as possible. Once identified, remediation should begin for the students before they leave high school. The primary goal is to prepare high school students for college so they need as few remedial courses as possible after they complete high school. Remedial course requirements tend to lessen the likelihood of a student's success at the college level. Assess students at the 10th grade level or before if possible. State grade-level tests may be helpful, but the actual placement test used by the college is the most meaningful assessment tool. When the scores are returned to the students, be sure to explain in detail what the scores mean in terms of remedial work and expense necessary at college. Work closely with partner high schools to have them take responsibility in whatever ways are possible for the remediation before the student enters the community college.

Transitions. This project has helped illuminate the need for better integration across school systems and commitments to working together in more effective ways to ensure successful student transitions. Each level of education has its own goals, objectives, and bureaucracy. Each system has its strengths, weaknesses, and problems. They all have in common a basic commitment to student success, but tradition and time often work against collaboration.

Cooperative programs. In North Carolina, the K-12 system and the community college system are beginning to make progress on cooperative programs. There is some experimentation with placing college programs on high school campuses (middle or early college) that is an example of this spirit of cooperation. The Career Pathway is a highly visible and effective practice that can also enhance cooperation among high schools and community colleges – and four-year colleges as well. The Career Pathway, with its documented and aligned courses and experiences, holds great promise for forging improved cooperation and alignment across the historically separate systems of education.

More information about Central Piedmont Community College and the CCTI Initiative can be found at http://www.league.org/league/projects/ccti/projects/summary.cfm?key=cpcc.

Corning Community College

Terry O'Banion

OCCUPATIONAL AREA: Information Technology
CAREER PATHWAY: Network Technology
CCTI PROJECT DIRECTOR: Linda Miller
PROJECT WEBSITE: www.corning-cc.edu/techprep/
PROJECT PARTNERS: Corning Community College
Campbell-Savona High School
Schuyler-Chemung-Tioga BOCES
Watkins Glen High School
Career Development Council
Corning, Inc.

The Project Partners

Today, the Corning region in New York has a population of approximately 13,000 people and is the home of two Fortune 500 companies: Corning, Inc. and the Dresser-Rand company. Corning has preserved much of its historical past, and the five blocks of Market Street, the community's downtown, has set a national standard for historic preservation and commercial vitality. The Corning Region, also known as the Southern Tier, has a very diversified economy and is home to major manufacturing companies from around the world. In addition, the Southern Tier boasts an extraordinary amount of intellectual property and well-educated personnel. For example, there are 6,400 scientists and engineers among the 342,000 members of the labor force in the Southern Tier. There are numerous museums, cultural and arts programs, educational institutions, research laboratories, and a wide array of sport and recreational facilities.

The Corning Region, also known as the Southern Tier, has a very diversified economy and is home to major manufacturing companies from around the world. In addition, the Southern Tier boasts an extraordinary amount of intellectual property and well-educated personnel.

As ideal as this region is for growth and development, however, in recent years, there has been a downturn in population and employment. Three counties make up the region, and between 1990 and 2000, Chemung County lost 4.3 percent of its population, Schuyler County gained 3 percent, and Steuben County lost .4 percent. The average unemployment rate in 2000 was 5.6 percent for the three-county region, but in 2003, that average had increased to 8 percent. The economy of the Southern Tier was severely affected when Corning, Inc. had to lay off a significant number of workers worldwide in 2000. Adding further economic duress to the region, the Shepard Niles Company closed; World Kitchen moved out of the state; and a number of leading companies downsized their workforces.

In this changing economic swirl, **Corning Community College** (CCC) plays an increasingly important role as a catalyst for economic development. When companies have reduced their workforces, the college has been at the forefront of retraining and counseling. It has also started new training programs for new businesses attracted to the potential of the region. Corning Community College is emerging as a key player in the economic and workforce development of the region.

In the early 1950s, the communities that make up the Southern Tier were experiencing a great deal of growth, and there were a number of studies on the need for expanded educational systems in the area. In 1951, a study commissioned by the Painted Post School Board recommended a number of alternatives, including joining with the Corning City School District for an enlarged consolidated district. Community leaders initiated another study by researchers from Harvard University that was published in 1954 titled *A Valley and A Decision*. That study specifically recommended that a community college be established in Corning that could be attached to one of the area high schools to share facilities and instructors. The State University of New York Board of Trustees officially granted approval for the new college in December of 1956, and on September 18, 1958, 118 students registered and began classes.

The college prospered and grew using temporary facilities offered by community leaders and sponsoring school districts. In 1960, the Corning Glassworks Foundation offered a gift of land and an additional grant of money to create a new campus. As a result, Corning Community College would become one of the few debt-free campuses ever built. The Houghton family of Corning Glassworks played an important role in the establishment of the new college campus. Arthur Houghton offered his home, Houghton House, as an intermediate facility for the college, the land on which the campus was built, and a residence adjacent to the campus, which has been used by college presidents as a home. The Arthur Houghton Library on the campus honors his early contributions.

Over the decades, the college has grown into an excellent institution and shares with most community colleges around the country the tensions that come from trying to create an institution that can be respected for both its commitment to liberal arts values and its commitment to the more practical arts of responding to community workforce and economic development needs. This dynamic tension between competing educational philosophies has characterized the community college movement for at least five decades. Corning Community College is a microcosm of these dynamic tensions, which influence college decisions, financing, and the general climate of the institution.

Today, Corning Community College is a dynamic player in the City of Corning and the surrounding region it serves. It is a well-respected institution of higher education in the State of New York and one of the leading institutions of higher education in the area. It has been successful in maintaining its commitment to core values of a liberal education while at the same time expanding its workforce and economic development programs throughout the three-county region. In the recent economic downturn, the college has made an elegant response to community needs and has prepared the way for a continuing expansion of its workforce and economic development mission.

Corning Community College has established a number of programs in response to area economic and workforce needs. The college has created a small business development center in the heart of Corning that addresses corporate needs for training through its Corporate, Community Education, and Services Division. In the academic year 2002-2003, the division provided training for 21 area companies, a 24 percent increase over the previous year. In the same time period, training was provided for 929 participants, a 94 percent increase over the previous year.

In addition, the college sponsors and houses the Central Southern Tier Tech Prep Consortium, one of the leading consortia of its kind. The CCTI project at Corning Community College has been successful, in great part because it is embedded in the structure and the culture of the tech prep program, which has achieved an astounding record of success. With Carl D. Perkins funds, the tech prep consortium was established in 1992, and today includes 12 secondary school districts, two BOCES centers, and two community colleges. Alfred State College is a postsecondary partner in the Building Trades career sequence. The consortium's mission statement reads, "The purpose of Tech Prep is to prepare students, Grades 9 through 14, for lifelong learning and workforce readiness through the development and implementation of applied academics, seamless curricula, and collaborative partnerships with business, education, and parents." The service delivery area for the consortium is the same as that for Corning Community College: the counties of Steuben, Chemung, and Schuyler.

The current career clusters in the Tech Prep Consortium include Business Management, Marketing, and Hospitality; Information Technology; Transportation, Architecture and Construction; Manufacturing Production; and Scientific Research and Engineering. Each Tech Prep student is provided a personal Tech Prep Portfolio that includes the selected career cluster or pathway and appropriate course proficiency profiles. Every course in the Tech Prep sequence is based on competencies, and it is the competencies, not the courses, that are articulated between the high schools and the community college. Usually, a student can earn up to 10 semester credits in the high school that can be transferred into Corning Community College. In the academic year 2002-2003, Tech Prep enrollments totaled 953 registered students, exceeding the goal of 450 by an astounding 212 percent. Four years ago, fewer than 10 students transferred from area high schools into Corning Community College through the Tech Prep program. Today, in one high school of 370, 105 are enrolled in Tech Prep; 17 are information technology (IT) students.

■ In the academic year 2002-2003, Tech Prep enrollments totaled 953 registered students, exceeding the goal of 450 by an astounding 212 percent.

All secondary academic curricula are aligned with the New York State Learning Standards. Following extensive development review by business advisory teams, the secondary career and technical programs have received New York State's Department of Education Career and Technical Education (CTE) endorsement. All CTE-endorsed programs incorporate state or national assessments and feature established articulations with postsecondary institutions.

Under the leadership of its coordinator, Linda Miller, the Central Southern Tier Tech Prep Consortium has become a model with exemplary materials and programs. In addition, the organization and governance of the consortium is exemplary. The Superintendents and President Team meets annually to review the Administrative Agreement and make necessary revisions. The Tech Prep Management Team is the regional advisory committee that guides and directs the implementation of consortium objectives. A site manager is appointed at each educational site to promote and disseminate Tech Prep information to all constituencies. A cluster advisor is also appointed at each educational site to provide support and resources for each registered Tech Prep student. Corning Community College serves as the fiscal agent for the Tech Prep Consortium, and the full-time coordinator reports to the vice president for academic affairs at Corning.

The information technology courses that are included in this CCTI project are formally based in the Business Administration Division and the Math/Physics/Technology Division. Information technology courses are spread across these two divisions, but they achieve their focus and organization within the framework of the Tech Prep Program.

The Tech Prep Consortium includes many partners among schools, business, and industry in the region. One of the major partners of the consortium involved in this CCTI project is the **Career Development Council** (CDC). In 1974, local employers, school superintendents, and union leaders wanted to include career development opportunities for youths and adults in the Corning region. A community partnership with business, industry, and education, the CDC serves Chemung, Schuyler, and Steuben Counties as a resource to link educators and students with local business and industry. Staff members are assigned to contracting school districts and visit schools regularly to provide a variety of services. In the 2002-2003 program year, CDC provided services for over 17,000 students and faculty, including classroom speakers, mock interviews, shadowing, career panels, field trips and business site explorations, career explorations, Tech Prep student career experiences, and special training programs for faculty. A school contracts with CDC for a basic career education package and may add additional programs including mentoring, student internships, community service learning, and a summer leadership institute. CDC also provides a student data tracking service for Tech Prep and the CCTI project. This arrangement is particularly advantageous, since CDC already tracks all the high school data pertinent to the project.

Several high schools, including **Campbell-Savona High School** and **Watkins Glen High School**, and the **Schuyler-Chemung-Tioga BOCES** also participate as partners in this CCTI project. **Corning, Inc.** is a central business partner in the CCTI project, and special staff members work with area schools to provide a variety of programs to encourage career development for area students, including shadow programs and paid internships for students in IT.

The Model Career Pathway

Corning Community College and the Tech Prep Consortium have developed eight Career Pathways under the Information Technology Career Cluster. Career Pathways include

- Computer Information Science,
- Computer Repair Technology,
- Computer Science,
- Computer Systems Technology,
- Microcomputers for Business,
- Network Technology,
- Web Technology, and
- Word Processing.

Corning Community College's Career Pathway in Network Technology, one of the eight career pathways under the Information Technology Career Cluster and the one featured in this CCTI project, is designed as a 4+2 pathway leading to an Associate of Applied Science (AAS) degree. Each Career Pathway aligns with 3 CCTI partner high schools and 13 additional secondary partners in the consortium. The Network Technology Career Pathway, designed under the Tech Prep CCTI program, offers students delayed articulation opportunities in addition to dual-credit options. Under delayed articulation, credits are awarded when the student enters CCC as a freshman and presents a compete portfolio for review. With a maximum of 25 credits available through delayed articulation, courses are outlined by competencies rather than exclusively mandated class structure. Articulated courses, identified by competencies on individual Course Proficiency Profiles, include

- Elements of Applied Mathematics (six credits);
- Computer Essentials (four credits);
- Network Fundamentals (four credits);
- LAN/WAN Networking (four credits);
- LAN Implementation and Configuration (four credits); and
- Network Project (three credits).

■ **With a maximum of 25 credits available through delayed articulation, courses are outlined by competencies rather than exclusively mandated class structure.**

Additionally, the Career Pathway template indicates dual-credit course opportunities for students. College Composition and Economics are available through CCC's Accelerated College Education (ACE) Program. CCC's dual-credit program is geared to academically advanced high school seniors.

Dual-credit, or ACE, courses are offered in the high schools by secondary faculty following training and approval by the college. ACE courses are primarily general education and liberal arts courses. They are available to students at reduced tuition cost, and grades are transcripted upon completion of the course. The majority of ACE credits easily articulate with four-year institutions.

Delayed articulation competency design enhances the pathway offering on a regional basis while reducing the spider-web effect of multiple articulations and specifications. Identification of competency mastery expectations enables individual school districts to design curricula in a variety of avenues to best meet the school's scheduling and delivery parameters.

The combination of delayed articulation and dual-credit opportunities makes it possible for a wider range of students to enroll in Career Pathways. Students in the mid-academic range are now able to envision and begin the transition to a college education and related career of choice.

Career Pathway development began with the identification of entry-level postsecondary program courses that overlapped secondary course content. Each identified postsecondary course curriculum was enumerated by competencies on Course Proficiency Profile templates. Registered Tech Prep CCTI students receive personalized portfolios that include their chosen Career Pathway, Portfolio Evaluation Criteria, and Course Proficiency Profiles for all applicable courses.

Identification of competency mastery expectations enables individual school districts to design curricula in a variety of avenues to best meet the school's scheduling and delivery parameters.

Upon high school graduation and enrollment at CCC, Tech Prep CCTI students present completed portfolios to the CCC Student Success Center for review and credit consideration by appropriate faculty members. Portfolios must contain required supporting documentation as outlined. Delayed articulation credits are transcripted as pass-fail and are not reflected in the grade point average (GPA). Under the delayed articulation agreement, portfolio review and awarded credits are provided at no cost to the student.

Each student understands that an inability to make satisfactory progress in an advanced course in the area for which articulated credit is awarded may require completion of a lower level course. Postsecondary and secondary faculty review Career Pathways and Course Proficiency Profiles annually.

Additional Career Pathways are available at www.corning-cc.edu/techprep/.

Curriculum and Instruction

To begin the development of the Career Pathway, secondary and postsecondary faculty met to compare existing curriculum from both levels and identify overlap and gap areas. CCC courses, which most closely aligned with articulation possibilities, were identified. The goal was to eliminate duplication of curriculum and to create a seamless series of objectives.

The next step was to itemize competencies for each course or curriculum on Course Proficiency Profiles, a standard formal documentation process for all Tech Prep courses. Subsequently, secondary courses are reviewed for existing and potential alignment with competency checklists for each course. High school courses are not required to match each postsecondary course verbatim. Students often need to take several or a series of high school courses to obtain a particular set of competencies eligible for articulated credit consideration.

Competency-based articulation provides distinct advantages for students as they learn specific competencies and skills within a comprehensive course curriculum. Identification of related competencies provides concept connections and strengthens mastery. Articulation rewards students for mastery and promotes the steady progression of learning.

While competency-based articulation provides secondary schools with internal control of curriculum design, it also elevates scheduling constraints since students need to secure appropriate and available courses containing specific competency sets. Multiple courses are often necessary to fulfill the range of particular competency sets. High school schedules have less flexibility and latitude to ensure inclusion of all related courses.

Development of customized Career Pathway templates for each secondary school in each Career Pathway is under way. Customized pathways will specifically indicate individual course titles particular to each school, while indicating the complete pathway opportunity and subsequent requirements. Specific, detailed pathways, as opposed to generic regional pathways, will enhance clearer choices and options for each specific student.

Each Career Pathway includes opportunities for ACCUPLACER assessment at the 10th and 11th grade levels. Early evaluation of college-level readiness enables students to logically connect secondary with postsecondary expectations. Effective counseling and guidance with appropriate course selections enhance each student's goal-oriented plan for success. As the ACCUPLACER initiative progresses, diagnostic data will be provided to the school to enable the implementation of Academic Intervention Services (AIS), as mandated by the New York State Education Department.

Bridges With Four-Year Programs

While CCC's Network Technology Career Pathway does not have direct program-to-program articulations with four-year-based Network Technology Programs, many students are able to package their courses and additional CCC courses for easy transfer to related bachelor degree programs. Efforts are under way to establish direct articulations and diverse transfer opportunities with four-year institutions.

CCC plans to participate in the National Student Clearinghouse by summer 2005, to enhance accurate data collection on graduate activities, transfers, and academic destinations. Current graduate surveys, dependent exclusively on self-disclosure, yield limited information. Between 1999 and 2002, CCC's information technology graduates reported transfer and continuation in baccalaureate programs at institutions of higher learning in New York State and surrounding states of the Northeast quadrant. Some of the colleges listed included Binghamton University, Mansfield University, State University of New York (SUNY) College at Fredonia, SUNY College at Oneonta, SUNY College at Geneseo, Rochester Institute of Technology, Connecticut University, Excelsior College, and Elmira College.

Student Support

Levels of student support vary among schools and student needs. Each secondary school has identified a site manager and a cluster advisor who are focused on ensuring program design, alignment, and student success. Site managers act as the foundational conduit of information and as links between the secondary faculty and staff and the Tech Prep CCTI Coordinator. Site managers are the Career Pathway leaders in the school. Peer influence has proven to be the most effective method of connecting with counselors, faculty, and staff.

Cluster advisors have the primary responsibility of ensuring that students are aware of, enrolled in, and comfortable with the requirements and expectations of the Career Pathway. Together, site managers and cluster advisors schedule classroom presentations, organize parent forums, and assist students with personal portfolio requirements. Career counseling and advising responsibilities lie with the guidance counseling staff, of which several assume the roles of site manager or cluster advisor. Otherwise, teachers in those roles coordinate with counselors to optimize each student's career choices and pathway.

Each enrolled student receives a *Student Handbook* designed as a monthly organizer of activities intended to encourage consistent awareness of program requirements and completion expectations. The *Student Handbook* supports goals and encourages documentation of progress and mastery. While the *Student Handbook* is a hardcover tool that includes general information and activities, current and changing information is not able to be included on a regular and timely basis. Thus, the Student E-BOARD, an electronic bulletin board on the website, provides current specific details and information. E-BOARD is updated monthly and is included as a specific activity in the *Student Handbook*.

The Career Development Council, the region's school-to-career cap organization, ensures that each student receives the opportunity to participate in individual and group work-based learning experiences. Postsecondary Tech Prep CCTI students receive specialized attention through the CCC Student Success Center. In addition to an array of established student orientation and transition services, Tech Prep CCTI students receive assistance with portfolio processing and program connections.

Special Features

A combination of two initiatives with complementary leadership has created a Tech Prep CCTI program with support and accentuation. Tech Prep, traditionally a secondary-to-postsecondary focus, emphasizes the leadership role of the secondary partners. CCTI, administered by the League for Innovation in the Community College, emphasizes the leadership role of the postsecondary partner. With both CCTI and Tech Prep blueprints focused on the development of Career Pathways, the combined energy, commitment, and leadership has made the program an influential model in the region.

Tech Prep CCTI initiatives have received public commendations from the SUNY Mission Review II Team and the Middle States Reaccreditation Team visit to CCC during March 2005. The regional partnership linking secondary with postsecondary efforts was recognized as an exemplary model.

Tech Prep CCTI Career Pathways is distinctive, with a competency-based design that optimizes seamless curriculum opportunities for students throughout the region. Students use personalized portfolios to document competencies and skill sets throughout high school to ease transition to the postsecondary setting. The *Student Handbook* includes a series of activities that keep students focused and organized as they work toward their goals.

With both CCTI and Tech Prep blueprints focused on the development of career pathways, the combined energy, commitment, and leadership has made the program an influential model in the region.

The Implementation Strategies

Most Effective Strategies

Corning Community College has identified, developed, and launched several strategies designed to ease student transition, enhance student success, and expand learning opportunities. With varying degrees of progress and success due to staggered stages of implementation, each strategy addresses the CCTI goals and objectives. Several of the strategies are in early stages of development and have not been fully tested in practice in this project, but they have been selected for implementation on the basis of their success in other settings. In addition, there is some research-based evidence of their success, especially the First Year Experience, as strategies that will assist students in making successful transitions.

First Year Experience Course. Following an extensive year-long planning effort by a cross-campus committee, CCC introduced a new First Year Experience (FYE) course for first-time college students in the fall 2005 semester. The FYE course emphasizes life skills and adaptability skills that affect and influence retention and success. Plans include offering the FYE course as a dual-credit, dual-enrollment course in the senior year in the partner high schools beginning in fall 2006.

Based on extensive national data that highlights the positive retention effects of such courses, coupled with the impact of On Course training – developed by Skip Downing, principal facilitator of On Course Workshops and the author of *On Course: Strategies for Creating Success in College and in Life* – the CCC Student Success Committee committed to designing and implementing a collegewide FYE course, crossing divisions, programs, and curriculum. Effective communication of the documented and anticipated value of such a course was integral to faculty and staff support. CCC administration was strongly supportive of the initiative from the beginning. However, successful development and implementation of the concept was dependent on support from faculty and staff.

A panel of FYE Experts from other New York State colleges was invited to CCC by the Student Success Committee to introduce the concept and address improvement and challenges encountered elsewhere. College leaders experienced in FYE from Genesee Community College, Jamestown Community College, and Monroe Community College provided a foundation on which the Student Success Committee was able to build.

To introduce the student success concept to secondary partners, one of the consultants from Genesee Community College was invited to return to CCC for an introductory presentation for secondary administrators, counselors, and faculty. As a result, 17 educators from partner high schools registered for the On Course training to prepare for the FYE Course. An intensive three-day training program, cosponsored by Tech Prep CCTI and CCC, will provide training for 47 secondary and postsecondary individuals in preparation for the implementation of the FYE Course.

The First Year Experience moniker was specifically selected by the Student Success Committee as the best representation of the goals and objectives of the Career Pathway approach: career plan + preparation = informed choices, increased retention, and success! Since FYE is a trademarked term owned by the University of South Carolina, permission for use of the course name was requested and obtained.

Information Communication Technology Reform. Efforts are under way to redesign, realign, and expand the CCC IT programs under an Information Communications Technology (ICT) umbrella or concentration. IT is expanding to ICT in order to position the college on the forefront of the emerging technology. The demand for communications technology and the convergence of data, voice, and visual media are increasing at exponential rates. A focused ICT emphasis by the college will provide students with a viable and enticing career pathway with multiple opportunities for specialization.

A common first-semester curriculum, crossing divisional barriers and administrative structures, is in the development stage. This concept of cross-divisional program administration and faculty sharing was relatively untested at CCC prior to this initiative. To date, the high levels of cooperation and flexibility are unprecedented and notably impressive. The common first semester will enable students who have selected the ICT Pathway, as well as students who are entering college with unclear career goals, to begin their journey on common ground. Students will have ample opportunity to then select a more specialized program without backtracking. This approach will provide solid entry and transition for students while encouraging effective career planning.

The umbrella concept is being developed with the involvement and support of local economic development entities. Data from a cooperatively developed survey, provided by Chemung-Schuyler-Steuben Workforce New York and Southern Tier Economic Growth, will guide the development and alignment of the ICT initiative.

Individual Career Plan. Efforts are under way to design and institute a comprehensive and effective Individual Career Plan (ICP) for each student. The ICP will become the "key academic resource and career-planning tool" for students, parents, and schools outlining career goals, pathway opportunities, and academic and technical requirements for success.

While New York State requires K-12 Student Career Plans, in many cases, schools are meeting mandatory compliance issues but, unfortunately, are not optimizing the Career Plan as a student-friendly tool. ICPs should be the focal point of every student counseling program. Together, a student, parent or guardian, and counselor should create a personalized yet flexible roadmap, *i.e.*, career pathway, that provides career goals and steps to reach those goals. Course selection, work-based learning activities, and postsecondary program opportunities will reflect the roadmap or pathway to the selected career field.

To be effective, each ICP needs to become an active and living working plan for students, parents, and counselors on which all educational decisions and choices are based. An ICP, simply designed for administrative compliance, is ineffective in a filing cabinet. An ICP that is used as a focus tool becomes a guiding beacon for students in the haze of educational and career planning.

■ **A focused ICT emphasis by the college will provide students with a viable and enticing career pathway with multiple opportunities for specialization.**

Several specialized workshops have been held in the consortium to assist secondary counselors in the development of an effective ICP program. Progress, albeit slow, has been noted as counselors address the issues and challenges surrounding change and restructuring associated with such a major shift.

Scheduling and time allocation for parent-student-counselor meetings and follow-up, alignment of all sections of effective career pathways, and redevelopment of integrated procedures provide numerous challenges to counselors and administrators. While agreement with the ICP concept, potential benefits, and advantages is generally consistent, the strategies and plans for gradual and radical change vary widely among the project partners.

Administrative support and efforts toward an effective user-friendly ICP system are continuing.

TALK TIME. Coffeeklatsch-style sessions provide opportunities for secondary and postsecondary faculty to engage in topic-specific conversations, develop and align curriculum, and, most important, build relationships and communication. After-school TALK TIME sessions, scheduled at least once monthly, are discipline, program, or content specific. This format enables college and high school faculty and staff to discuss topics and ideas pertinent and specific to their areas. This face-to-face interaction and sharing significantly enhances actions and results. Common issues, as well as challenges, restrictions, and requirements particular to each institution, become the basis for change and growth.

TALK TIME has become the preferred avenue for communication and sharing among secondary and postsecondary faculty and staff at Corning Community College. The open and inviting atmosphere enables academic colleagues of various levels to share ideas, discuss pedagogy, and design implementation strategies.

TALK TIME sessions are scheduled and coordinated by the Tech Prep CCTI office. The intermediary nature of the Tech Prep CCTI office enhances the consistent communication with all partners across the consortium.

Student Portfolio*, Student Handbook, *and E-BOARD. Dynamic communication tools and program materials significantly shape program quality and effectiveness. Strong, accurate, and informative materials are vital to optimizing program involvement, participation, and completion for students, parents, counselors, faculty, and administrators.

■ TALK TIME... enables college and high school faculty and staff to discuss topics and ideas pertinent and specific to their areas.

Student portfolios, currently in hard-binder format, are personalized for each student indicating name, school, career cluster, Career Pathway, site manager and cluster advisor contact information, and Tech Prep Program contacts. Portfolio contents include the selected Career Pathway and all related Course Proficiency Profiles, indicating appropriate course competencies. E-portfolios or electronic versions are currently being explored to determine effectiveness and student access issues.

Student Handbooks, structured as program organizers, provide a series of tethering activities per grade level. Activities include Student Events, E-BOARD, Portfolios, Work-based Learning, Goal Planning, ACCUPLACER, College Search, and an *Annual Student Survey*. Handbooks are designed to be a formal method by which students are reminded, at least monthly, of program information and requirements.

The E-BOARD is an electronic bulletin board on the Tech Prep website designed to provide current and changing information and news to students in an easy-to-access format. Electronic communication is the tool of choice for students today and provides a cost-effective means to share up-to-date information. An E-BOARD activity in the *Student Handbook* reminds students to access the electronic newsletter monthly and to document participation.

Least Effective Strategy

ACCUPLACER. While this strategy cannot be considered least effective regarding expected results, the implementation of this strategy has been the most problematic. The delayed establishment of ACCUPLACER in the high schools according to the projected timeline has created a significant void of useful student data. Thus, this strategy is considered the least successful effort of the project to date.

In conjunction with the National Bridge Partnership Program, Tech Prep CCTI-registered students will take the online ACCUPLACER assessment in 10th and 11th grades to determine academic readiness levels for postsecondary study. Student diagnostic data from the ACCUPLACER assessment will assist secondary schools in providing Academic Intervention Services to students, as mandated by the New York State Department of Education. Efforts to implement the initiative have been slow due to unforeseen time constraints and scheduling issues. To accommodate the needs for segmented data and student assessment costs, Tech Prep CCTI established a new account with the ACCUPLACER assessment service. This approach will enhance the distinction of the initiative and highlight direct impact and results.

An instructional manual for proctors is under development, with proctor training to be scheduled. Procedural issues regarding data collection, interpretation, reporting, and evaluation are under examination. Measurable goals for the initiative are to be identified prior to implementation. Implementation of the initiative experienced delays throughout the 2004-2005 school year. Fall 2005 was established as the new start date for the ACCUPLACER in the High School Initiative.

Lessons Learned

Shared vision. The first step to implementing a successful Career Pathway model is to establish a shared, universally accepted vision, highlighting expected benefits and outcomes of that systemic change. The common purpose must be clearly defined with mutually beneficial outcomes. Each partner will be expected to experience some level of change, which usually results in resistance and rigidity. The common vision with obvious positive outcomes will power the change and adaptability. The vision must constantly focus on student success.

Overcoming barriers. Genuine success for students is the goal of every serious educator. Achieving that success is the continuing challenge. While artificial barriers – such as scheduling, budgets, and administratively imposed requirements – exist in every environment, the challenge is not why but how to improve the educational opportunities for students.

The Career Pathway needs to emerge as a solution to the needs of students, not as an additional task or duty with no relevance to existing processes and patterns. Identifying and designing the Career Pathway as a realistic and effective connection of secondary to postsecondary to career enhances the value and potency of each segment of the pathway. Thus, it is critical that all partners be actively involved and well informed from the beginning of the initiative. Philosophical buy-in from all partners is necessary to generate the creativity, flexibility, and adaptability required for permanent and substantial change.

Leadership. A strong catalyst is essential in spearheading the effort and maintaining momentum. Change requires massaging, team building, methodical planning, and step-by-step implementation. A pivotal leader who can clearly articulate the vision and orchestrate the efforts of all partners guides the progressive change. Establishing trust through honest communication, attention to detail, and effective follow-through should be the hallmark of the leader and the leadership team. Insistence on unwavering quality elevates the initiative in priority by all partners.

■ Establishing trust through honest communication, attention to detail, and effective follow-through should be the hallmark of the leader and the leadership team. Insistence on unwavering quality elevates the initiative in priority by all partners.

Collaboration with business and industry. Education partners need business partners and business needs education. The disconnect often occurs because of the differing timeframes of operations involved. Business and industry, operating on a time-sensitive nature with profit-impacting repercussions, differ from the educational structure of the traditional school calendar, established curriculum, and mandated assessments. Education deals with human development, business deals with human capital. Bridging that divide is critical to the success of the career pathway project and critical to the success of any initiative. Education needs to realize that all students are preparing for the workforce at some perhaps undetermined point in their lives. The pathway to that career will vary with each individual. However, education is the means to reach that goal. Education is not the goal in itself. Conversely, business partners need to invest in the future workforce while analyzing and realizing the short and long-term effects of their decisions. Clearly, business expedites the change process. Active business-partner involvement will enhance the Career Pathway development process and spur the timely implementation and assessment of the process. Again, the establishment of a mutually beneficial atmosphere is paramount.

College as leader. Dynamic, committed leadership from the college is critical to true systemic change. CCTI has spawned the Career Pathway development by challenging the community college with leadership responsibilities and actions. Postsecondary administrators and faculty need to clearly and actively establish the creative atmosphere and solid foundation for new strategies and initiatives focused on vision and goals. Casual involvement is not enough; continued active participation and leadership by the college is necessary to effectively initiate change.

High school counselor and faculty roles. Career Pathway development and success is heavily dependent on counselors and faculty at the secondary levels. Daily emphasis and procedural embedding are essential to program success. Positive feedback and constructive suggestions should be frequent and genuine.

Language. Throughout the development and implementation process, leaders should make a conscious and concerted effort to remove the words *but* and *can't* from conversations and discussions. Logistics and obstacles contain hidden and often unexpected solutions when presented in an environment of possibility and creative nurturing.

More information about Corning Community College and the CCTI Initiative can be found at http://www.league.org/league/projects/ccti/projects/summary.cfm?key=ccc.

Southwestern Oregon Community College

Terry O'Banion

OCCUPATIONAL AREA: Information Technology
CAREER PATHWAY: Programming and Software Development
CCTI PROJECT DIRECTOR: Brenda Brecke
PROJECT WEBSITE: www.socc.edu
PROJECT PARTNERS: Southwestern Oregon Community College
Oregon Department of Education
North Bend School District
Marshfield High School
ORCA Communications
Bay Area Hospital
Affiliated Computer Services

The Project Partners

Our CCTI site partnership in Southwestern Oregon, a joint venture with the Oregon State Department of Education, will allow us to design a program of study to prepare IT professionals that aligns with national standards and will be a design for a statewide Pre-K-14/16 model.

Brenda Brecke, CCTI Project Coordinator, Southwestern Oregon Community College

Southwestern Oregon Community College (SOCC) is a rural community college struggling to serve an economically depressed area on the Oregon coast. The college is providing leadership for a number of innovative programs created by a state that is one of the nation's leaders in educational reform. Given the added burden of reduced budgets, Southwestern Oregon is doing remarkably well with the challenges and is leveraging the CCTI project as a pivotal element in meeting those challenges.

In 1991, Oregon's state legislature, to raise expectations for education, passed the Oregon Educational Act for the 21st Century, which set the state on a course of educational reform in K-12 that has had significant impact on the state's community colleges and universities. And it has made Oregon the place to visit for innovative and substantive practices to improve the educational enterprise. The law, strengthened and clarified by the legislature in 1995, calls for rigorous educational standards to evaluate student performance and progress.

Oregon is developing two types of educational standards for secondary school students:

- ***Academic Content Standards*** define what students are expected to know and establish competencies in English, mathematics, science, history, geography, civics, economics, the arts, and a second language.
- ***Performance Standards*** define how well students must perform on classroom assessments and state assessments leading to the Certificate of Initial Mastery and the Certificate of Advanced Mastery.

The Certificate of Initial Mastery (CIM), ideally to be achieved by the 10th grade, is designed to certify the achievement of basic academic skills. CIM is articulated with a set of proficiencies required by the universities for admission through Proficiency-Based Admission Standards System (PASS).

The Certificate of Advanced Mastery (CAM), ideally to be achieved by the 12th grade, is designed to certify the achievement of applied and contextual learning. In the *Oregon Standards* newsletter issued for the 2002-2003 school year by the Oregon Department of Education, it is noted that "many of the cornerstones of the CAM design are aimed at helping students identify their particular aptitudes, use their learning styles to their best advantage, and envision and plan toward a fulfilling future."

These initiatives are being piloted in various high schools and are still in development. The framework for these innovations will continue to expand into the future, requiring high school graduates by 2006-2007 to develop an education plan and build an education profile, demonstrate extended application through a collection of evidence, demonstrate career-related knowledge and skills, and participate in career-related learning experiences as outlined in the education plan.

There are real challenges in Oregon in achieving the grand design of this reform plan:

1. The legislature continues to adjust the overall design.
2. The plan changes as necessary to meet the federal requirements of the No Child Left Behind Act.
3. There are insufficient funds to implement the special programs of the reform effort, and there are almost no funds for staff development to help teachers and administrators implement the new reforms.
4. Interviews with a few selected educators in Oregon reveal that it is difficult to understand the reform plan and to communicate its various and complex components.

The Oregon Department of Education provides detailed information on elements of the reform plan at its website, www.ode.state.or.us/cimcam/index.htm.

While Southwestern Oregon is adapting to changes brought about by the state's reform efforts, and indeed playing a central role in the area of information technology programs, it is at the same time coping with profound change in the community it serves. The college's 2002 *Institutional Self-Study* summarizes the economic and social challenges of this region.

The local economic situation reflects a 20-year shift from a production economy based on wood products to a service economy. Family-wage jobs in the wood products industry have been replaced by low-wage service jobs. Since 1976, jobs in lumber and wood products have declined by 4,500 positions, or 82 percent. The loss of jobs continues in the fishing, timber, and cranberry industries. The unemployment rate is one-third to two times higher than state and national percentages. It is only now, in the midst of a national recession with Oregon holding the highest jobless rate in the nation, that the state unemployment level has risen to match the unemployment level South Coast residents have endured for 20 years.

The economic decline is reflected in social decline: One-fourth of the population of the area is functionally illiterate; 39 percent of children age 17 and under within Coos and Curry Counties received emergency food assistance in 2001; Coos County ranked first of 36 Oregon counties in child abuse; one in five children under the age of 5 in Coos County live in poverty, and 22 percent of the mothers in Coos County have less than 12 years of education.

The declining social and economic conditions are also reflected in the declining student population. From 1999 to 2002, enrollments in K-12 districts served by the college decreased from 13,935 to 12,796 – a loss of 1,139 (8.2 percent) students. The population of the 1st grade in these districts is approximately one-half the population of the current 12th grade – a dramatic illustration of the decline in the school population and an indicator of the challenge faced by Southwestern Oregon Community College in attracting enrollments in the future.

The budget at the college is based on an enrollment-driven formula. For the college to survive, it must be very creative in attracting students from a base of declining population. Undaunted by these overwhelming challenges, the leaders of the college understand and accept their crucial role in this community. Southwestern's president, Stephen Kridelbaugh, has responded to the challenge stating, "One of the goals of the college is to revitalize the economy and the workforce in this area. We do what we have to do to bring family-wage jobs into our area. If we don't have a trained workforce, we cannot attract industry to move here."

■ For the college to survive, it must be very creative in attracting students from a base of declining population.

The college is aggressive in pursuing new industries and is unabashedly entrepreneurial in creating arrangements that will attract new students. On-campus housing, unusual for public community colleges, is provided for 400 students and attracts a number of out-of-district students. A culinary arts program, with tuition set at $19,000, will enroll 100 students from around the nation in the fall of 2005. Through an aggressive recruiting program, 1 percent of all high school graduates in the state of Alaska (42 students in 2003) attend Southwestern Oregon. The college has spent more than $40 million on new facilities in the last 10 years, at no cost to taxpayers. The loans are being paid off with revenue streams from some of the programs cited.

As part of the plan to address the challenges of the region, the college strongly encourages college faculty and staff to pursue grants. The college has a philosophy of supporting successful and promising programs, and the Department of Computer Information Systems (CIS) is one of the most successful at SOCC.

The CIS department at SOCC has become a primary source of training in information technology on Oregon's south coast. The program is staffed with a core of very active and innovative IT faculty who collaborate, in a very challenging environment, to create programs and opportunities for students. Although enrollments in the IT programs have not met expectations, the faculty continue to seek grants, design alternative instructional strategies, create models, and play a major role in Oregon's development of IT offerings.

Encouraged and supported by the college leadership, the CIS department has applied for and been awarded a number of grants that provide the basis for expanded programs. The department has had a partnership with Cisco Systems since 1997, and is a Cisco Networking Academy and a regional academy for Cisco instructor training. There are four corresponding courses in the Advanced Cisco Lab for the Cisco CCNP.

The department was selected in 2000 as one of only eight recipients in the United States of a $250,000 grant from Microsoft for the Working Connections project managed by the American Association of Community Colleges. The grant provided funds for faculty release time to create new curricula to reflect changes in IT. During the first year of the grant, Microsoft also provided $900,000 worth of software; in the second year, Microsoft added additional software valued at $780,000.

There have been nine additional grants from various sources over the past few years for specific programs and services, and the CIS department has meshed and leveraged this grant support to create model programs and services. A hallmark of the programs is that they have been created using national standards from a variety of sources, including

- National Center for Emerging Technologies (www.nwcet.org);
- International Society for Technology in Education (www.iste.org);
- Association for Computing Machinery (www.acm.org);
- International Technology Education Association (www.iteawww.org);
- State Educational Technology Directors Association (www.setda.org); and
- Oregon Department of Education (www.ode.state.or.us/cifs/newspaper/).

Using these various standards for reference, the CIS department has created 4 AAS degrees and 10 certificates based on a career-ladder approach. The AAS degrees are in Technical Support, Computer Networking, Web Development and Administration, and Software Support. The career ladder is designed for multiple points of entry for students. Courses are modularized, and some, such as the beginning course CS101, are offered in a variety of formats, including lecture, self-paced, challenge-test, and skills courses.

There is also a computer science transfer program for students who want to complete degrees beyond the community college. Southwestern partners with a number of Oregon universities through the Southwestern Oregon University Center and has a dual-enrollment agreement with the Computer Science and Engineering departments at Oregon State University. The college is an active member of the Oregon Computer Science Chairs Committee, a statewide group that develops articulation agreements among the various educational institutions.

The CIS department was fortunate to receive two complementary grants at about the same time, and, in their usual fashion, the faculty meshed and leveraged these two grants to form the framework for this CCTI partnership. The CCTI grant from the League for Innovation provides a larger umbrella for a challenge grant to create a Career Pathway for IT awarded in the winter of 2003 by the Oregon Department of Education (ODE) and the Oregon Department of Community Colleges and Workforce Development (CCWD). The challenge grants addressed four areas of "great economic and workforce development need" in the state of Oregon, including information technology. The purpose of the project is "to design integrated, articulated, and statewide secondary/postsecondary pathways that provide students with a smooth and seamless transition to further education and employment." The purpose of the State Challenge Grant could be a page taken from the national CCTI project purpose.

Southwestern has received four additional grants with similar pathway goals to the CCTI grant. The coordinators of these grants have become partners in collaboration, sharing best practices, what works, what doesn't work, and lessons learned in career pathways. The Oregon Incentive Grant partners the college with the WIA agent, South Coast Business Employment Corporation, to create an IT pathway for retraining dislocated workers. The Oregon Opportunities Grant is a planning grant to design five career pathways for adult re-entry. The Federal Department of Labor Pathways Grant designs custom pathways for dislocated workers as they work to complete the Employment Skills Training Certificate, a Southwestern program. And the Carl Perkins Challenge Grant is working with local high schools in the area of health care to establish a career pathway for high school graduates and career-related learning opportunities.

Although not a formal partner, Southwestern became involved in the work of the High Schools That Work Initiative (HSTW). Several high school and college faculty and administrators attended HSTW conferences in 2004, and a site evaluation visit for the college and two high schools was held in 2005 by the HSTW program.

The **Oregon Department of Education** (ODE) has become an important partner as Southwestern's participation increases in the national and state career pathway initiative. As Oregon seeks to strengthen the impact and influence of the CIM (Certificate of Initial Mastery) and the CAM (Certificate of Advanced Mastery), the pathways project will increase in importance as well. Additionally, Southwestern regards other Oregon community colleges as partners in this endeavor, seeking their input and sharing the outcomes of these related grants and initiatives.

K-12 partners in this project include the South Coast Education Service District, which provides access to the 10 school districts in the college's service area. The primary school partners include the **North Bend School District** and the Gold Beach High School in the Central Curry School District. Both of these schools are creating charter-magnet technology programs that will play major roles in this CCTI project. **Marshfield High School**, located in Coos Bay, Oregon, became an affiliated member of the CCTI grant in 2004.

Operational in the fall of 2003, the Gold Beach Technology Charter School is a school-within-a-school concept. The North Bend School District's program is a magnet school with a new technology building built with local bond-levy funds. The new facility, located between the middle school and the high school, will house five special classrooms for IT. The first classes were offered in the fall of 2003 for students in the 6th to the 10th grades, and classes for the 11th and 12th grades will be added in the next two years. Due to budget considerations, Gold Beach terminated the formal partnership at the end of Year 2 of the project.

At the end of Year 2, Coos Bay School District's Marshfield High School (MHS) became interested in participating with CCTI and the other grant work, being included in the HSTW visitations and evaluation, and increasing the collaboration with the college in general. MHS does not have a separate technology school and has inactivated its Cisco Academy and Tech Support A+ classes as a budget reallocation measure, but is seeking alternate avenues to make these courses available. The school district is extremely interested in the five CTTI objectives, especially reducing the need for remediation at the postsecondary level.

Southwestern regards other Oregon community colleges as partners in this endeavor, seeking their input and sharing the outcomes of these related grants and initiatives.

In addition to these two technology schools, local employers have important roles in the project. **ORCA Communications** is a broadband service provider owned by the Coquille Indian Tribe, with a need for networking and technical support workers. The **Bay Area Hospital**, the largest hospital on the Oregon coast, needs IT workers in all areas in which the college offers programs. **Affiliated Computer Services** was persuaded by the college to locate in the Coos Bay area through offers of special training and space. ACS is a worldwide provider of diversified business and IT outsourcing solutions, and hires software and technical support workers.

There are other partners in the CCTI project, but the two high schools and the Oregon Department of Education are the primary players to create a Career Pathway that will meet the requirements of both the state grant and the national grant. Three employer partners provide local business perspective.

Curriculum and Instruction

Five official CCTI templates have been developed in this project:

- Computer Science transfer template for students seeking a B.S. degree
- Networking Design and Administration Career Ladder
- Technical Support Career Ladder
- Software Support Career Ladder
- Web Development and Administration Career Ladder

Although the Oregon Department of Education prefers the CCTI official style for the templates, staff at SOCC designed a customized template that is more student and parent friendly. These templates will be distributed to students and parents during special academic advising sessions. The templates demonstrate the gap between high school graduation requirements and college-level preparedness, and another template demonstrates the North Bend High School ORCO Tech School graduate requirements in relation to college-level preparedness.

Curriculum and instructional approaches at the secondary level. ORCO Tech is North Bend High School's school within a school, with a focus on providing a technology-infused curriculum. Students are encouraged to explore one or more IT pathways through the selection of their tech electives. The freshman and sophomore required technology courses have been designed to align with Southwestern Oregon Community College computer literacy requirements, thereby providing a transfer-credit opportunity. Southwestern has been collaborating with ORCO Tech faculty to make available at least two additional transfer-credit opportunities in each of the four pathways. In addition to providing the technology-infused education, ORCO Tech has strengthened its academic standards by increasing the math, science, and foreign language graduation requirements beyond those of the high school.

■ ...the high school has initiated a series of staff development activities that include faculty advising techniques, classroom methodologies, assessment strategies, engagement, and college alignment.

Staff development opportunities have been offered to the K-12 faculty and staff through focused workshops based on high school faculty requests. In response to attending the High Schools That Work conference, the high school has initiated a series of staff development activities that include faculty advising techniques, classroom methodologies, assessment strategies, engagement, and college alignment. The HSTW visit allowed faculty and staff from two high school districts, ESD, and the college district to share information, to gain an understanding of the different systems, and to explore collaboration options.

The Southwestern CCTI project developed a minigrant program called the CCTI Teachers Using Technology Program, designed to promote excellence in teaching and professional growth of high school teachers through the use of technology. The program supported initiatives in teaching and service or enhancements in existing courses and programs. A successful applicant was typically awarded a $500 stipend, with an additional $250 available for hardware, software, materials, and supplies. Instructional teams applying for larger requests were also considered. In Year 2 of the CCTI grant, five high school faculty received the minigrants. The minigrant program was suspended in Year 3 due to lack of funds.

The Asset test has been used to test all sophomores at North Bend during the spring of the last two years. Recently, Coos Bay School district agreed to participate as a partner school and tested all sophomores, as it will continue to do each year. The test results provide counselors, teachers, and staff with data to guide students and their parents to help them set realistic short- and long-term goals. These data, when coupled with other activities like Connect to Your Future – ORCO Tech parent night at North Bend – will help parents and students understand the pathway opportunities and options available. Other topics covered at parent night include an overview of the Career Information System (CIS); career pathways at SOCC; available scholarships; credit-based transition courses; and dual admission and enrollment with the University of Oregon, Oregon State University, and other four-year colleges and universities.

Curriculum and instructional approaches at the postsecondary level. The CIS Department was one of the recipients of the Microsoft-AACC Working Connections Grant, Class of 2002. One of the major projects of the grant was curriculum development. The cluster areas are Networking, Technical Support, Software Support, and Web Development. All programs were developed using the NWCET Skill Standards for Information Technology, ACM curriculum recommendations, Oregon Employment Department information, CIS Advisory Committee recommendations, and other sources. The CCTI grant is an excellent follow-up project, as the high school students are able to exit high school with certificates and even an AAS.

The CIS Department used the Career Ladder model in designing the new programs. The model is one in which one or more certificates ladder to the AAS degree. Each degree and certificate includes the appropriate coursework for the knowledge and skills necessary for identifiable entry-level jobs. This allows students to complete a certificate, acquire a job, and continue their education. Additionally, many students are completing a certificate from one cluster while majoring in an AAS from a different cluster; this is similar to obtaining a minor in a bachelor's program. Southwestern Oregon Community College was the first school in the state to develop entire programs using the career-ladder model.

The staff of the Oregon Education and Workforce Development Department has supported the career-ladder model and has promoted its use as a promising practice statewide. The following graphic shows the steps in the Networking Career Ladder.

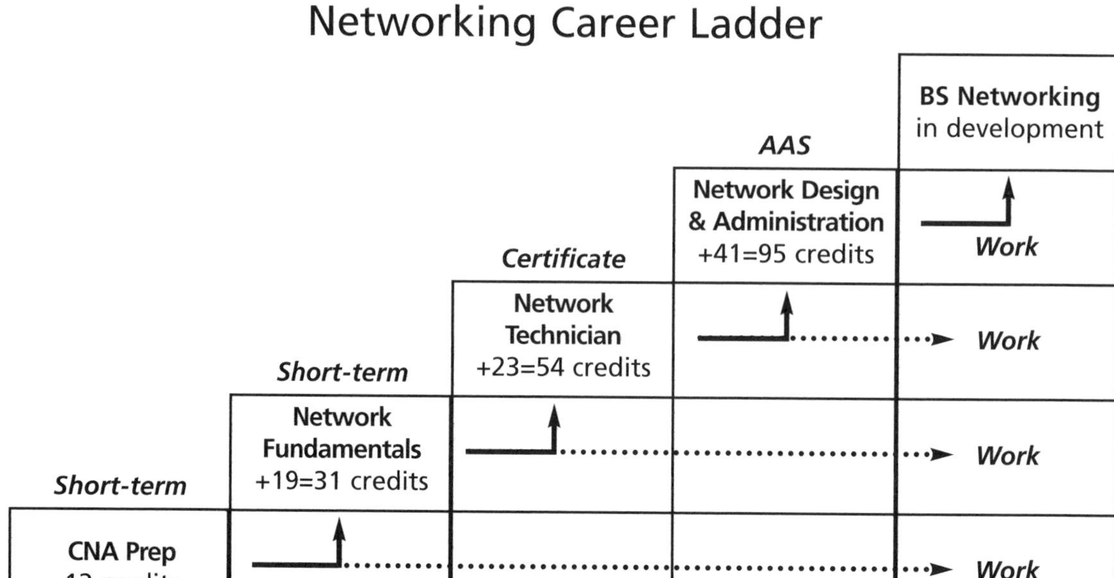

Multiple-entry points exist to allow students to enter the program with credit for prior learning or experience. The student may have gained the skills and knowledge from high school 2+2 programs, industry certifications, self-study, work experience, and other college programs such as Adult Learning Skills Program (ALSP) or short-term training. The following graphic depicts the multiple-entry points into the A+ courses.

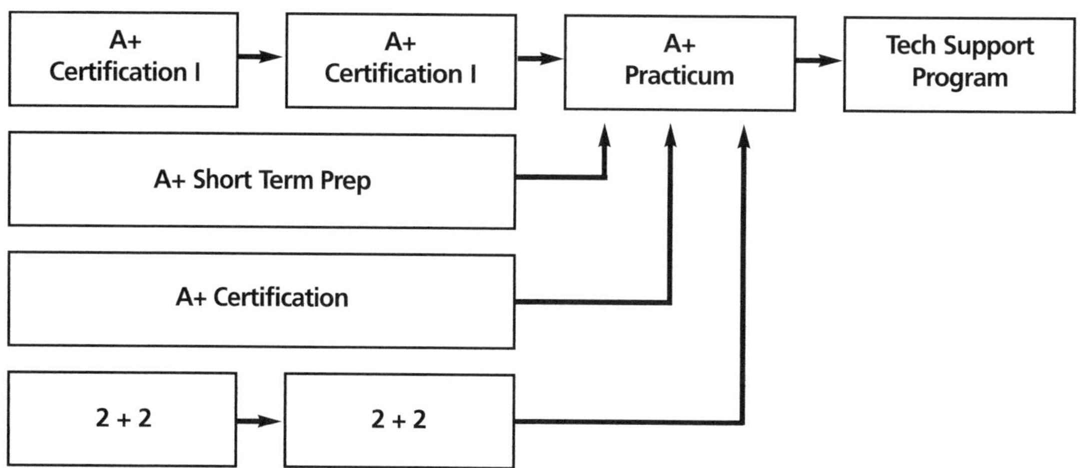

The LENs (Learning Exchange Networks) Program, the internationally acclaimed program available from the League for Innovation, is faculty development curriculum based on extensive research and best practices. The program consists of six modules and addresses topics and skills essential for quality teaching and learning. The CCTI team and campus administration have cooperated to offer LENs modules for academic year 2005-2006. This effort has received strong administrative support with a variety of incentives for faculty to participate in the LENs modules. Special emphasis on new and part-time faculty will help ensure professional development for faculty.

As a result of several faculty and staff attending an intensive Noel Levitz training program, a collegewide Noel Levitz training workshop was provided on student retention and success during fall 2004. This two-day training placed emphasis on improving student contact and communication through advising and other faculty and staff contact. Anecdotal data suggest that this service was useful to many faculty. The training session also helped the campus retention committee better focus its efforts to improve student advising and retention across campus.

As a result of the Community College Survey of Student Engagement (CCSSE) report, the Campus Retention Committee, with the assistance of the CCTI team, generated a draft of collegewide student competencies based on those recommended by the League for Innovation. This draft was approved by the general faculty and will be incorporated into course outlines, class syllabi, and programs. The plan is to refine competencies as needed, with a periodic review at least once annually.

Bridges With Four-Year Programs

The Associate of Arts Oregon-Block Transfer (AAOT) completion ensures that the student has met the general education core requirements for all universities in the Oregon University System and has completed 90 quarter credits. The student will transfer to the university with junior status. Additionally, many private schools and out-of-state universities recognize the AAOT. Southwestern CS students are advised to complete the AAOT with the CS program's required courses. Beyond the generic AAOT, there is a special dual-enrollment program with Oregon State University and a computer science articulation agreement with Western Oregon University. The college has had many successful transfers to Oregon universities.

At Southwestern, students are provided a number of options in the career pathways. One pathway option is designed for students planning to complete a bachelor's degree with or without attendance at the community college.

Student Support

Recruiting. The CS department is an active participant in the college's student recruiting effort. The recruiting department selects programs each year for aggressive and focused recruiting outside of the college district. During the 2003-2004 academic year, the CS department was one of the selected programs.

College information was distributed to about 1,500 schools in several states and resulted in an increase of students. The college also has an active in-district recruiting and advising program in which the department participates in many ways. Staff members in the CS department have provided student support by presenting at the Day at Southwestern for high school juniors and seniors and advising at each high school's special Southwestern registration day.

Retention efforts. Concurrent with initiatives associated with the CCTI grant, the college president established a campuswide Retention Committee. The strong support of the administration has helped ensure more coherent and successful efforts by the committee and faculty. The heightened recognition of the need for more effective retention efforts resulted in a number of initiatives, including an all-staff Noel Levitz in-service workshop, a year-long schedule for advising, increased hours in the writing lab, increased opportunities for students to meet with their advisors prior to the start of classes, better diffusion of the results of the CCSSE survey, and three intensive advising nights during spring 2005 to highlight degree changes and dual-admission and enrollment initiatives for returning students. The retention committee will remain a long-standing committee, continuing to research best practices to refine current activities or frame new ones that enhance student retention.

Academic advising at the high school. The North Bend High School has modified its academic advising model to include cohort advising by a faculty member. The cohort meets once per month for current advising information. This information has included the CCTI pathways with special emphasis on the high school requirements and the college entrance gap. At this time, the high school reports that students are taking more mathematics and science courses in the 2005-2006 academic year.

Career exploration. The Oregon Career Information System (CIS) is Oregon's career information delivery system. Developed at the University of Oregon, it is a consortium organization administered by the university (oregoncis.uoregon.edu). The objective of CIS is to provide a comprehensive and state-based resource to help all Oregonians become aware of work and educational options, connect education and work, and make successful career decisions and transitions throughout their lifetime. Oregon CIS software and materials are user friendly and are used in schools and colleges to support career development. The system allows users to build their own educational and career profile and modify it over time. One of the CCTI activities is to encourage parents to use the system by learning to use the CIS with their students. CIS includes career information, college information, scholarship information, labor market information, and college and course prerequisite requirements.

■ **The strong support of the administration has helped ensure more coherent and successful efforts by the committee and faculty.**

Special Features

The Southern Regional Education Board (www.sreb.org), through its High Schools That Work (HSTW) program, is a partner in the CCTI project, and the college took advantage of this opportunity for a consultation. High Schools That Work has gathered information and data from some of the most successful high schools in the nation and uses this information to help other schools improve. HSTW provides a technical assistance visit (TAV) to high schools to provide an assessment of the current practices and make suggestions for improvement. HSTW agreed to visit the partners (two high schools and the college) in the CCTI grant and pay special attention to the partnership. The visit, in February 2005, was designed to help project partners and the college assess the current status of important research-based practices. During the TAV, local teams observed classroom practices, reviewed school data, and held in-depth interviews with teachers, administrators, guidance and advisement personnel, students, board members, and parents.

The purpose of the visit was to help sites improve the quality of learning for students by working with teachers, counselors, and administrators to raise expectations for student achievement; refine what is taught; improve how students are taught; improve how the high schools and college relate to students; improve how teachers relate to each other; improve how the high schools and college communicate with parents, employers, and each other; collect and use data for making continued improvement; and improve strategies for building transitions from secondary to postsecondary institutions. A final report addressed the five outcome goals of the CCTI grant and the objectives of the HSTW project. The education partners of the Southwestern CCTI grant used the reports to draft a preliminary strategic plan for Year 3 of the CCTI grant. The partners met in August 2005 to finalize the plan.

The Implementation Strategies

Most Effective Strategies

Design pathways by alignment with national standards, recognized business and industry standards, or other relevant standards. Using ACM, NETS, ALA, NWCET, and ISTE Standards, Southwestern developed an IT Career Pathway using the credit-based transition model employing a variety of techniques, such as 2+2, course challenge, online courses, hybrid courses, and internet protocol videoconferencing (IPV) courses. Southwestern is partnering with a newly formed tech high school in the college district and plans to add each of the 10 high schools in the district.

The strategy was successful because it was educationally sound and research based. Students value an education that is based on national standards and not just regional requirements, thus giving them mobility in their education and career.

In addition to the CCTI grant, Southwestern has received five complementary grants from the Oregon Department of Education: the Oregon Challenge Grant to develop a model IT pathway for Oregon; the Oregon Adult Re-Entry IT Career Pathway Grant to develop an IT-concentrated program for adults seeking retraining; the Pathways to Advancement Grant, with six career-learning areas; and the Carl Perkins Capacity Grant, focused on health-occupations pathways.

As part of a statewide initiative through the Oregon Challenge Grant, Southwestern developed the IT-focused career pathway from Grade 9 through Grade 14. The pathway will be a credit-based transition model from secondary to postsecondary and is being developed in conjunction with the Oregon Department of Education. Similar models are being developed in engineering, health, and education in the State of Oregon. The Oregon Department of Education will coordinate the rollout of the final models developed for the four focus pathways.

Support the high schools in bridging the gap between the state requirements for high school graduation and the entrance requirements for college-level curriculum, to reduce the need for remediation of all students entering college. The college is improving and enhancing relationships with district high schools by facilitating high-school-to-college transitions through collaborative efforts. Creative methods are being devised to maximize the high school and college resources in these financially hard times, benefiting the student with smoother transitions to college as well as affordable and relevant education. Special emphasis is given to increasing the success of high school and college students in mathematics and language arts. The goal is to improve the academic performance at both levels and decrease the need for remediation. High school and college teachers are working as teams to achieve this goal. The teams are participating in the High Schools That Work Initiative.

■ Understanding and acknowledging the gap between high school graduation requirements and college-level requirements has been an awakening for many parents and students.

The college has implemented a program to provide advising to parents and their high school students on the need to prepare to meet the requirements in math, English, and reading prerequisite standards for admission into college-level courses. By increasing availability and advisement of transfer-credit opportunities, the college encourages high school students to stay on track in taking those prerequisite courses, with the goal to advance into the transfer-credit courses while still in high school. This effort is designed for IT pathway participants, but all college-bound high school students could benefit from this strategy.

This effort has been successful because students and their parents want it to be possible to exit high school ready for college-level work. Understanding and acknowledging the gap between high school graduation requirements and college-level requirements has been an awakening for many parents and students. Already, North Bend High School reports that more students are taking more math and science courses for the 2005-2006 academic year.

Use formative academic and employability assessments to alert students to academic or skill deficits they may have, and begin remediation as early as necessary to ensure success in a rigorous program of study. College placement tests will be given in the sophomore year of high school to alert students to their current academic standing in comparison to college-level work. This will give students two years to gain identified skills and knowledge needed to make the transition to college or the workplace. Academic and career counseling will be provided to assist the students and their parents in making informed schedule decisions. The HSSSE will be used to determine current student engagement and help guide the high school's selection of activities to increase engagement. Ultimately, the project hopes to make the senior year productive for all students, resulting in students entering college without the need for remedial coursework.

The success of this strategy is directly related to the timing of the college placement tests. The tests are given early enough in the students' high school career to fix and fill the gaps. The advising process includes information about what students need to do to meet college requirements, especially in the area of math. Again, involving the parents is a requirement to make this a successful strategy.

The CCSSE survey was used in Spring 2004 to assess how Southwestern met five national benchmarks associated with student engagement. The results were thoroughly reviewed by college trustees, administration, faculty, and support staff. As an outcome of the CCSSE survey, various campus groups, including the Campus Retention Committee and the Faculty Senate, increased their efforts to generate greater student engagement in the educational experience. Initiatives so far include direct strategies to foster better advising, adoption of core competencies by the faculty, and a comprehensive set of faculty in-service activities based on the LENs materials and technology needs. Changes for advising students included a pizza-party group-advising night for transfer students, increased promotion of advising and early registration, and raffle items for students who register early.

As part of the High Schools That Work initiative, the college sent teams of math and writing teachers to summer intensive programs in remediation techniques. Additionally, Southwestern requested a High School to College and Careers Technical Assistance Visit (TAV) sponsored by the Southern Regional Education Board. The three-day site visit occurred in February 2005. During the visit, three locally generated teams observed classrooms; reviewed school data; and held in-depth interviews with teachers, administrators, guidance and advisement personnel, students, board members, and parents in North Bend and Coos Bay

School Districts and at Southwestern. Final reports were sent to each of the three partner institutions, along with a general report about how all three are collaborating as a group. This report has provided a framework for future planning and collaboration among the three partners. The high schools are planning to use teacher in-service days to create senior-year math and language arts curricula.

Implement instructional strategies based on learning-centered practices such as collaborative learning, contextual learning, and active learning. Southwestern's Adult Learning Skills Program developed a Career Pathways project for an adult IT cohort that draws from recent high school graduates, high school students, and an adult population (TANF, Adult Basic Education, ESL, dislocated worker, and other unemployed and underemployed adults). Creating an adult IT cohort as the first step in re-entering the educational system is especially successful with adult re-entry students who have been out of the classroom for several years. This eases students back into the academic setting and helps them prepare for more traditional courses. The cohort's activities were in the context of information technology, with lessons and topics flowing from one class to the next. The math, reading, and writing examples and exercises were focused on IT topics. The Oregon Adult Re-Entry IT Career Pathway Grant has developed an IT concentrated program for adults seeking retraining.

At IT Educator's Workshops on instructional design, methods, and strategies using electronic technology, participants focus on contextual learning, active learning, and other learning-centered practices. Instructional experts deliver these workshops, which are open to high school and college teachers in all disciplines. The workshops were the result of a survey of high school faculty that identified areas of interest. The IT Educator's Workshops helped ORCO Tech faculty infuse technology into the curriculum by providing needed technical training. For several high school teachers, this was their first introduction to effective use of technology in the classroom. The most important results of the workshops were the connections made among faculty and the establishment of relationships between the college and the high school, as well as the internal relationships. More workshops open to both college and K-12 faculty, are planned for 2005-2006 and will use the LENs materials.

In summer of 2005, a cohort of high school students enrolled in 12 credits of IT coursework. The accelerated delivery included instruction, supplemental lab time, and assistance in IT career planning.

Increase the use of computer-based and internet-based technology to enhance learning. For both college and high school students, the college has increased the number of online and internet-enhanced courses. The partner schools are working together to design alternate-delivery curriculum materials to provide technical-skill coursework for 11th and 12th grades that culminates in dual-enrollment credit. CCTI is supporting this effort through the Distance Education department's initiatives to create more hybrid and fully online classes hosted by the college.

Several IT Educator's Workshops have been and will be developed and delivered that focus on technical skills using IPV and web-based delivery methods to enhance instruction. Compatible workshops focus on instructional design, methods, and strategies using electronic technology. These workshops are open to high school and college teachers in all disciplines.

The college developed a minigrant program called the CCTI Teachers Using Technology Program to promote excellence in teaching and professional growth of high school teachers through the use of technology. The program supports initiatives in teaching and enhancements to existing courses and programs. Projects supported by the CCTI Teachers Using Technology Program benefit the teaching function by infusing technology into coursework. The program, although successful, has been terminated due to a reduction in funds for the CCTI project.

Success comes when faculty are provided in-service training that is just-in-time training: what they want to know when they need to know it. In addition to the initial training sessions, the college created an ongoing position of technical support for faculty. A technical facilitator is available for questions and solutions, facilitates user groups, and hosts online discussions. Three IT courses have been developed and delivered online with a complete one-year certificate offered in 2005-2006. The majority of IT courses now have elements of technology integrated into the teaching methodologies as well as the course content.

Least Effective Strategies

Include all partners in the creation of the pathways and other grant work. In the beginning stages of the grant, and especially in the pathway creation, business partners were included in the discussion of educational objectives for their input and employer perspective. The business partners were overwhelmed by the amount of detail in these discussions, and the college had to change the way it involved these partners. Now the college is more selective in how it schedules involvement of the business partners and the amount of material recommended for their review. Additionally, Gold Beach High School did not have the administrative commitment to follow through on the long-term project, and subsequently withdrew from the project after Year 2. This further reinforces the need to be clear and direct about the role of each partner.

The primary partners in this project include the high schools and the Oregon Department of Education. In addition to the overall project site committee, focused subgroups meet regularly to work on targeted strategies. Business partners are invited only to meetings that are applicable to their involvement in the project.

Build a bridge program for a cohort of recent high school graduates to prepare them for transition into the college CIS programs. A summer cohort was formed with instruction for recent high school graduates. The program would have been more successful had the students been grouped on the basis of their college placement test results. All students significantly increased their placement scores at the end of the project, but some were not ready for college-level coursework. This diversity in the cohort made it more difficult to organize group activities applicable and appropriate to all participants. To benefit from a cohort experience, students need to be grouped on the basis of placement tests.

Lessons Learned

Faculty and staff learned the value of follow-up activities. To ensure that faculty and staff will use new teaching strategies with information technology, it is imperative that they are trained and that there are opportunities for continued training throughout the year. Project leaders at Southwestern have learned that follow-up activities to training help keep the learning momentum alive. Follow-up activities may include a user's group, online discussion group, help desk, and demonstrations of individual success. In general, the goal of the follow-up activities is to maintain the energy and interest in the newly learned techniques and knowledge. Interestingly, the follow-up activities are similar to the activities used with traditional students to reinforce their learning and cohort building.

One example of a campuswide staff development activity is the Turn It In software to aid in reducing plagiarism. In the fall of 2004, Southwestern conducted a traditional fall in-service training workshop on the Turn It In software that included classroom tips and techniques presented by an English teacher and software information presented by a computer science teacher. Along with the original training teachers, several early adopters have created a user's group to help members use the product, and they have become the campus experts. The Turn It In User's Group presented to the general faculty during the annual fall 2005 in-service week. The early adopters are from nursing, history, political science, writing, computer science, and biology. An added benefit to what they are learning in the user's group is that faculty from very different disciplines are discovering the commonalities of their courses, sharing teaching techniques, and building new collaborations.

Ultimately, the goal of faculty and staff training is to recognize teaching as a craft and to support the faculty in honing that craft. At Southwestern, there is a growing interest in creating a Teaching and Learning Center or Faculty Resource Center. This center would be a comfortable place for all members – faculty, staff, and administrators – to receive training on technology as well as on teaching strategies, techniques, and research.

Reaching admirable goals takes planning, time, and trust. The grant partners have come to realize that reaching shared and admirable goals takes considerable time and the building of trust between the partners. The education and business partners in the CCTI grant recognize the value in the goals of the grant and the idea of a seamless education, where students navigate a clear pathway to their career and education goals.

However, there are many barriers that make implementation of these shared goals difficult and complex. Some of the variables are different schedules, existing courses, existing personnel, budgets and state funding models, competing priorities, physical distance between schools, culture at each school, and the autonomy of each school.

Similar barriers exist in the building of partnerships between community colleges and the state systems, but these barriers can be overcome. As one example, five Oregon community colleges, including Southwestern, have assumed a statewide leadership role in promoting and facilitating planning for integrating career pathways into current systems. The five colleges recently held a two-day pathway academy attended by all 17 Oregon community colleges. Each college sent a team to create a pathways action plan for the college. Additionally, a statewide team developed strategies to eliminate barriers and provide support as colleges plan and implement pathway strategies. This project required six months of planning and capitalized on the statewide Workforce Strategies Council as an existing framework to launch the efforts.

Southwestern and its partners have invested time and resources in building human connections and collaborations by appreciating, respecting, and understanding each partner's goals and limitations. With time, planning, and trust among the members, this partnership can create projects and opportunities for students to succeed that surpass anything a single member could do alone.

More information about Southwestern Oregon Community College and the CCTI Initiative can be found at http://www.league.org/league/projects/ccti/projects/summary.cfm?key=socc.

■ The education and business partners in the CCTI grant recognize the value in the goals of the grant and the idea of a seamless education, where students navigate a clear pathway to their career and education goals.

Law, Public Safety, and Security

- Fox Valley Technical College (WI)
- Prince George's Community College (MD)
- San Diego Miramar College (CA)

Fox Valley Technical College

Terry O'Banion

OCCUPATIONAL AREA:	Law, Public Safety, and Security
CAREER PATHWAY:	Criminal Justice/Law Enforcement
CCTI PROJECT DIRECTOR:	Mary Hansen
PROJECT PARTNERS:	Fox Valley Technical College Area high schools Local law enforcement agencies Four-year colleges and universities

■ Officers from our partner law enforcement agencies are actually teaching the college's transitions courses in criminal justice to high school students via our interactive television network. Students are able to examine firsthand the fields of law, public safety, and security from professionals in those fields....and are better prepared for the realities of these careers and the skills they will need to be successful.

Susan A. May, Executive Vice President and Chief Academic Officer, Fox Valley Technical College

The Project Partners

The project of the College and Career Transitions Initiative at **Fox Valley Technical College** (FVTC) reflects the values and practices of a state system, a local college, and a career program recognized nationally for commitments to and leadership in quality occupational education.

The Wisconsin Technical College System (WTCS) includes 16 districts, 47 campuses, and hundreds of outreach sites. The principal purposes of the technical college system are to (1) provide occupational education and training and retraining programs, including the training of apprentices, that enable residents to obtain the knowledge and skills necessary for employment at a technical, paraprofessional, skilled, or semi-skilled occupation; and (2) provide customized training and technical assistance to business and industry in order to foster economic development and the expansion of employment opportunities.

With this strong emphasis on occupational education, it is not surprising that 58 percent of the students in the statewide system are enrolled in associate degree programs leading to careers, 14 percent in technical diploma programs, 12 percent in basic education programs, and only 8 percent in liberal arts transfer programs. Even though the system has increased its emphasis on transfer programs in recent years, it is interesting to note that since 1991, more students have transferred annually from the University of Wisconsin System into the Wisconsin Technical College System than the other way around, reflecting in part the aspirations of students, but also the quality of occupational education offered at the WTCS. In 1999-2000, 2,979 students from the University of Wisconsin System transferred into the WTCS; 2,576 students transferred from the technical system into the university system.

Fox Valley Technical College, the third largest of the 16 colleges in the state system, serves over 50,000 students a year in courses offered in more than 70 different occupational programs. The college also provides an extensive service to business and industry by contracting with 1,300 employers a year for training and other services. Fox Valley graduates more than 1,500 students a year, with 92 percent employed within six months. In an annual survey, 96 percent of employers are satisfied with the skills of FVTC graduates. For its excellent programs, the college has won the Wisconsin Forward Award and the national Pacesetter Award for Quality in Education.

Fox Valley's mission statement reflects the strong emphasis on workforce training mandated by the statewide system: "The mission of Fox Valley Technical College is to help individuals reach their potential by providing cost-effective education and training which meets their objectives for employment, continuing higher education, and personal enrichment. We seek to build and maintain a diverse and effective work force that supports the economic growth and stability of our communities."

The Criminal Justice Program at Fox Valley is a microcosm of the mission and values of the college. The leaders constantly apply continuous quality practices to their work; collaboration among leaders and program units and with area agencies is the norm; entrepreneurship has been honed to a fine degree; and data are gathered on students and program outcomes on an ongoing basis. The program is aligned with the goals of the college and enjoys a great deal of support and flexibility from college leaders in achieving and expanding those goals.

The word microcosm suggests a smallness very different from the reality that has been achieved by this program. The program has been around for decades, building a strong base of community support and involvement of leaders from local law enforcement agencies. In the last 10 years, the program has built on this foundation to become one of the eminent Centers of Excellence in criminal justice in the United States. Several achievements highlight the strengths of this program:

- Largest law enforcement training program in the Midwest (In 2002, there were 45 full- and part-time employees, 122 independent consultants, and 425 adjunct instructors.)
- Largest recipient of grants for Criminal Justice Programming – more than $40 million in the last 10 years
- Associate degree program ranked third in the nation for police graduates
- Anticipated growth rate for programming of 20 percent a year
- Programs offered in every state in the U.S., Canada, and Puerto Rico

The Criminal Justice Program has become a national and, increasingly, an international leader in preparing students for careers in law enforcement, but also in training and retraining current employees in evolving areas such as homeland security and the protection of children. As the primary subcontractor

■ The mission of Fox Valley Technical College is to help individuals reach their potential by providing cost-effective education and training which meets their objectives for employment, continuing higher education, and personal enrichment.

for the National Missing and Exploited Children Foundation, the Criminal Justice Program provides all of that organization's training. The program houses the National Training Center for Crime Prevention and Community Leadership, cosponsored by the National Crime Prevention Council and Fox Valley Technical College, as one indication of its national leadership.

The vision of program leaders is to expand the program into a worldwide center. In the 2003 Criminal Justice Strategic Planning Process, a model of self-assessment that examines strengths, weaknesses, opportunities, and threats with unusual candor, program leaders have proposed a new vision statement that reflects their past success and values and their future ambition:

> We will be working from our new flexible, innovative complex delivering training worldwide. We will be one team utilizing an integrated data system and seamless processes. We will provide and receive the finest customer service.
>
> We will have choices in what we do, engaging in sophisticated partnerships. The Criminal Justice Center planners of today will lead us to our status as the premier Criminal Justice Center in the world. Like the internet, we will be everywhere and nowhere.

When a local program becomes a nationally recognized leader, there is always the danger that local needs may be overlooked in favor of national needs that bring more recognition and resources. The leaders of the Criminal Justice Program at Fox Valley appear to have a very realistic understanding of this dilemma. In interviews with both the former and current directors, the same basic philosophy for managing the program was articulated: "Don't ever forget where you came from," and "We don't know the word *no.*" The leaders understand that their success is based on the reputation that has been created with support and partnerships with local law enforcement agencies working together to create opportunity. They have been astute in leveraging their national success and connections to benefit the local agencies providing opportunities to bring in national consultants and resources and helping connect local agency leaders to national opportunities. It has been a classic win-win situation.

It is not surprising, therefore, that the Criminal Justice Program was selected by college leaders as the venue for this CCTI project. The program already embraces, by philosophy and practice, the elements supported by OVAE related to ensuring that students make successful transitions from high schools to postsecondary education and on to work or further education.

Responsibility for coordinating the project is housed in the Office of High School and College Transitions, an office that serves all programs in the college, including the Criminal Justice Program. The philosophy of this office is captured in a school-to-work mission statement that reflects all the central elements supported by this OVAE project:

> To meet the needs of the changing workplace, Fox Valley Technical College's High School and College Transitions team, in cooperation with the K-12 system, universities, and colleges, will provide students with an opportunity to participate in applied/integrated, sequential, nonduplicative coursework. This will lead to a seamless transition into postsecondary education and the world of work. Efforts will link educators, employers, and the community to prepare local youth for life and work in a more competitive global economy.

The office and the CCTI project are coordinated by Joanne Pollock, director of the Office of High School and College Transitions and Tech Prep curriculum specialist, in cooperation with other professional staff who have responsibilities for youth options and youth apprenticeship programs, four-year articulation programs, and KSCADE, a network of area high schools and other institutions of higher education that has delivered ITV courses to more than 5,000 high school students in the last five years.

These leaders in the High School and College Transitions office selected the Criminal Justice Program because assessments had identified a need to expand opportunities for high school students to explore career options in criminal justice. Currently, high school juniors and seniors in area schools can enroll in a KSCADE ITV course in Introduction to Criminal Justice, a popular course that provides many students with their first understanding of what is involved in a law enforcement career. Most of the students enrolled in the course have indicated they would like more information on law enforcement, and especially on the variety of career opportunities in the field. Instructors have also indicated a need for students to become more aware of the realities of the jobs to offset their sometimes romantic notions of law enforcement reflected in popular TV shows and other media.

■ Instructors have also indicated a need for students to become more aware of the realities of the jobs to offset their sometimes romantic notions of law enforcement reflected in popular TV shows and other media.

The Model Career Pathway

To some extent, Career Pathways in Wisconsin have been around since the early days of Tech Prep. While there was rarely uniformity or consistency in what was developed, many of the technical colleges, along with their secondary partners, developed pathways that defined a recommended sequence of courses for transition from secondary to postsecondary coursework.

The pathways were college specific and incorporated the secondary requirements as defined by the Wisconsin Department of Public Instruction. Colleges identified their program requirements and created a semester-by-semester matrix by which students could visualize their chosen program from beginning to end. The colleges suggested high school course offerings in both the academic and elective areas that would be beneficial to students in preparing for their careers.

While these pathways were well received by all the stakeholders, they proved to be both labor intensive and costly. Since the major mission of the technical colleges is to graduate students with skills that are workplace relevant, curriculum, programs, and program requirements must change to keep pace. This meant that the published hard-copy pathway guides required annual revision. The staff time and cost became a burden, and the guides soon became outdated.

In developing the Criminal Justice/Law Enforcement Pathway for the CCTI grant, Fox Valley staff looked to the past as a place to begin. They started with the secondary requirements as defined by the Wisconsin Department of Public Instruction as the first layer of the new matrix. The second layer included program requirements, a suggested course sequence, course descriptions, and prerequisites, and identified "helpful high school courses" as defined by the Fox Valley Technical College Criminal Justice/Law Enforcement Division.

Within the matrix, staff identified and highlighted the required postsecondary courses articulated at the secondary level for technical college credit and advanced standing and included postsecondary courses available for dual credit. The college placement exam, ACCUPLACER, was incorporated into the pathways as a reminder that students needed a specific competency level for program entrance or required remediation to continue. Finally, staff used several of the example pathways provided by the CCTI partners to create an initial pathway.

Since the original Criminal Justice/Law Enforcement Pathway was developed, it has been reviewed by representatives from all the stakeholder groups and has undergone many changes and redesigns. The final pathway will be available on the FVTC website www.fvtc.edu and will remain dynamic, with regular updates.

Simultaneous with the development of the Criminal Justice/Law Enforcement template for CCTI, but for entirely different reasons, FVTC was looking at presenting degree and diploma program information in a career-cluster format. Traditionally at FVTC, the presentation of programs in printed material and on the web was in alphabetical order. Program brochures each presented one program and the brochures were organized and displayed alphabetically. With more than 70 degree and diploma programs, the resulting display was often referred to as the "wall of confusion": A student interested in welding and foolish enough to look under *W* would walk away disappointed and would certainly not think to look under *M*, where Metal Fabrication/Welding was cleverly hidden.

■ A student interested in welding and foolish enough to look under *W* would walk away disappointed and would certainly not think to look under *M*, where Metal Fabrication/ Welding was cleverly hidden.

The college began organizing programs into 14 career clusters to help customers find their areas of interest in a more expeditious manner. While creating the Criminal Justice/Law Enforcement Pathway template at the same time, the CCTI and High School Transitions teams were inspired to examine the national career clusters created by the National Association of State Directors of Career Technical Education Consortium to see how the college's new organization efforts matched with this national effort and how they both matched with the CCTI model.

Comparisons revealed that the CCTI pathways are highly specific, while the national career clusters are broader and more inclusive. With the input of the FVTC instructional deans, it was determined that the most logical and manageable first step for FVTC would be to concentrate on creating a broader pathway model for the newly organized career clusters. This model incorporates FVTC programs within cluster pathways that overlay the individual program pathways.

The CCTI and High School Transition teams worked with division staff across the college to develop Career Cluster Pathways as a tool to provide the high school audience – students, teachers, counselors, and parents – with information about coursework and career exploration options that create a broad-based seamless pathway to a successful career. The short-term goal was to develop a pathway for each college-defined career cluster by the end of the 2004-2005 school year. A long-term goal is to create program-specific pathways for all specializations in the career clusters. The opportunity to create a Criminal Justice/Law Enforcement Career Pathway in the Law, Public Safety, and Security cluster for this CCTI project has provided a laboratory for college leaders to experiment with these goals.

Curriculum and Instruction

For the past six years, Fox Valley Technical College has offered a number of introductory-level courses to high school students as part of the state-legislated Youth Options program. With support from their school district, students are given the opportunity to pursue coursework relating to a career field of interest, providing them the chance for in-depth career exploration.

Each year, FVTC has seen Youth Options enrollments increase, both for the students attending classes on campus and those receiving programming via the interactive television network, KSCADE. Over time, the FVTC classes that have become most popular on KSCADE have been the criminal justice courses. Staff who are working or have worked in the field of law enforcement teach classes for both the on-campus students – whether in a full-time program or via Youth Options – and the students enrolled in KSCADE. This real-world approach to instruction provides the students with a solid understanding of the many facets of law enforcement and what is required on the job each day. Courses such as Introduction to Criminal Justice and Law Enforcement Issues have prepared many students for the process of deciding whether this career field is right for them.

As part of the CCTI initiative at FVTC, the KSCADE instructors have used this real-world approach in developing a new course called Careers in Criminal Justice. As development for the course began, instructors saw the benefit of using both technology and face-to-face contact to allow students to gain the best understanding of the many criminal-justice-related careers available to them. Early in curriculum development, a computer-based learning object (http://www.wisc-online.com/objects/index_tj.asp?objID=CRJ104) was developed to be used simultaneously with text information and guest speakers. The interactive learning object directly engages learners in exploring the many branches of law enforcement and provides the instructor a basis on which to relay similar information for each branch of the career field. Guest speakers for each branch reinforce the class discussions and homework assignments.

The most effective information-retention tool developed for this course may be the research element that is required of each student. While learning about the many careers in criminal justice, students learn how to make contacts on their own to gain more information on careers and develop a rapport with local law enforcement officials. By meeting with staff from fields like forensics, community policing, corrections, and the court system, students make a much deeper connection to the information covered in class and often find these contacts to be the most valuable contribution to their decision-making process.

CCTI records for the 2003-2004 school year show that 77 students participated in the project, while in 2004-2005, approximately 130 students participated. Each cohort will be tracked in the FVTC student-records system to determine ultimate numbers enrolling in the college and, specifically, those who choose to enter the field of law enforcement

Bridges With Four-Year Programs

In 2000, Fox Valley Technical College leaders identified a need to build student transfer opportunities. A full-time Coordinator of Articulated Programs and Credit Transfer position was created, whose role is to develop and expand articulation agreements with four-year colleges. The ultimate goal is to partner with four-year colleges and universities so FVTC associate degree graduates are granted junior status, creating a seamless transition for associate degree students to pursue a bachelor's degree.

■ ...Criminal Justice associate degree graduates can continue their baccalaureate education in a traditional program on a local campus, an online learning environment, or a degree-completion program that provides flexibility for working adults.

The Criminal Justice Department at FVTC aggressively sought credit-transfer opportunities for Criminal Justice-Law Enforcement associate degree graduates. Articulations with colleges in the community and online colleges across the country were pursued. As a result, Criminal Justice associate degree graduates can continue their baccalaureate education in a traditional program on a local campus, an online learning environment, or a degree-completion program that provides flexibility for working adults. Institutions that have developed articulations with FVTC include the University of Wisconsin-Oshkosh and Concordia University in Wisconsin, as well as Northern Michigan University.

In addition to these articulation agreements, FVTC offers a Criminal Justice Executive Development Institute. This leadership development program is designed to address the professional growth needs of law enforcement personnel pursuing a career as a management executive in criminal justice agencies. Credits earned in the Executive Development Institute are accepted by several graduate programs in Wisconsin.

The Criminal Justice Pathway at FVTC can lead students on an educational journey that begins in high school, and takes them to a bachelor's degree, and through to a graduate program.

Student Support

Student support is essential to any college student's success. As the CCTI cohorts have evolved, FVTC has implemented a number of strategies to provide support for students taking criminal justice courses on KSCADE.

All schools participating in KSCADE are required to provide facilitation services daily for enrolled students. KSCADE facilitators assist students each day with instructor communications, technical support, and scheduling coordination. For example, facilitators work with CCTI students to administer ACCUPLACER testing on site, which includes proctoring the test and submitting scores. They may also recommend remediation to school administration and provide additional resources and assistance.

The KSCADE school administrators provide other support to CCTI students as well. Principals and other administrators meet monthly as the KSCADE Programming Committee to collaborate on programming issues related to KSCADE. As part of their role, this group determines guidelines and policies that affect the daily activities in the KSCADE classrooms. Programming committee members and site facilitators work together to establish an environment of success for these students who have chosen to participate in a nontraditional way of learning.

Because the Fox Valley Technical College CCTI cohort includes students from a number of high schools, the college's KSCADE network manager assures that services and support contacts of the college are available to students and staff, assists with technology needs, and keeps lines of communication open between the college and the high schools. The network manager meets periodically with FVTC instructors and high school staff, as well as students, to provide updates and coordinate additional resources focused on success for all involved in the project.

Special Features

The FVTC program provides opportunities for students to begin a Career Pathway in high school and follow it through a master's degree. A high school student may earn up to six FVTC credits in the Criminal Justice/Law Enforcement program prior to enrollment at the college. Additionally, students who attend high schools with comprehensive articulation agreements are eligible for several advanced-standing credits. Upon completion of the associate degree program, students who are interested in continuing their four-year degree may choose among several institutions where there are formal transfer agreements, including the opportunity to acquire a master's degree.

The Implementation Strategies

Most Effective Strategies

ACCUPLACER administration and follow-up. Students in the Fox Valley Technical College Law and Public Safety cohort complete the ACCUPLACER assessment as juniors and seniors to determine readiness for the Criminal Justice Associate degree program. All students are notified in writing regarding their individual scores, and suggestions for remediation are included if applicable.

As part of the CCTI Career Pathway assessment process, FVTC has developed a follow-up process for students who wish to improve their skills. The KSCADE office contacts each student and provides a test summary and comparison of the student's test scores to the required scores for the Criminal Justice Program. Included in the summary is information on an optional remediation program called GOAL-to-Go. FVTC Basic Skills staff worked with KSCADE to design GOAL-to-Go, an optional remediation program, specifically for the CCTI cohort.

In its pilot semester, GOAL-to-Go is designed to allow students to participate in necessary remediation without leaving their high schools. An FVTC basic skills instructor takes the GOAL-to-Go courses for math and English to the students via a traveling laptop lab. The guidance office at participating schools schedules dates and times for the traveling program, and students participate by enrolling in a structured eight-hour class for each subject area either to prepare to take the ACCUPLACER college-entry test or to remediate after taking the test prior to retesting or program entry.

Introductory courses offered on distance education network. High school juniors and seniors in the FVTC district interested in law enforcement may enroll in Introduction to Criminal Justice, offered on the KSCADE distance education network. This introductory course provides students a broad overview of the field of criminal justice and allows them to earn both high school credit and three college credits.

In addition, high school juniors and seniors interested in more detailed information about law enforcement careers may enroll in a follow-up course, Careers in Criminal Justice, also offered on the KSCADE distance education network. This class primarily deals with a career-oriented study of various federal, state, and local criminal justice departments and agencies. The course focuses on both the organizational structure and personnel policies of the respective departments and agencies. Some of the major areas of concentration include recruitment and selection procedures, minorities in law enforcement, minority recruitment within the criminal justice system, computerization within the criminal justice system, various areas of specialization within departments and agencies, and interagency relationships within the criminal justice system. The course identifies the importance of specific recruiting policies and interagency relationships within law enforcement and satisfies the elective requirements of the Wisconsin Training and Standards police-recruit learning objectives.

Much of the class time is devoted to guest lectures from federal, state, and local departments and agencies. Classes also include video presentations, distribution of department and agency booklets and instructional material, and class participation and discussion. In every class session, time is set aside for in-depth discussion about course topics and current issues within the spectrum of the criminal justice system, whether on a local, state, national, or global scale.

In addition to guest lectures and class participation and discussion, the student is required to complete several career critiques. In the career-critiques project, each student selects a specific criminal justice field and applies for a position. The student contacts a specific agency and gathers information about the field and the opportunities in the field. Then the student creates a résumé and cover letter as part of an application that is handed in to the instructor for review, and on which the student makes an oral report to the class. This process provides an opportunity for the student to make a realistic assessment of personal skills and abilities for selected positions and to learn about the requirements of specific fields.

Secondary and postsecondary articulation agreements. Fox Valley Technical College offers all district high schools the chance to articulate courses for advanced standing and has developed articulation agreements for almost 90 FVTC courses. Courses are offered from divisions across the college and include both technical studies and general studies courses; some of these are relevant to the Law, Public Safety, and Security Career Cluster Pathway. Students can receive tech-prep credit through Advanced Standing (Articulated) Agreements or Technical College (Transcripted) Credit Contracts.

Advanced Standing (Articulated) Agreements are established when technical college competencies are taught in one or more high school course and are taught by a high school teacher. A junior or senior who successfully completes the high school course is eligible for advanced standing credit at FVTC. In the 2003-2004 school year, FVTC offered almost 90 courses at 35 high schools through Advanced Standing (Articulated) Agreements. The student must receive a B or better in the course to be eligible for advanced standing credit upon enrollment in an appropriate program at FVTC or at another college in the Wisconsin Technical College System.

Technical College (Transcripted) Credit Contracts are established when a technical college course is delivered at the high school and taught by a high school teacher. A successful student receives an official technical college

■ **Fox Valley Technical College offers all district high schools the chance to articulate courses for advanced standing and has developed articulation agreements for almost 90 FVTC courses.**

transcript. In the 2004-05 school year, FVTC offered eight courses at three high schools for Technical College (Transcripted) Credit Contracts. The Office of High School and College Transitions is working with division deans to expand the number of courses available under this option. The Criminal Justice/Law Enforcement Pathway specifies the courses that are articulated and are required in the Criminal Justice Program.

In Wisconsin, Youth Options, a state-legislated initiative, is also available to qualified juniors and seniors as an opportunity to explore a career while still in high school. FVTC offers a wide range of courses that students can access at any FVTC location, over the KSCADE ITV network, online, or through other distance education formats.

Articulation opportunities from two-year to four-year institutions. Fox Valley Technical College has collaborated with a number of four-year institutions to develop program-to-program articulations for the Criminal Justice associate degree program. Transfer opportunities exist in areas of Public Safety Management, Management of Criminal Justice, Law Enforcement Administration, Sociology-Criminal Justice Emphasis, and Public Services Administration. In addition, FVTC's Criminal Justice Executive Development Institute has articulation agreements for a Master of Public Administration program and a Master of Science in Management and Organization Behavior. Institutions that have developed articulations with FVTC include the University of Wisconsin-Oshkosh and Concordia University in Wisconsin, as well as Northern Michigan University.

Opportunities for real-world experiences. The college's CCTI initiative has developed two resources that provide students in the cohort with the opportunity to learn about day-to-day skills needed in many law enforcement career settings.

■ **A *CCTI Resource Guide* is provided to all students to enable them to contact law enforcement agencies to obtain firsthand information, get their questions answered, and, in many cases, meet someone in a specific job they find interesting.**

A *CCTI Resource Guide* is provided to all students to enable them to contact law enforcement agencies to obtain firsthand information, get their questions answered, and, in many cases, meet someone in a specific job they find interesting. Some of the areas covered in the *Resource Guide* include parole, corrections, community policing, the court system, and dispatch. Both state and local agencies are included.

In the spring of 2004, students were also given the opportunity to work with law enforcement officers during a Day in the Life capstone event. During the event, students participated in a number of scenarios designed to teach them about the many skills required in the line of duty. Officers facilitated each scenario and provided many opportunities for hands-on activity. A courtroom scenario at the end of the day provided a forum for instructors to summarize the day and field questions from students.

As a follow-up to the 2004 capstone, another day-long event is planned for 2005. Homeland Security: An Emergency Perspective will be the theme for this event, designed to educate students on the many aspects of homeland security and provide hands-on activities that clearly demonstrate the vast law enforcement resources involved. Scenarios planned for the 2005 event include search techniques, water rescues, and K-9 mobilization, and scenarios that illustrate the communication system required by state and federal agencies in response to a homeland security crisis.

Least Effective Strategies

Mentoring. One project goal included a mentorship relationship for the CCTI cohort, but there has been some difficulty in establishing such a program. There is a challenge in creating opportunities for students to participate in criminal justice/law enforcement activities that could be dangerous; the young age of most of the students in these kinds of activities is also a challenge. To ameliorate this situation, staff created a *Resource Guide* with lists of approved career-focused opportunities available in the various communities where students live. Annual capstone experiences that simulate real-life criminal justice/law enforcement experiences are also being created to provide students hands-on practice.

Remediation. Identifying the need for remediation in cohorts has been possible through the administration of ACCUPLACER at all area high schools. College test-center staff analyze scores, and students are informed about remedial needs. However, identification of need does not always translate into successful remediation in the high school setting. A potential solution to this problem may be GOAL-to-Go, a set of short-term ACCUPLACER preparation or brush-up courses in math, reading, and language skills brought to the high schools by an FVTC basic skills instructor.

Lessons Learned

Strengthening high school programming. Career Pathway models are highly likely to be successful in a college environment that champions good relationships with area high schools across numerous programs and offices. Fox Valley Technical College's administration recognizes and supports partnerships with area high schools and includes strengthening high school programming and activities as part of a strategic direction. Staff from across the college come together to brainstorm ideas, and the synergy at these meetings results in a wide variety of successful projects. Division deans are very interested in working with the Office of High School and College Transitions to provide transition programming for area high school students. Grant writers from FVTC's Institutional Advancement office are always searching for appropriate grant-funding opportunities.

Connecting through Tech Prep. The technical colleges in Wisconsin administer the state Carl Perkins Tech Prep dollars at the local level, and since 1990, FVTC has actively offered Tech Prep Career and Technical Education (CTE) programs, as well as joint secondary and postsecondary staff development opportunities. All area high schools participate in the Fox Valley/K-12 Joint Tech Prep Council, where the appropriation of local Carl Perkins funding is determined. The opportunity to come together on an annual basis under the umbrella of Tech Prep provides an excellent forum for K-12 and college staff to review existing programs and design new ones for students.

For example, the annual Tech Prep Organization meeting brings both secondary and postsecondary staff together to share curriculum and other articulated and transcripted credit course updates, as well as to discuss questions and concerns. The counselor meeting, which features an agenda planned jointly with the transitions office and high school counseling staff, brings together staff from both levels to discuss and offer student support. An Educator Externship provides K-12 participants with a week-long immersion experience at FVTC, including an ACCUPLACER test-taking session. The Tech Prep Summer Series features CTE courses such as Culinary Arts and Wood Technologies, providing high school tech-ed teachers a state-of-the-art experience in their field. These and other experiences assure both teacher and student success in the CCTI program.

Partnering for CTE programming. Where two-year community and technical colleges provide transitional education such as career-cluster pathways, students are more likely to pursue baccalaureate degrees and become lifelong learners. The Fox Valley K-12 culture has long held a preference for preparing students for four-year postsecondary education; but more and more, area high schools are recognizing the value of partnering with the college in CTE programming for their students. FVTC's Office of High School and College Transitions, in collaboration with Criminal Justice Division staff, has established advanced standing and transcripted credit agreements with all 29 area high schools, as well as some out-of-district schools. Well-established secondary-to-postsecondary transition opportunities enhance and facilitate the development of Career Pathways.

■ The opportunity to come together on an annual basis under the umbrella of Tech Prep provides an excellent forum for K-12 and college staff to review existing programs and design new ones for students.

Dual credit and credit transfer. FVTC came to CCTI with the advantage of having well-established transition opportunities with almost 90 general-studies and technical courses articulated for advanced standing at area high schools. To that number have been added some FVTC technical courses taught for transcripted credit by high school teachers at the high school. An additional opportunity for area high school students is Youth Options, a Wisconsin-legislated initiative that allows qualified high school juniors and seniors to participate in postsecondary courses for transcripted (dual) credit at the college via instructional television (ITV) or on the internet. FVTC has formal agreements with many private and some public four-year colleges for credit transfer opportunities for associate degree completers.

Career selection. Before embarking on a career they think they want to pursue, high school students need to understand the realities of the demands of careers, not just jobs, in the real world. A transitional approach to career decision making, through context-based courses, can help clear up perceptions and misperceptions about the ideal career and help students select the right career path early in their search. The technical college philosophy has always emphasized training for employment that is the right fit for its students. Enlisting the expertise of career professionals in providing this training is an important part of that philosophy.

For example, well-established partnerships with experts in the criminal justice field, men and women who are willing to lend their expertise through the site partnership and other venues, have been a critical component of the success of the CCTI career-cluster pathway. These partnerships, along with collaboration among college and high school staffs through KSCADE, have both emphasized the reality of the job through the integration of technical and academic skills and helped take the initiative to students who would likely have been unable to participate, had the ITV network not been in place.

Clarifying paths for student success. Through developing the career-cluster pathways, we have discovered that we better serve secondary schools when we are more prescriptive about identifying the secondary courses, electives, and activities that enhance student success in postsecondary programs. FVTC has articulation agreements with most area high schools, with these articulated courses carefully aligned to FVTC courses and programs. But by not identifying other secondary courses, electives, and activities useful to students, we missed an important part of the message. In many instances, absence of dissemination of this information translated into a message at the secondary level that, because they weren't written down, there must not be any standards for program entrance at the college. In collaboration with division staff, we are developing Career Pathways for all FVTC career clusters, giving all the stakeholders much more comprehensive information, from secondary through postsecondary, including four-year transfer and career opportunities. In the past, we had marketed all this information to students, parents, and high school staff, but we had not developed a comprehensive package of information to include all the career pathway information.

Remediation. In projects such as the CCTI career-cluster pathway, education-provider partners may need to take on nontraditional roles to ensure successful student transitions between educational entities – for example, postsecondary institutions providing secondary services. FVTC has placed ACCUPLACER in area high schools, which has allowed the college to test students, analyze scores, and identify remediation needs. While the college has been able to offer high school students limited remediation courses in basic skills labs during evenings and summers, a gap remains between the identification of the need for remediation and the ability of secondary students to acquire remedial help at their high schools. That awareness led to the creation of an eight-hour math course that is delivered as *ACCUPLACER* prep or brush-up by college faculty at the high school. Additional curriculum for eight-hour courses in reading and sentence structure is being piloted on high school campuses in 2005-2006.

Capstone experience. A capstone event that incorporates academic and technical skills in reality-based scenarios with a hands-on emphasis is an effective way to demonstrate job reality. In May of 2004, FVTC's site partnership collaborated on an end-of-year capstone event, Day in the Life, that moved the students through several reality-based scenarios: a traffic stop, an accident scene, firearms and use of force, and problem solving. Students indicated that the day met their expectations, that they appreciated the hands-on aspect of the event, and that an experience like this would affect their decision regarding a career.

More information about Fox Valley Technical College and the CCTI Initiative can be found at http://www.league.org/league/projects/ccti/projects/summary.cfm?key=fvtc.

Prince George's Community College

Terry O'Banion

OCCUPATIONAL AREA:	Law, Public Safety, and Security
CAREER PATHWAY:	Law, Public Safety and Security – Criminal Justice
CCTI PROJECT DIRECTOR:	Donna Gaughan
PROJECT WEBSITE:	http://www.league.org/league/projects/ccti/projects/summary.cfm?key=pgcc
PROJECT PARTNERS:	Prince George's Community College Potomac High School Northwestern High School Bowie State University Laurel City Police Department

The Project Partners

In 1967, the President's Commission on Law Enforcement and Administration of Justice, in a seminal report, *The Challenge of Crime in a Free Society*, recommended that an ultimate goal was the B.A. degree for all police personnel with general enforcement powers. In 1973, the National Advisory Commission on Criminal Justice Standards and Goals recommended that as a condition of initial employment, every police agency should require, by no later than 1975, two years of education at an accredited college or university, and by no later than 1982, four years of education at an accredited college or university.

None of the more than 20 police agencies within Prince George's County – including the largest among them, the Prince George's County Police Department (PGCPD) – adopted these recommendations at the time. However, the PGCPD did institute a program of salary incentives for personnel who earned an associate's, bachelor's, or master's degree. In spite of the stipends, however, no requirements for formal education beyond the traditional high school diploma were put in place for any of the several police agencies in Prince George's County. And unfortunately, the educational incentive program no longer exists within the Prince George's County Police Department. This lack of commitment to higher education for police personnel throughout the county creates conditions that make this CCTI project a particularly challenging one.

■ CCTI has been the catalyst for bridging across many existing silos: business and education, secondary and postsecondary, academic and career, credit and noncredit. For the first time in many years, we are witnessing business leaders, educators, and elected officials working cohesively to address the learning needs of county businesses and residents alike.

Daniel P. Mosser, Vice President for Workforce Development and Continuing Education, Prince George's Community College

Prince George's County, Maryland, is a large suburban county that borders Washington, D.C. It is the second most populous county in Maryland (816,791 in 2001) having grown 12 percent in the last decade. It is also one of the most affluent of all counties in the United States, ranking 28th in annual per capita income of 3,087 counties. One of its distinguishing features is the nature of its racial and ethnic population. Sixty-three percent of the population is African American, 27 percent Caucasian, and 4 percent Asian. The county is the home of the highest concentration of Black enterprise families – wealthy African-American householders – in the country. Minorities own 50 percent of the firms in the county.

There are several troubling indicators, however, that suggest a more precarious socioeconomic situation than the one painted by this rosy picture of minority wealth. Between the last two censuses, for example, the county's mean annual household income in constant dollars has dropped by 3 percent. Residents living in neighborhoods with household incomes between $45,000 and $75,000 declined by 30 percent while those above and below in incomes increased by 35 percent and 37 percent, respectively. There is a squeeze beginning on the middle class in Prince George's County.

The county's population has always been very mobile, reflecting the constant moves in and out of the nation's capitol. But since 1990, most of the new families have been from lower socioeconomic groups with single mothers, rather than the previous prosperous out-of-state residents that cycle through Washington, DC, following elections. As a result, there are emerging pockets of poverty that create concern for political leaders and educators. Now, 10 percent of all households in the county fall below the poverty line, and 20 percent of households are headed by females. This change in socioeconomic conditions is also reflected in the county's crime statistics: Crime rates in Prince George's County are typically three to four times the rates of other counties in the region.

The county's split personality is also manifested in the pattern of occupations and the levels of education achieved by residents. In 2000, 40 percent of all county employers and 60 percent of all jobs were in professional services. A high-tech corridor is emerging along Route 1 between NASA headquarters and the University of Maryland-College Park. The county boasts five additional institutions of higher education: Bowie State University, the University of Maryland University College, Capitol College, and Prince George's Community College. In spite of the accessibility of higher education, only 25 percent of the county's residents hold a baccalaureate degree or higher, compared with 55 percent in nearby Montgomery County. Forty percent of the residents have never attended a college class of any kind.

■ The county is the home of the highest concentration of Black enterprise families – wealthy African-American householders – in the country. Minorities own 50 percent of the firms in the county.

In the environment created by the socioeconomic conditions of the county, law enforcement is a growing occupational area that provides high-demand, high-wage opportunities. Data from Maryland's Office of Labor Market Analysis and Information document that police patrol officers are among the 50 occupations in highest demand in the county, averaging 106 openings annually. Between 1998 and 2008, across Maryland, there will be need for more than 540 correctional officers. In Washington, D.C., there will be numerous opportunities for law enforcement personnel of all kinds, with attractive salaries. The challenge and the opportunities for increased training and employment of law enforcement personnel in this region make this CCTI project very timely.

Prince George's Community College was established in 1958, and rode the wave of that great period of community college development during the 1960s when more than half of the current community colleges in the nation were created. It is a textbook community college: open-door philosophy, community-based programs, comprehensive curriculum, student and teaching centered. Today, the college consists of three campuses, enrolling over 40,000 students in 60 different programs of study. The college's creative faculty has established many excellent programs, services, and centers to provide rich educational experiences for students, in spite of considerable budget limitations. Prince George's County provides the lowest level of support for the college of any county support for area community colleges in the state.

After 27 years under the same president, who retired, Ron Williams was appointed in 1999. Under the leadership of the new president, a new vision statement for the college was approved by the Board of Trustees: "Prince George's Community College will excel as a nationally recognized, intellectually vibrant institution which is accessible, community-centered, technologically advanced, and responsible to the educational needs of a richly diverse population and workforce."

Prince George's Community College is an excellent community college with a dedicated faculty and staff strongly committed to serving the citizens in its district. The following highlights some of the distinguishing characteristics of the college:

- The college was named one of 16 national models for undergraduate education by the Association of American Colleges and Universities, a distinction shared with Duke University, the University of Michigan, Colgate University, and the U.S. Air Force Academy.
- In competition with leading four-year colleges and universities, the college was the recipient of the Theodore M. Hesburgh Award for Enhancing Undergraduate Teaching and Learning granted annually by TIAA-CREF.
- A study released in 2003 noted that the college accounts for $146.7 million of all annual earnings in the county's economy.
- The Center for Academic Resource Development is a nationally recognized program at the college that sponsors innovative academic programs and faculty development. During 2000-2001 the center received approximately $3,750,000 in grants.
- The Outstanding Community College Professor of the Year for 2002, named by the Council for the Advancement and Support of Education and The Carnegie Foundation for the Advancement of Teaching, was Alicia Juarrero, a philosophy professor at the college.
- Of the 60 community college students chosen for the *USA Today*/Phi Theta Kappa All-USA Academic Team in 2005, 2 were from Prince George's Community College. One of these students made the first team, and the other made the second team.
- Fifty students are chosen annually to be New Century Scholars, one from each state. In the first year of this program (2002), the Maryland student was from Prince George's Community College.

The demographics of the college reflect the demographics of the county. In the fall of 2004, 76.9 percent of the students were African American, 10.3 percent were Caucasian, 4.3 percent were Asian, 3.5 percent were Hispanic, 4.1 percent were nonresident alien, .03 percent were American Indian, and .04 percent were unknown. Slightly more than half of the college's students (50.4 percent) receive financial aid. Of the first-time freshmen who took the placement test in the fall of 2003, 71.4 percent needed developmental coursework in mathematics, 59.4 percent in reading, and 32.9 percent in English.

The faculty demographics do not reflect the composition of the student body. Prince George's Community College, like many of the community colleges established in the 1960s, is still dominated by the White faculty hired in the late 1960s and 1970s. Over the ensuing decades, the faculty did not change, but the ethnic composition of the student body did, creating today's mismatch of culture and backgrounds. In 2005, 67 percent of the full-time faculty were White, 25 percent African American, 2 percent Asian, 2 percent Hispanic, 2 percent Native American, and 2 percent nonresident alien. The part-time faculty is a little different: Forty-three percent are White, 52 percent are African American, 2 percent are Hispanic, 2 percent are Asian, and 1 percent are Native American. In the last five years, the college has made excellent progress in increasing the minority representation on its faculty. In 1995, 16 percent of the full-time faculty were African American; in 1999, the number had increased to 19 percent. Recognizing the need for a faculty that better reflects the students they serve, the board of trustees established a benchmark of 25 percent of the full-time faculty to be African American by 2004; that goal has been achieved.

The Criminal Justice, Forensics, and Paralegal Studies Department offers 50 courses in support of four degrees, two certificates, and one Letter of Recognition:

- AA Degree in Criminal Justice (Transfer Option)
- AAS Degree in Forensic Science Technology
- AS Degree in Forensic Studies (Transfer Option)
- AAS Degree in Paralegal/Legal Assistant Studies
- Certificate in Forensic Science Technology
- Certificate in Paralegal/Legal Assistant Studies
- Letter of Recognition for Paralegal/Legal Assistant Studies

Recognizing the need for a faculty that better reflects the students they serve, the board of trustees established a benchmark of 25 percent of the full-time faculty to be African American by 2004; that goal has been achieved.

Two programs illustrate the quality and impact of the training offered in this department. The forensic science program is one of the most comprehensive in the country, offering 14 forensic disciplines taught by 42 adjunct faculty who are all professionals in the field. In recognition of the quality of this program, the National Science Foundation awarded the college a grant to develop case-based forensic science curricula that can be tailored for postsecondary and secondary students. Currently, 485 students are enrolled in the program, with 81 percent female and 78 percent minority.

Based in the continuing education department, the Criminal Justice Institute has trained more than 300 law enforcement officers who are working in 150 different law enforcement agencies. The program is designed to prepare officers for initial entry and to provide continuing education for career officers; the placement rate for entry-level officers is 100 percent.

Given the need and opportunity for improved law enforcement training in Prince George's County, and given the quality of the Criminal Justice, Forensics, and Paralegal Studies Department, this CCTI project was a natural for Prince George's Community College.

Potomac High School (PHS) is a key partner in the project. PHS enrolls approximately 1,150 lower- to middle-class students; 99.7 percent are African American. The school has been recently restructured into learning communities around 6 schools containing 13 career academies. The Criminal Justice Academy will be the primary focus for the high school activities in this project. Another key partner is **Bowie State University**, although the students can transfer to any four-year college or university in the State of Maryland with which PGCC has an articulation agreement. The employer partner is the **Laurel City Police Department**. Laurel City Police Department provides paid summer internships for high school seniors in the program. If the students are interested in local law enforcement, they can enroll in the PGCC municipal police academy and be hired by the Laurel City Police Department.

Northwestern High School is shadowing the PHS program and is creating a criminal justice program that might become part of this project. Its students are taking part in a summer program at Prince George's Community College. Northwestern enrolls 2,512 students, 57.13 percent of whom are African American and 35.03 percent of whom are Hispanic.

Key leaders at Prince George's Community College visited nine additional high schools in the college's service area in the fall of 2005 to invite them to participate in the CCTI project.

The Model Career Pathway

The career pathway for students in the criminal justice program begins at the high school. This template was originally initiated at Potomac High School in October 2002 as a result of a grant, Academies – A Tool for High School Reform. It was expanded with the PHS-PGCC partnership. The template is used as a guide to direct students on the core curriculum necessary to obtain an AA degree or transfer to a four-year college. It specifies required general education courses at both the high school and community college level, recommended courses, and courses for the criminal justice major.

Curriculum and Instruction

The core of this curriculum at the high school level is the usual series of required general education courses in English, mathematics, science, and social studies. It also includes a foreign language, reading, and ROTC. In addition, the career pathway includes recommended electives. What is distinctive about this high school curriculum is the inclusion of four college-level criminal justice courses. The first two are Criminal Justice I and Criminal Justice II. These two courses were in the academy curriculum prior to the PHS-PGCC partnership. Students who take these courses have an opportunity to test out of two of PGCC's criminal justice courses: Introduction to Criminal Justice and Criminal Investigations. The two courses are not identical to Introduction to Criminal Justice and Criminal Investigations, but there is so much overlap in content that the college did not want the students to have to take these courses if they could test out.

The students also have the opportunity to enroll concurrently in two additional courses, Law Enforcement and the Community (Cross-Cultural Relations) and Juvenile Delinquency. These two courses are identical to the PGCC courses. Potomac High School students who are concurrently enrolled at PGCC and pass these courses will receive college credit from PGCC, and the credits will also articulate to a state four-year institution. The courses are taught by high school teachers who received training by PGCC faculty on how to teach the courses. The teachers are, in effect, hired by the college to teach the courses, but are paid theirl salary by the school system and not by the college.

When the students progress from PHS to PGCC, they take additional courses in English, mathematics, science, humanities, social science, physical education, and computer literacy. They also take additional criminal justice courses: Police Operations, Criminal Law, Criminal Evidence and Procedure, and two criminal justice electives. The following criminal justice courses are required in the Career Pathway.

CJT 152 – Police Operations. The purpose of this course is to help students understand the duties, authority, responsibilities, and rights of the uniformed police officer. Emphasis is on the function of the patrol officer as it relates to criminal investigation, intelligence, vice units, and traffic administration.

CJT 153 – Law Enforcement and the Community. This course is a study of the relationship between police and the community, with recommendations for ways of working together to reduce crime. Emphasis is placed on policing in a culturally diverse society.

CJT 155 – Juvenile Delinquency. This course examines studies of youth crime: its volume, causes, and trends. The prediction, prevention, treatment, and control of juvenile delinquency by social control agencies is examined relative to social policies needed to reduce its incidence. The organization and procedures of the juvenile justice system are explored.

■ **Potomac High School students who are concurrently enrolled at PGCC and pass these courses will receive college credit from PGCC, and the credits will also articulate to a state four-year institution.**

CJT 151 – Introduction to Criminal Justice. The introductory course is a survey of the history, philosophy, and social development of police, courts, and corrections in a democratic society. The course covers the identification and operations of local, state, and federal agencies.

CJT 251 – Criminal Law. This course is a study of substantive criminal law as applied to the local, state, and federal systems. Court decisions are used to address various sources and types of criminal laws. Students will learn legal terms and will be able to identify and evaluate the elements of the most commonly committed misdemeanors and felonies, as well as the most common defenses.

CJT 253 – Criminal Investigation. This course focuses on the fundamental principles and procedures employed in the investigation of crime. Emphasis is placed on the investigation of specific crimes, the identification of sources of information, and the procedures necessary for the proper handling of evidence. The course is designed for students to develop a working knowledge of the steps of investigation, beginning with the initial security of the crime scene and concluding with the presentation of evidence and proper testimony in court.

CJT 254 – Criminal Evidence and Procedure. This course presents an examination of the principles and techniques of criminal procedure employed during trials to determine the admissibility of physical and testimonial evidence. An analysis of laws and court decisions relating to admissibility is emphasized.

In the academies grant, PHS implemented strategies from Walbrook High School in Baltimore, which has had a history of fires being set inside the 1,290-student school by rogue students. To address this issue and others, the school created a Maritime Industries Academy, a public military school, that is partially funded by the Navy. The students in the academy take courses in earth science, biology, physics, oceanography, English, algebra, geometry, precalculus, and social studies, as well as SAT prep classes. University and college faculty work with the high school to create the curriculum and teach the students. These faculty meet with the students and their parents to inform them about selecting and preparing for a postsecondary school. At a time when absenteeism and the dropout rates are high among African Americans, the attendance record for the academy students has been nearly perfect.

Modeling programs on the Walbrook experience, Potomac High School created three schools: Health and Science, the School of Business, and the School of Public Service. Law and Public Policy is in the School of Public Service. Instructional methods include weekly quizzes, homework assignments, class projects, and class papers (final and midterms). These instructional approaches are similar to those employed at the community college. Thus students taking the two concurrent enrollment criminal justice courses at PHS will be prepared for the instructional methods employed by their teachers at the college.

Bridges With Four-Year Programs

Prince George's Community College has articulation agreements with many of the four-year programs in the State of Maryland, including University of Maryland-College Park, University of Maryland-Baltimore County, University of Maryland-University College, and Bowie State University. The State of Maryland requires that all community college programs articulate to four-year institutions in the university system. No individual articulation agreements are required. While technically Bowie State is the four-year partner in this project, it is not the only school to which graduates can transfer.

Student Support

Guidance and support are provided at both the secondary and postsecondary institutions. ACCUPLACER has provided an accurate diagnostic assessment targeting remediation needs for college students for a number of years. The 2003 fall placement tests indicated that 71.3 percent of newly admitted students at PGCC required remediation in reading, English, or mathematics. As PHS has one of the lowest success rates of any high school in the county, it was anticipated when planning this project that PHS students would require remediation. To ensure that students could participate in the program as a cohort in this project, ACCUPLACER was administered to PHS students in the 11th grade to allow for remedial interventions prior to their entrance to the college. They were assessed on college readiness skills in English, reading, and mathematics.

The original placement test was administered by a PGCC counselor. Each student was given a copy of his or her test results, and PGCC counselors reviewed the test results and advised each student individually. PHS counselors also met with the students concerning the *ACCUPLACER* tests. For the CCTI high school students, remedial intervention is offered during the summer (see Implementation Strategies). If further intervention is required when the students progress to the college, students are advised into developmental courses. Counselors from PGCC work with high school students planning to transfer to the college, and students can also access information on the assessments and other information they need on the PGCC web page.

Once they progress to PGCC, students can visit PGCC's counselors, who help students with learning skills, academic choices, career assessment and planning, and four-year college or university transfers. PGCC also offers courses on techniques, skills, attitudes, and behaviors associated with effective learning; math confidence building; effective test taking; career assessment and planning; learning to learn; and getting a job and keeping it. Minority students can also enroll in PGCC's nationally recognized program for mentoring minority students, A.L.A.N.A. (African, Latin, Asian, Native American). A.L.A.N.A. is a retention program designed to improve academic success, retention, and transitions to other institutions. The primary focus is to provide structured, trusting mentoring relationships to students that facilitate academic and personal growth. Each student participating in A.L.A.N.A. is assigned a faculty mentor who meets with the assigned student based upon an agreed schedule; assists in the development of skills necessary for the student to succeed in college; monitors the student's academic performance; assists the student in developing realistic career, academic, and personal goals and expectations; refers students to appropriate support services; attends program-sponsored activities; and attempts to follow up with students. The student signs an agreement to attend classes regularly, be prompt and keep scheduled appointments, contact the mentor if experiencing difficulty in classes, meet in person with the mentor at least four times a semester, take responsibility for the relationship, identify short-term goals, and attend program activities.

The Implementation Strategies

Most Effective Strategies

Summer Criminal Justice Academy. The PHS students in this project were offered an opportunity to attend a two-week Criminal Justice Academy at PGCC in the summer of 2004, prior to their advancing to the 12th grade. The focus of the academy was remedial education and topics in criminal justice. The five students who participated in the program were also offered the opportunity to visit the Career Counseling Center, Student Services, and the college library.

Project managers felt the summer academy was successful in that it exposed PHS students to the campus atmosphere and learning environment. And the students clearly enjoyed it. However, the managers decided the summer program needed more hands-on learning. In the summer of 2005, another Criminal Justice Academy was offered with more hands-on learning as well as role playing. The two-week summer 2005 program was a dual effort funded by both NSF and the CCTI grants and included both CCTI students and Forensic Academy students. The first week included lectures on First Responder, Crime Scene Processing (by Forensic Science faculty), and Courtroom Testimony. During the second week, students responded to a mock crime scene as law enforcement officers the first day, then as crime-scene technicians on the second and third days; they conducted a mock trial the third and fourth days of the second week. An individual from the local forensic lab assisted the students at the crime scene when they gathered and recorded evidence. Police from the county police force, lawyers, and a judge acted their parts in the exercise. The last day of the academy included debriefing, survey, and discussion.

■ A.L.A.N.A. is a retention program designed to improve academic success, retention, and transitions to other institutions. The primary focus is to provide structured, trusting mentoring relationships to students that facilitate academic and personal growth.

Dual-enrollment courses. Five PHS students enrolled in Law Enforcement and the Community in the spring of 2005. Juvenile Delinquency was not offered, because the students had to pay tuition and their parents could afford only one college course. The PHS teacher of Law Enforcement and the Community said that the course was initially a shock to the students. They were surprised by the amount of work and by what they were required to do on their own. The course required more independent reading and analysis than the students were accustomed to. But all five students passed with a C or better. By exposing students to postsecondary education while still in high school, and providing them the opportunity to earn college credit while still in high school, it was hoped that the enrollments at the postsecondary level would increase.

The first small cohort experience is promising. Four of the five students in the cohort enrolled at PGCC in fall 2005; however, three of them did not score high enough on the ACCUPLACER reading placement test to enroll in any PGCC criminal justice courses yet. One student from Northwestern High School is enrolled in two criminal justice courses. The fifth PHS student received a four-year scholarship from Kent State University.

Currently there are 10 12th grade students enrolled in the Criminal Justice II cohort at Potomac High School, and the counselors are identifying other students who have expressed interest in the academy. The scheduler left the school; another came this year but left due to illness. Thus scheduling was done offsite by someone not familiar with the academy, and records on 10th graders who had expressed interest in the academy are missing. PHS is planning to offer one or both of the concurrent enrollment courses, depending on what the students want.

Professional development opportunities for secondary and postsecondary faculty. High school faculty are hired as PGCC Criminal Justice adjunct faculty to teach the concurrent criminal justice courses. To maximize the success rate of students enrolled in these courses, PGCC faculty hosted a one-week seminar in Teaching College-Level Courses during the summer of 2004 for two PHS teachers and two Northwestern High School teachers. As part of the seminar, the secondary school teachers were provided information on topics regarding syllabus development, multiple lecture strategies, responding to a diverse student population, using instructional media and technology, appropriate classroom assessment, and testing and grading techniques. As incentives, the secondary school faculty were provided with materials to be used in their courses, including textbooks, sample syllabi, sample quizzes and tests, website references, and a stipend.

On the survey at the conclusion of the training, one of the teachers wrote, "This was an excellent training opportunity. The instructor is quite knowledgeable about the subject area of the training and was very good at making connections that tie to her classroom and professional experiences. The discussions were helpful, but the sharing of information and experiences is invaluable. We all get paid to teach, but it is great to be around an educator who has passion for what she does. She is a natural and an asset to her students and this college."

Another wrote, "Initially, I thought the purpose of the course was to learn more about the content of the courses we'd be teaching rather than developing teaching skills. However, the material covered was very relevant and helped a lot to prepare us for the community college setting and to relieve some of the anxiety related to teaching on this level. The ideas and strategies discussed were creative and helpful. The resources provided, particularly on syllabus, were excellent."

Law Enforcement and the Community was taught in spring 2005 by one PHS faculty member, and he used the PGCC syllabus, textbook teaching methods, and sample quizzes and exams.

Secondary and postsecondary articulation agreements. An articulation agreement with PHS was developed for the two Criminal Justice courses, Law Enforcement and the Community (Cross-Cultural Relations), and Juvenile Delinquency, though students can test out of Introduction to Criminal Justice and Criminal Investigation. Criminal Justice I and II were offered in the fall of 2004. Law Enforcement and the Community was offered as a concurrent enrollment course for the 12th grade cohort in the spring of 2005. As mentioned, four of the five students in the cohort enrolled at PGCC in fall 2005; however, because of placement scores, three of them are not enrolled in any PGCC criminal justice courses yet.

Site-based experiences. During the summer of 2004, three students were offered paid internships with the employer partner, the Laurel City Police Department. The internship consisted of a two-week period where students shadowed employees of the Laurel Police Department to experience a law enforcement atmosphere and develop a better understanding of the internal organization of a municipal police department and its daily activities including communications, administrative duties, patrol duties, and special assignment duties. A PHS faculty member was involved in the management of the internship to assure the quality of the experience for the students. Surveys were conducted at the conclusion of the internships. Students said they "learned a lot about real police work" and that there was a lot more paperwork than expected. One student said that "...they [the police] go to work not knowing what to expect every working day." Students were successfully witnessing, firsthand, the day-to-day activities of an actual police department and thus are more likely to understand the reality of the job. This internship experience was not offered in the summer of 2005 because the project director was on leave.

■ Students were successfully witnessing, firsthand, the day-to-day activities of an actual police department and thus are more likely to understand the reality of the job.

Opportunities for parents to meet with students and advising faculty. In August 2005, PGCC hosted a Parent-Student Night for secondary students involved in the project and their parents. During the evening, college faculty and staff provided information about Prince George's Community College, including admissions and testing, career counseling, student services, vocational services, the Criminal Justice Department, and degrees offered in the field of criminal justice.

Least Effective Strategies

While students felt they learned a lot in the remediation program in the summer of 2004, three of the four who made the transition to PGCC did not meet the minimum score on the ACCUPLACER placement test in reading. Therefore, they are now required to take a full semester of remedial reading before they can continue in the Law, Public Safety, and Security Criminal Justice Pathway. Since Potomac High School has one of the lowest performance levels in the county, and since about 80 percent of all students who enter the college straight from high school require some remediation, it is not surprising that the students required remediation. Furthermore, several weeks of part-time instruction is not sufficient to prepare students in these areas.

Lessons Learned

Partner relationships. Probably one of the most important lessons learned is that the relationships among the partners are crucial. There has to be complete buy-in by the high school principals in any pathway program. While the Potomac High School principal was willing for her school to be a partner in the project, she was concerned about finances. The college agreed to assign college staff to cover the high school courses, but she still had concerns, so her staff did not participate in the conference.

Cost to students. Another issue is related to the cost of college tuition for dual-enrollment courses. The parents in this low-income neighborhood do not have the resources to pay for these extra benefits, and therefore, only one course, Law Enforcement and the Community, was taught. College staff recognize that special funding might be located to support these courses, but they are concerned about how to sustain such funding.

Remediation. Another lesson is that a brief summer remediation experience is not sufficient to help students with poor reading, English, and mathematics skills to score high enough on the ACCUPLACER to go straight into credit courses. However, testing them early helps alert students to their skill deficiencies. Solutions to the remediation problem need to be addressed by the county school system. The college is willing to help, but students need to be taught to read, write, and do mathematics from an early age.

Future lessons. Probably the most important lessons are yet to be learned. The students in the Criminal Justice Academy progressed to PGCC in fall 2005. Will they succeed in their English and mathematics courses? Will their training in study skills serve them well? Will they complete their training and eventually progress to the Police Academy or to a four-year institution? Time will tell.

More information about Prince George's Community College and the CCTI Initiative can be found at www.league.org/league/projects/ccti/projects/summary.cfm?key=pgcc.

San Diego Miramar College

Terry O'Banion

OCCUPATIONAL AREA: Law, Public Safety, and Security
CAREER PATHWAY: Paralegal and Law Enforcement
CCTI PROJECT DIRECTOR: Robin Carvajal, rcarvaja@sdccd.net
PROJECT PARTNERS: San Diego Miramar College
Public Safety Training Institute
Crawford High Educational Complex School of Law and Business
Multiple Business Partners

The Project Partners

The city of San Diego and San Diego County represent a region used to superlatives: the best year-round climate in the U.S., the best of Southern California, the best access to Mexico and the Pacific Rim. The superlatives are collectively expressed in the city's motto, "America's Finest City." Many residents and visitors would agree that these superlatives are not overstatements; the region is climactically, geographically, educationally, and economically blessed.

There is a spirit of cooperation in the region that is also one of the key characteristics of San Diego and San Diego County. That cooperation has led to the creation of one of the top regional training centers in the country, housed at Miramar College, that provides the home for this CCTI project.

San Diego's Gross Regional Product (GRP) was $120.1 billion in 2001. In 2002, the GRP increased by 5.1 percent, to 126.2 billion. Part of the reason for this growth is San Diego's abundant and diverse supply of labor at competitive rates. The total civilian labor force is about 1.5 million. In March of 2003, the unemployment rate was 4.3 percent, far below the state's rate of 6.7 percent and the nation's rate of 5.8 percent. The area's climate and quality of life are major factors in attracting a quality workforce. San Diego companies do not have a hard time attracting and retaining workers.

In addition, local colleges and universities, with a population of over 230,000 students, augment the region's steady influx of qualified labor. Higher education institutions in the region include the University of California at San Diego, San Diego State University, and California State University at San Marcos. The University of California at San Diego ranks sixth in the nation for total university

The affiliation with...CCTI has been of strategic importance to all of us in the San Diego Community College District because of the opportunities for networking nationally with other institutions facing similar challenges and [because of] the best-practices information exchange it has provided us.

Henry Ingle, Vice Chancellor, San Diego Community College District

research and development expenditures. San Diego's education institutions graduate nearly 1,600 students annually with bachelor's, master's, and Ph.D.s in engineering, computer science, information systems, mechanical engineering, and electronic technology. The business schools annually graduate more than 1,000 students, and more than 2,500 students annually receive advanced degrees in business administration. In addition, there are approximately a dozen world-renowned research institutes in the area that provide the building blocks for new industries, including the Salk Institute for Biological Studies, the Scripps Research Institute, the Burnham Institute, Howard Hughes Medical Institute, Palomar Observatory, the International Thermonuclear Experimental Reactor Project, and Scripps Institution of Oceanography.

In addition to the universities and four-year colleges, there are five community college districts with a total of eight institutions serving San Diego County. These institutions play a significant role in addressing workforce needs in the county and serve as major resources for other community needs. The San Diego Community College District, which includes San Diego City College, San Diego Mesa College, and San Diego Miramar College, sits in the heart of the county and is the largest community college district.

San Diego is strategically located for access to Mexico and the Pacific Rim, and the local economy has profited enormously because of this geographical access. The San Diego-Tijuana border crossing is the world's busiest land border crossing, and Tijuana Economic Development Corporation promotes development in the region. In addition to investments from European and other international firms, San Diego benefits from investments from Japan, Taiwan, Korea, and China. The Japan External Trade Organization, established in 1958, is a nonprofit Japanese government-supported organization dedicated to promoting mutually beneficial trade and economic relationships with the San Diego region. TradePort is designed as an easy-to-use tool offering central access to comprehensive information, trade leads, and company databases.

In 2001, a military population of 292,235 accounted for 10 percent of the total county population in San Diego. Ten Navy and Marine Corps installations are located in San Diego County, each with its own family housing program. NCAS Miramar, occupying more than 23,000 acres 15 miles north of downtown San Diego, is the Marine Corps' largest aviation facility and hosts the largest military air show in the world. The Marine Corps base at Camp Pendleton is the nation's busiest military base and occupies 250,000 acres 38 miles north of downtown San Diego. Because of these military bases, San Diego County is one of the leading counties in the nation for Department of Defense wages and salaries and Department of Defense procurement contract awards.

Miramar College is a comprehensive two-year public community college that offers educational programs spanning both academic and technical fields of study. The college is located in the rapidly growing northeastern part of the city of San Diego, just north of the Miramar Marine Corps Air Station. In the fall of 2002, the student population numbered 10,899, a 10 percent increase in enrollment over fall 2001. This student enrollment is 47 percent White, 13 percent Latino, 11 percent Philippino, 12 percent Asian-Pacific, and 6 percent African American.

Miramar College's mission statement reflects the leadership provided by its president, administrators, and faculty:

> Our mission is to prepare students to succeed in a world of dynamic change by providing an environment which values excellence in teaching, learning, innovation, and partnerships in a setting that celebrates diversity.

Central to this mission statement, a 2001 strategic plan sets out goals with related measures, intended outcomes, and strategies that set Miramar apart as a leading community college. That leadership has been recently confirmed by Miramar's selection as one of 15 colleges to participate in this CCTI project and earlier selection by the League for Innovation as one of a small group of colleges to participate in a national project on 21st century learning outcomes.

The college has a long history related to the creation of public safety training programs in San Diego County. In the 1950s, the San Diego County Sheriff's Department, San Diego Police Department, and San Diego Fire Department conducted basic academy lecture classes in classrooms at their individual agency locations, but physical lab activities related to law enforcement training were held in San Diego Community College District facilities when space was available.

In the late 1960s, the San Diego Community College Board of Trustees made a commitment to the public safety agencies to develop a dedicated site for their specialized training needs. A 125-acre site was selected adjacent to what was then the Miramar Naval Air Station. This surplus military property had been used as an emergency auxiliary landing field during World War II and was commonly known as Hourglass Field.

Miramar College opened as a training center for law enforcement and fire services in 1969. Instructional facilities included an outdoor firing range, a forensics lab, a mock courtroom, and a vehicle operations course. The training divisions from the San Diego County Sheriff's Department, San Diego Police Department, and San Diego Fire Department were located on campus to supervise employees during their coursework. Full-time faculty were assigned on campus as well to provide instruction in courses related to the Associate Degree Programs in Police and Fire Science.

As the population in San Diego County grew between 1960 and 1990, many of the smaller incorporated city law enforcement agencies were hiring new personnel who needed training. In 1971, there were new state laws requiring continuous training of law enforcement and other safety personnel, and small enforcement agencies could not afford to provide their own training. Miramar College was the ideal answer for these growing agencies, and as a result, the number of public safety students at the college increased rapidly.

Beginning in the early 1990s, changing economic conditions and negative recessionary periods created a need for all public safety agencies to maximize training funds. Through the leadership of the San Diego County Police Chief's and Sheriffs' Association, San Diego County law enforcement CEOs elected to support a regional training center that became the San Diego Public Safety Training Institute at Miramar College. Consequently, a joint powers agreement was structured among the San Diego Community College District, County of San Diego, and City of San Diego. This document is authorized under the California Government Code and outlines a governance structure for the training institute that is unique to public safety training centers in Southern California.

Currently, the **Public Safety Training Institute** provides training and education to personnel in 18 incorporated cities. These personnel include the San Diego County Sheriff's Department, San Diego County Probation Department, San Diego Port Authority, Harbor Police Department, San Diego Fire Department, Hartland Fire District, and California Department of Forestry. Limited training is conducted for the San Diego County District Attorney's Office and the federal agency local offices of the DEA, FBI, INS, and Border Patrol.

The Public Safety Training Institute at Miramar College serves approximately 10,000 sworn and nonsworn students annually, delivering instruction in topics ranging from basic academy training to advanced technical skills. Technology-supported lab facilities feature vehicle operation simulators and a laser-assisted firearms training simulator. This and other special equipment was funded under a grant from POST, the California Commission on Peace Officer Standards and Training. It is estimated that 90 percent of law enforcement personnel in San Diego County train at the Public Safety Training Institute at Miramar College.

■ It is estimated that 90 percent of law enforcement personnel in San Diego County train at the Public Safety Training Institute at Miramar College.

The future for the Public Safety Training Institute is bright. With the closure of military bases in the San Diego region, 25 surplus acres at the Naval Training Center have been allocated to the institute for the development of an instructional facility. This site includes lecture-lab classrooms for public safety training. Additionally, an application was made with the Marine Corps Air Station, Miramar, for 80 acres to develop a Public Safety Vehicle Operations Course. This application is in the final stages, and as drafted, will be a partnership between the Public Safety Training Institute and the United States Marine Corps. The site will include classrooms and the ability to deliver courses beyond mandated public safety vehicle operation courses in topics such as Driver Awareness, Driving Under the Influence, and required driver license coursework, which will allow military personnel to operate a variety of vehicles on federal military enclaves. An array of courses will also be available for military dependents.

Founded in 1957, Crawford High School is a comprehensive high school in the San Diego Unified School District. It is located in an economically disadvantaged urban area of San Diego and houses a large immigrant population. According to the California Department of Education, Crawford is the most diverse high school in the state. The school serves approximately 1,500 culturally and linguistically diverse students, 600 of whom are English language learners. Of the 437 students in the Legal and Business School (LAB) in 2005, 49 percent were Hispanic/Latino, 30 percent were African American (including African), 8 percent were Cambodian, 4 percent were Vietnamese, 2 percent were White, and 7 percent were of other ethnicity.

In the fall of 2003, Crawford High School established a Legal and Law Enforcement Academy, a partnership project with the American Legal Administrators (ALA) under ALA's Project Leap. In the fall of 2004, the school again changed its organizational structure, establishing the **Crawford High Educational Complex School of Law and Business** (LAB). The vision of Crawford's School of Law and Business is "to inspire passion for learning, prepare students for postsecondary options, and ensure that all students develop the skills needed to meet the social, cultural, and economic demands of our society."

The LAB is a comprehensive education program that integrates rigorous standards-based academic curriculum, career-exploration activities, and vocational education. Students participate in the LAB as a cohort from the 10th through the 12th grade. The format of the LAB offers a small learning community and personalized support services to ensure student success. The advisory board, made up of many legal and law enforcement agencies in the community, provides professional guidance on curriculum, industry standards, and program operation, as well as opportunities for students to intern.

The San Diego chapter of the American Legal Administrators organization, in concert with other legal and law enforcement professional groups in San Diego County, created Project Leap in early 2000. The primary purpose is to recruit high school students into the many high-demand, high-wage careers in the legal and law enforcement professions in San Diego County. Crawford LAB is one of the major projects of Leap, but the organization also provides a variety of services to area high schools, including opportunities for students to interview leaders in the legal field and to participate in career days, job fairs, job shadowing, and internships.

Curriculum and Instruction

This CCTI project, orchestrated by Miramar College, was launched with great enthusiasm and great promise. In the past two years, however, there have been a number of significant, unanticipated changes that have been challenging for project leaders. Crawford High School initiated and is still going through a major structural change from a general high school to one that includes four small schools in the same system. The San Diego Community College District appointed a new chancellor; Miramar College appointed a new president. The CCTI project director at this site was also reassigned, and a new project director was appointed and has since been replaced by another.

These are major changes in school systems, with a huge impact on policies, programs, practices, personnel, and students. External projects, such as this CCTI project, often get lost in this sea of change or are relegated to such low priority that they disappear from the screen. That is not the case here. The project has survived and has emerged under new leadership as a viable national model that can inform the practices of others; in addition, it serves as an example of how excellent leaders in excellent institutions can address the challenges of enormous change, and address those challenges in creative and innovative ways.

■ **The project has survived and has emerged under new leadership as a viable national model that can inform the practices of others; in addition, it serves as an example of how excellent leaders in excellent institutions can address the challenges of enormous change, and address those challenges in creative and innovative ways.**

At the College

Upon receipt of the Career Pathway template designed for this CCTI project, Miramar Community College (Miramar) and Crawford High Educational Complex (Crawford) faculty identified and developed articulated courses for a Law Enforcement career pathway. Crawford then identified interested eligible candidates to fill the classes. The Law Enforcement pathway leads to an Associate of Science Degree in Administration of Justice (ADJU) with Miramar. Initiatives are under way to diversify pathways leading to San Diego City College degree programs.

The many changes at Crawford High School and at Miramar College have required a refocus on the career-pathways concept for this project. In the fall of 2005, new arrangements were made to introduce and reintroduce the Career Pathway to Crawford High School teachers. Considering the degree of change that has occurred at Crawford in the past two years, a reintroduction of the pathways model is critical to laying the foundation for its use and full appreciation. These staff-development activities focus on implementation, appropriate use, and strategies related to the Career Pathway.

Miramar and Crawford faculty work together to provide smooth transitional opportunities for students. The Summer Career Institute (SCI) held on the Miramar campus is one example. The primary goal of SCI is to provide students with a college campus experience during the summer months. In the summer of 2005, SCI focused on Diversity and Community Relations, a course offering Crawford seniors college credit in a tailored setting sensitive to their cultural and educational needs and using project-based learning strategies in its delivery.

The Diversity and Community Relations course focuses on developing a greater student understanding of the need for police and other legal and law enforcement agencies within a community. Through interactive mock trials, interviews, and presentations from a multitude of community professionals, students are provided a fresh perspective on service officials. To illuminate the complexity of community relations work, the class also includes a review of behavior and personality types as well as demographic and linguistic challenges with which law enforcement personnel have to deal.

At the High School

The California State University (CSU) system recently created an Early Assessment Placement (EAP) test to be administered to all potential high school graduates. It was developed using questions from previous California State Testing (CST) products. CSU borrowed sample questions and concepts from CST and compiled a comprehensive EAP test, which was administered to the entire 11th grade class at Crawford during the last months of the 2004-2005 school year. The results from this test provide Crawford seniors with an accurate snapshot of their current ability to achieve English and math success at the postsecondary level. The results of the EAP will be used to alert students about their academic deficiencies. This, in turn, will endow both high school administrators and students with an opportunity to focus on remedial needs.

Summer Career Institute staff at Miramar worked closely with Crawford's Employer Outreach Specialist to identify local business and internship opportunities for students in the Law Enforcement pathway. Students can earn up to two college credits for summer internships working in the local business community. Internship credit varies, depending on whether or not students are paid and number of hours worked. Students earn one credit for 60 hours of unpaid or 75 hours of paid intern time. Two credits are available for 120 hours of unpaid time or 150 hours of paid time.

Bridges With Four-Year Programs

The Diversity and Community Relations course offered to Crawford juniors in the summer of 2005 has been matriculated with the California State University (CSU) system. Miramar worked with CSU to ensure a seamless transition to four-year universities. Additional matriculation efforts are being considered and will continue to be addressed as pathway development diversifies and is institutionalized.

Student Support

SDCCD worked closely with advisory boards and businesses to ensure seamless student support. SDCCD is partnering with CSU to develop and deliver "How to Get to College" presentations for high school students. These presentations will define the pathway and review additional products involved in the getting-to-college process (*e.g.*, FAFSA, College Application information). Offering such presentations in the classrooms and in grade-level assemblies allows working relationships to be strengthened and students to become more aware of the CCTI partners, goals, and products.

Several fundamental initiatives have aided student support. The full-time employer outreach professional at Crawford is able to assist with internship development and business advisory issues. Crawford's principal is actively engaged in supporting pathway development and has helped align CCTI initiatives with student needs. Crawford's student counselor and dean of students have also been heavily engaged in assisting pathway support and development

College campus visits were successfully coordinated, and future trips are currently being planned. Campus visits heighten student awareness and exposure to college life. These visits will include exposure to application, financial aid, and typical entrance requirements and processes. Multiple campus and college visits offer a comprehensive perspective on the entire educational experience and opportunity.

Special Features

SDCCD is a vital member of Crawford's Business Advisory Board, and the CCTI coordinator chairs the advisory board. This facilitates the development of strong relationships and a deep understanding and integration of CCTI goals and objectives. It allows for a closer functioning relationship between Crawford's school goals and the goals of CCTI. And it provides a forum where representatives from local business and industry can learn about and participate in the CCTI project.

This advisory committee provided project leaders an opportunity to embed the goals of the CCTI project into institutional structures. The local CCTI Improvement Plan is now reflected in Crawford's mission and vision, and in institutional action plans for achieving school goals. Crawford's strategic plan includes identified tasks, expected outcomes, and deadlines for achieving results, and these reflect the goals and strategies of the CCTI Improvement Plan. This opportunity to merge common goals met with everyone's satisfaction and greatly minimized the duplication of effort.

Multiple San Diego businesses also partnered in promoting CCTI initiatives. The Career Pathway on Law Enforcement identified opportunities to earn credits via internships, which placed students in law firms and business and resource centers throughout San Diego. The internships served as a catalyst to bring the local CCTI players together for increased collaboration. Corporate and student needs were addressed through the internships and provided a practical application for sound learning for the educators at Crawford and Miramar.

The Career Pathway in Law Enforcement also served as a catalyst to link existing programs and projects that share common goals with the CCTI project. Existing programs in Tech Prep and Jump Start were tapped for resources to assist the development of CCTI. For example, the Summer Career Institute, a creation of the District's Tech Prep initiative, was adapted for the CCTI project as one of the key learning experiences for students in the Law Enforcement Career Pathway.

The Implementation Strategies

Most Effective Strategies

Alignment of high school and college curriculum. SDCCD, Miramar, and Crawford worked collaboratively to articulate curriculum in the creation of the Law Enforcement pathway. Miramar shared course outlines and curriculum with Crawford and supported efforts to integrate courses with college-prep activities. College-prep activities built awareness of expectations and introduced concepts covered in college.

Articulating coursework for students has many benefits. By earning postsecondary credit early and using the pathways, students are given a head start in developing and sustaining productive career interests. In addition, the more credit students have, the less likely they may be to drop out of postsecondary instruction. Aligning high school and college curriculum into pathways early helped bridge the gaps for potential at-risk students in earning college degrees.

Following are articulated courses for the Law Enforcement Pathway:

- ***Legal Office Procedures***. The Legal Office Procedures course was introduced during the fall 2004 semester as a Tech Prep articulated course. Students participate in theme-based learning activities related to office roles, communication skills, organization and records, and management procedures.
- ***Computer Applications***. Students receive instruction in keyboarding techniques and basic hardware. In addition, students are introduced to Microsoft Office products and additional software.
- ***Diversity and Community Relations***. This course offers Administration of Justice (ADJU) students the opportunity to analyze, develop insights, and effectively handle face-to-face street contact between peace officers and the public. Subject matter emphasizes the major cultural groups in California and the community relations problems facing law enforcement personnel. The course fulfills degree, certificate, and multicultural requirements and is transferable to various four-year institutions. The Diversity and Community Relations course, while not offered at Crawford, is typically taken by 11th grade students in the summer before they enter the 12th grade. The course is held at Miramar's campus and is available to all high school students throughout San Diego.

■ ...the Summer Career Institute, a creation of the District's Tech Prep initiative, was adapted for the CCTI project as one of the key learning experiences for students in the Law Enforcement Career Pathway.

Early college exposure (Summer Career Institute). The SCI goals for Crawford students were designed to provide high school juniors with exposure to postsecondary education and to make meaningful connections to the business world. Students also had an opportunity to gain exposure to a college campus for the first time. The SCI provided centralized points of contact for employers interested in offering internship experiences.

The SCI specifically targeted incoming high school seniors interested in careers in law and law enforcement. High school students enroll in a three-week, three-credit summer course held on the Miramar campus, followed by an internship that allows students to earn up to five units of college credit that can be used toward an AS degree in ADJU at Miramar.

Students were challenged with practical experiences addressing the needs of their community and of service workers as a whole. A tailored learning environment combined with real-world career-field exposure proved to be a successful tactic. The exposure to theme-based learning environments provided students with distinctive practical experiences. It also allowed students to see and more fully understand available career avenues.

College placement exams for juniors and seniors. The CCTI staff is coordinating the administration of college placement exams to Crawford students during their junior and senior years. Successful implementation of this activity was interrupted during the 2003-2004 academic year because of the significant changes in Crawford's educational structure. Their conversion from a comprehensive high school into small targeted schools temporarily delayed testing. Efforts to implement this strategy have resumed, and placement tests were administered during the 2005-2006 academic year for the senior and junior classes.

The high school principal and college and high school counselors agreed that early assessments provide students with a helpful overview of the postsecondary entrance process as a whole. In addition to identification of students' readiness for postsecondary instruction, remediation techniques tailored to student needs can be made available for students who are identified as needing additional preparation.

College-prep remediation courses. A remedial class in one or both of the core subject areas (math and English) was offered at Crawford and open to both students and their parents during the 2005-2006 academic year. The remedial classes were offered based on the results of the EAP exams as well as the college placement tests administered in the fall.

Future opportunities to assist with remedial instruction are being explored. Assessment testing is suggested during the 9th and 10th grade years to provide students with more time for remedial work. Responding to placement testing deficiencies identified in juniors is challenging to address before entrance into postsecondary programs. According to current California High School Exit Exams (CAHSEE) and California Standards Testing (CST) figures, more than 80 percent of students will require some form of remediation, and only 37 percent of students passed both the math and the English sections of the CAHSEE. The test scores of the Crawford High School population pose significant barriers to the full use of the career pathway model. Given the significant diversity at the school and the below-grade test scores, this project is focusing on identifying student needs and building program support systems that bring students closer to moving along career pathways. In many cases, that means exposing the high school students to the potential of going to college. It also means testing them to clearly identify basic skill gaps that would prevent them from performing adequately at college.

Least Effective Strategies

Employing multiple strategies simultaneously. As multiple implementation strategies for CCTI were developed and implemented, Crawford reorganized into several smaller schools. Employing multiple strategies simultaneously did not work very well during such a dynamic time. It became too overwhelming for Crawford while the students were trying to adjust to a major school reform initiative. Postponing engagement in the project until Crawford had time to adjust to the new structure may have been more beneficial for those involved.

Considering challenges facing students. The SDCCD project chose to work with an intercity program that serves a highly diverse population. Crawford was chosen because of its participation in the LEAP project, not for the likelihood that the students would progress to college. This student population is comprised of a large percentage of new immigrants. Many of the students require extensive ESL instruction in addition to remediation of basic skills. The need for basic ESL instruction has prevented many of the students from being prepared to use the Career Pathway as a guide.

Some of the intensive strategies that were developed were not realistic for this population, given its current level of reading and writing abilities and limitations. The initiatives placed unrealistic pressure on the high school partners to implement a transition strategy prematurely. Current efforts are focused on implementing practical student support strategies after assessing the priorities and developmental needs of the students and the program overall.

Lessons Learned

Project-based learning is essential. Integrating an introductory college class with project-based learning techniques has been a very successful strategy when working with students who would not typically be considered college bound. Helping at-risk students understand learning themes and principles through real-world experiences was a huge success.

Consider culturally relevant instructional strategies. The learning strategies that were employed during the Summer Career Institute class offered to high school seniors were tailored to the cultural dimensions of its audience. Coursework considered the potential for writing and reading levels below those expected at the collegiate level. Writing focused on life experiences

■ **Integrating an introductory college class with project-based learning techniques has been a very successful strategy when working with students who would not typically be considered college bound.**

versus the more abstract focus typically found at the postsecondary levels. Students examined issues of diversity and law enforcement relevant to how such issues may have affected them personally.

The San Diego City Schools Race and Human Relations Office currently employs Culturally Relevant Instructional Strategies (CRIS) in its advocacy and intervention services. CRIS strategies consider the cultural context of the learner and employ modified instructional methods accordingly. Such strategies focus on potential differences in learning styles among ethnicities and inform and enable educators to be better equipped to communicate effectively in a diverse arena. Coordination with diversity experts in advance will maximize instructional content, time, and overall program efficiency.

In the Summer Career Institute, the instructor provided numerous opportunities for project-based learning, with great consideration given to the culture of each student. For example, students were provided an array of culturally diverse reading materials from which they were allowed to select the readings they felt were more relevant and appropriate to their own backgrounds. In addition, the assignments focused on a demonstration of understanding of concepts rather than a grammatically correct presentation of concepts. This was particularly important given the basic skill challenges of the group. In this way, students have an opportunity to be exposed to higher educational opportunities, which in turn provides incentives for them to pursue those opportunities.

Clear MOUs are necessary. During this project, the senior management of every educational entity involved changed. At times, so did overall project support. Shifting priorities for all players disrupted the overall synergy of the partnership. Memorandums of Understanding (MOU) should have been drafted by key players to officially identify, declare, and maintain the roles and responsibilities of those associated in the partnership. MOUs can serve as the backbone for support during shifting leadership roles and priorities. MOUs should be agreed to at a level high enough to be supported in case of turnover.

Any college considering adapting the career pathways models should thoroughly plan for strategic barriers. Project leaders should identify expected or potential major changes such as new senior leadership, organizational structure changes, and changes in resources and support, and be prepared to adjust as necessary. Once potential barriers are identified, implementation strategies should be continuously reviewed for efficacy and realistic attainment. Flexibility, communication, and common goals must be mandatory components of a successful College and Career Transitions Initiative.

More information about San Diego Miramar College District and the CCTI Initiative can be found at http://www.league.org/league/projects/ccti/projects/summary.cfm?key=sdmc.

Science, Technology, Engineering, and Mathematics

- Lehigh Carbon Community College (PA)
- Sinclair Community College (OH)
- St. Louis Community College (MO)

Lehigh Carbon Community College

Elisabeth Barnett

OCCUPATIONAL AREA:	Science, Technology, Engineering, and Mathematics
CAREER PATHWAY:	Nanofabrication Manufacturing Technology
CCTI PROJECT DIRECTOR:	Deanna Quay
PROJECT PARTNERS:	Lehigh Carbon Community College Carbon Lehigh Intermediate Unit Lehigh Career and Technical Institute Other area high schools Penn State University Temple University Lehigh Valley Business Education Partnership

■ Improving high-school-to-college transition is about changing both high schools and colleges. For high schools to improve student preparation for college means that colleges must be very clear about the specific knowledge and skills students need...to enroll in credit-bearing courses. Improving college completion rates is not just about getting better prepared students from high school, it is equally about colleges doing a better job to help students earn a degree or certificate.

Gene Bottoms, Senior Vice President, Southern Regional Education Board, High Schools That Work, CCTI Advisory Working Group Member

The Project Partners

While Lehigh Carbon Community College (LCCC) and its partners are involved in educating students for employment in a wide range of STEM career areas, it selected nanofabrication manufacturing technology as the focus of its work under the CCTI grant. The decision to emphasize this occupational area was based on the emerging demand in local industry for workers with an understanding of nanofabrication manufacturing techniques and the principles underlying them. Nanofabrication manufacturing, which deals with the production of extremely small items of various types, can be applied in the creation of products ranging from computer components to medical devices. Its principles can be taught within the context of a number of science disciplines, including biology, physics, and chemistry.

This CCTI project has had a three-fold focus: (1) The project has emphasized improvements in the articulation and quality of the Career Pathway leading to a degree in nanofabrication manufacturing technology. (2) To reduce remediation and improve the academic skills of students, teachers have been trained in the Reading Apprenticeship (RA) program, developed by the WestEd Strategic Literacy Initiative. (3) Work has been done to expand STEM-related dual-credit course offerings to high school students.

Lehigh Carbon Community College is a comprehensive community college established in 1967 under the sponsorship of the local school district. It offers 15 transfer programs, 52 career associate degree programs, 33 certificate programs, and 10 specialized credit diploma programs, in addition to continuing education and other noncredit offerings (Bragg, 2003). Lehigh's nanofabrication manufacturing technology program was established in 2003, and has served up to 12 students a year.

The **Carbon Lehigh Intermediate Unit** (CLIU), a regional service coordination agency, serves 15 school districts in Carbon and Lehigh counties. The CLIU provides a broad range of services to the schools, including assistance with curriculum and instruction, staff development, educational technologies, and special education and behavioral health services. It is very supportive of career technical education, including CCTI, and has also taken strong leadership in bringing the Reading Apprenticeship program to the area.

The **Lehigh Career and Technical Institute** (LCTI) is an area vocational center and future comprehensive high school located adjacent to the college in a state-of-the-art facility that is currently undergoing massive enlargement and renovation. LCTI has played a major role in preparing students for local employment opportunities, as well as in establishing a sophisticated approach to career-technical education intended to prepare all students for both further education and employment. Its nanotechology curriculum serves as the basis for the secondary part of the CCTI career pathway. Other high schools, including Northwestern Lehigh High School, Salisbury Township High School, Emmaus High School, Southern Lehigh High School, and Whitehall High School, send students to LCTI for career-technical training while providing most of the academic coursework in the home school. The total number of schools participating in the CCTI initiative increased from three to six in the past year.

Postsecondary partners **Penn State University** and **Temple University** have articulated programs that allow students to progress from the nanofabrication manufacturing technology at LCCC into four-year degrees in engineering. In addition, the LCCC program ends with a capstone semester at Penn State University's Nanofabrication Facility.

Finally, business partners are very active in supporting local education through their involvement in the **Lehigh Valley Business Education Partnership**. There is regular communication with the education community about the workforce needs of local business and industry.

The CCTI partnership grew out of the Lehigh County Career Pathways Steering Committee, a group that formed nine years ago to enhance the area's education system, especially in the area of career-technical education. The committee's involvement with High Schools That Work (HSTW) was an important aspect, and all of the schools participating in the CCTI grant are HSTW schools. Members of the partnership, with the leadership of Clyde Hornberger and the Lehigh County Superintendents, developed a detailed competency-based career pathway system that leads to multiple national certifications in each career area. This system has received recognition by the Pennsylvania Department of Education and the Pennsylvania Department of Vocational Education as a state model and has served as the basis for the development of numerous additional pathways.

History of the Partnership

The partnership has aggressively pursued grant funding to enhance career-technical education in the region, and each of its grant-funded initiatives is integrated into the overall system. They include:

- Three middle colleges developed under Tech Prep demonstration grants within existing area vocational centers;
- A 2+2+2 grant from the state designed to support the development of pathways spanning secondary schools and two- and four-year colleges;
- National Science Foundation support for the nanofabrication manufacturing technology program; and
- Local industry-funded technology grants.

To complement these initiatives, and with particular interest in obtaining support for the dissemination of RA training, the committee submitted a successful proposal for funding as a CCTI site in 2002. Since receiving the grant, it has worked to align the local CCTI initiative with the national CCTI framework. To do this, it has refined the nanofabrication manufacturing technology curriculum so that it more adequately reflects CCTI guidelines and provides better articulation between the high school and college levels. In addition, the committee has undertaken the development of new dual-enrollment courses.

The Model Career Pathway

The Nanofabrication Manufacturing Technology Pathway was developed through the integration of two existing, well-aligned programs. At the secondary level, it reflects the current curriculum in nanofabrication offered to students at LCTI along with courses in English, math, science, and social studies that students take at their home schools. Students in this pathway typically spend half a day at the LCTI and half a day at the home school where they take their academic courses and may participate in extracurricular activities. Beginning next year, LCTI students will have the option of staying for the full day and taking both career-technical and academic courses at LCTI's new expanded campus. This is expected to be particularly beneficial for students who live some distance from LCTI.

The postsecondary portion of the pathway reflects the proposed revised Nanofabrication Technology (A.A.S.) curriculum that LCCC faculty completed and submitted for approval to the college curriculum committee in February 2005. The changes were designed to

- Incorporate a broader platform of applications beyond the semiconductor industry that has been in decline in recent years,
- Provide a more extensive foundation of skills that will prepare students to take full advantage of the Penn State University capstone semester, and
- Create an Introduction to Nanoscience course that will be available on campus and also offered for dual enrollment by high school students.

Curriculum and Instruction

At the secondary level, all students in the district choose a traditional or technical course of study through high school, with both courses designed to be college preparatory. Students in the Nanofabrication Manufacturing Technology Pathway, along with other career-technical students, take courses such as Applied Biology and Applied Communication. These are rigorous academic courses appropriate for students wishing to go to college, but they emphasize applied and contextual learning to increase their relevance to students with a career-technical education focus. These courses are normally taken at the home high school. The Nanofabrication Manufacturing Technology Pathway at the high school level includes a total of four English courses, four math courses, four science courses, and four social studies courses.

Plans are for the new college-level Introduction to Nanoscience course will be available to high school students as an 11th grade elective in the near future. The course introduces students to the field of nanoscience and microtechnology. This is accomplished in a progression from understanding basic material properties to fabricating such materials into useful devices on a nanoscale, and an overview of the functionalities that can be obtained. The student gains an understanding of how nanoscience integrates and unifies knowledge from many branches of science and engineering (LCCC course outline, 2005). The course is to be offered as a dual-enrollment option. Other dual-enrollment courses in the pathway include DC Circuits and Digital Fundamentals.

The curriculum at LCTI is individualized, with students progressing at their own pace through a series of competencies tailored to specific job descriptions and certifications, based on those detailed in the O'Net system, formerly the *Dictionary of Occupational Titles*. Some learning activities are done in groups, while others involve students working alone at their own pace. To progress, students show evidence of accomplishment of the competencies to the instructor, who documents their progress in booklets, noting that items have been completed or need additional work. Both technical and professional development – soft or SCANS skills taught using Skills USA module-based software – are emphasized and assessed. All students are expected to work toward industry certifications. In addition, all students are considered to be on their way to postsecondary education at either a two- or four-year college. In fact, 60 percent of the graduates attended college in 2003-2004, up from 23 percent in previous years.

The curriculum at LCTI is individualized, with students progressing at their own pace through a series of competencies tailored to specific job descriptions and certifications...

The experience at LCTI with this individualized, competency-based curriculum has resulted in a lessened emphasis on designating the program as a high school or college-level experience. Students are encouraged to complete progressively more certifications, which may build upon one another or may be in new but related areas. In general, the competencies are keyed to industry standards rather than to beliefs about what constitutes high school or college-level work.

In addition to the focus on nanofabrication manufacturing technology, a major change in teaching and learning in the region has occurred through the introduction of Reading Apprenticeship training. This program was originally adopted when a group of local superintendents became concerned about reading, especially reading comprehension, in the high schools. After extensive research on alternatives, local education leaders deemed this approach to be the most effective and the most respectful of teachers' diverse ways of managing classrooms.

The RA program is designed to provide teachers with a framework to understand and implement strategies that help students comprehend reading materials in the context of any course. It is considered to be useful at the middle school, high school, and college levels. The stated goals of the program are to

- Train teachers to use reading literacy strategies that help students learn content more effectively;
- Help high school students increase their independence and effectiveness with reading and learning;
- Create greater awareness among students about science and technology careers;
- Provide juniors and seniors access to college courses while they are still in high school; and
- Prepare students for the transition from high school to college, lessening the need for remediation courses upon entry into college (Bragg, 2003).

■ **Students are encouraged to complete progressively more certifications, which may build upon one another or may be in new but related areas. In general, the competencies are keyed to industry standards rather than to beliefs about what constitutes high school or college-level work.**

Training for local teachers in RA methods began in 2002, with participation gradually increasing each year. Under the CCTI grant, teachers at participating high schools and at LCTI have received the training, with priority given to science, math, and technology teachers. In addition, during the past year, the opportunity to be trained has been offered to college faculty across many disciplines. College President Dan Snyder expressed his appreciation for the leadership that the CCTI project has taken in expanding professional development opportunities for college faculty. The training is also supported by the director of the college's Teaching and Learning Center.

A solid core of teachers has become highly enthusiastic about the RA strategies, especially with the way they help students become engaged, participate more, and make connections among ideas. Several instructors are tracking groups of students to see if their grades and standardized test scores improve over time, with promising early results. Their enthusiasm has infected many other teachers, with increasing numbers enrolling in the training programs each year. The most devoted have formed a study group in which they exchange ideas for applications of the strategies, and several have become certified as trainers. In addition, based on discussions with representatives of the CLIU, the

Pennsylvania Department of Education has shown interest in recommending RA to school districts across the state for the improvement of reading, as part of a current statewide emphasis on improved literacy and numeracy.

In addition, the CCTI project has made available a new resource, the Achieve3000 system, to teachers trained in Reading Apprenticeship. Participating teachers can arrange to have the students in their classes receive an emailed daily article on a topic of current interest that is keyed to the students' individual reading levels. In this way, students can discuss common topics while progressing in reading at their own speed. To increase its appeal, it is called KidBiz for middle school students and TeenBiz for high school students. Teachers and students have responded very positively to the availability of this resource.

Bridges With Four-Year Programs

The Nanofabrication Manufacturing Technology Pathway is one of a group of LCCC Career Pathways with strong articulation agreements with Temple University and Penn State University. Students graduating with A.S. or A.A.S. degrees in engineering, manufacturing, industrial maintenance, or nanofabrication are able to transfer into B.S. programs in electrical, mechanical, or civil engineering with several different specializations. As mentioned, LCCC students in nanofabrication attend Penn State for their final semester.

Student Support

To enhance student guidance in selecting a career and learning about the education needed to prepare for it, the CCTI project is supporting the introduction of Career Cruising, career guidance software that can be used in both high school and college. It includes interest surveys and information on colleges and careers and allows students to develop individual portfolios.

In addition, staff of LCTI spend time in middle schools to inform students and parents about the range of career education pathways available beginning in the 9th grade. Marketing materials developed in conjunction with the Tech Prep demonstration project are used in explaining the features of the Career Pathways.

Younger students also learn about career options, including nanofabrication manufacturing technology, through participation in summer camps offered at LCCC. Several of these camps are designed to encourage students to enter STEM careers, and include opportunities to learn about nanoscience.

Special Features

The Lehigh Carbon Technical Institute, the principal secondary partner in this CCTI project, is clearly a leader in career-technical education. A number of elements give evidence of LCTI's approach.

- An assumption by the school leadership that all students will go on to college
- A large number of graduates who enroll in postsecondary education, reflecting increases of about 260 percent over the past eight years
- State-of-the-art teaching facilities and labs in many career areas, including the only secondary school Clean Room in the country
- A detailed curriculum guide for each career pathway that includes progressively more difficult tasks, leading to readiness to earn national industry certifications (the curriculum is self-paced, meaning that students can move at a speed commensurate with their interests and skills)
- Soft skills integrated into the curriculum
- The provision of rigorous academic courses, taught using contextual and applied methods relevant to students' career areas
- An individual learning plan developed for each student, updated annually

The use of Reading Apprenticeship across a wide variety of schools, school levels (middle school, high school, and college), and disciplines is bringing increasing numbers of teachers together to talk about teaching and learning. RA offers a series of specific ways to improve the classroom experience, but, just as important, its introduction has offered opportunities for teachers to reflect on their own teaching practice in ways that show promise for improving students' experiences throughout the region. First, the impact on students seems to go well beyond reading, with the focus on critical thinking and applying learning to new situations. Second, teachers are becoming energized. They are training each other; some are meeting in study groups to discuss ways to improve teaching and share materials. There is clearly a sense of excitement among those who have participated as they see students responding to the approaches. Finally, educational leaders speak of increased communication between the K-12 and college systems in response to the initiative.

RA offers a series of specific ways to improve the classroom experience, but, just as important, its introduction has offered opportunities for teachers to reflect on their own teaching practice in ways that show promise for improving students' experiences throughout the region.

The Implementation Strategies

The CCTI project uses a set of implementation strategies to attain the five CCTI objectives. These strategies are outlined in the table on page 163.

Most Effective Strategies

Among the specific implementation strategies, the CCTI project has identified five of which it is particularly proud.

Development of a career pathways system that begins with career awareness in first grade and continues through education and on-the-job career training. The system was first created as part of the involvement of local school districts with High Schools That Work and includes a detailed, self-paced, competency-based curriculum framework.

Widespread use of Reading Apprenticeship strategies. The CCTI project has focused on training high school and college science and math teachers in the use of this approach.

Lehigh Carbon CCTI Program

CCTI Objective	Key Strategies
Decreased need for remediation at postsecondary level	• Reading Apprenticeship training for high school teachers and college faculty, especially those in science, math, and technology • Administration of the COMPASS test in high school to assess student progress toward college readiness
Increased enrollment and persistence in postsecondary education	• Development of dual-enrollment courses • Continued improvement of student performance at LCTI through the use of individualized instruction and high expectations • Involvement of selected students in the middle colleges and the Academy for Science and Technology
Increased academic and skill achievement at the secondary and postsecondary levels	• Program in nanotechnology coordinated among secondary, community college, and four-year college partners • Reading Apprenticeship training for high school teachers and college faculty • Use of career-pathways curriculum and instructional methods at LCTI
Increased attainment of postsecondary degrees, certificates, or other recognized career credentials	• Increased communication and coordination among secondary and postsecondary teachers and counselors • Development of materials to market pathways to middle school students and their parents
Increased entry into employment or further education	• Creation and improvement of relationships with business and education partners • Development of new articulation and partnership agreements

Dual-enrollment opportunities for students, using different modalities. College-level courses are taught to high school students at the high school, on the college campus, and via distance learning. Through the CCTI project, a new course, Introduction to Biotechnology, has been created, and an introductory course in nanotechnology is under development.

A middle-college program, created under Tech Prep demonstration grant funding. The program enrolls cohorts of students within the area vocational centers who are working toward degrees in STEM careers and involves them in activities on the college campus.

Revision of the nanotechnology program with extensive input from industry representatives and secondary and college faculty. This was done in response to changes in local industry that decreased the importance of knowledge related to electronics and increased the importance of chemistry and biochemistry knowledge.

Least Effective Strategies

Students were tested with COMPASS during the 10th grade to assess for college readiness. This was believed to be too early, and there was also concern about how to interpret the results. Since the test is not designed for current high school students, it is hard to tell what the test scores mean for those still in high school.

Initial plans called for evaluating the effectiveness of Reading Apprenticeship teacher training by comparing the outcomes for students of trained teachers with students of teachers who were not trained. As more and more teachers have become trained, and because students are taught by many different teachers, this evaluation design has become unworkable.

Plans for the Future

The CCTI partnership, jointly and individually, is continuing to develop ways to build the Career Pathway and educational opportunities in the region that match the direction in which the economy is moving.

Faculty training. In the summer of 2005, a workshop will be offered to middle and high school science teachers, introducing the idea of integrating lessons on nanoscience into existing biology, chemistry, and physics courses. Teachers will be offered the opportunity to use kits developed by Penn State for high school instruction. The underlying assumption is that nanoscience is becoming increasingly prominent, and that all students should be introduced to basic principles.

Dual enrollment. LCCC President Snyder and others are working with the state on dual-enrollment legislation that will make it easier for colleges to offer dual-enrollment courses and improve funding streams. There is also discussion of appropriate quality standards and how to meet the needs of at-risk students.

Academy option. The college is also working on creating the Pennsylvania Academy for Science and Technology that would be located at the college, offering rigorous instruction for high school students interested in accelerating their progress toward four-year degrees in STEM areas.

Literary Challenge. Cathy Enders, a math teacher at LCTI, is developing a Literary Challenge course for all incoming high school freshmen based on RA strategies. This would give students a good foundation in reading and critical thinking that could then be reinforced by teachers across the curriculum. This is likely to become a model for other schools in the area.

Facility expansion. LCTI is in the process of adding on to its building and will open a portion of the facility as a comprehensive high school next year. Executive Director Clyde Hornberger is looking at ways to make the academic curriculum parallel the career-technical curriculum. Students will be taught in groups, but will be expected to master a series of tasks in each subject area before advancing to the next level.

Lessons Learned

The project partners have identified several lessons they have learned that may be useful to others implementing similar programs.

Reading Apprenticeship. In reducing the need for remediation among students entering STEM areas, Reading Apprenticeship strategies have proven very helpful. While they do not yet have data on the effectiveness of the program, teachers' early observations are encouraging. In addition, RA has served as an organizing tool, involving

Dealing with change. Major changes in course can be problematic. When a project's focus, expectations, or reporting requirements change, it may reduce the credibility of project leadership and dampen the enthusiasm of partners.

Dual-credit courses. The development of dual-credit courses requires working with many different people. Initial efforts to develop them are likely to be slow, as the planning process must take into account state requirements and standards, qualifications of faculty, and skepticism among some stakeholders. These problems may be overcome if the new course is shown to be important for students entering the local workforce.

Diverse options. Education should be designed to meet the needs of students who wish to attain different levels of education. Multiple pathways and credentials appropriate to the needs and interests of different students are useful.

Placement testing. While testing of students for college readiness using college placement tests is a good idea, students should not be tested before the 11th grade. In addition, it would be helpful to have norms for high school students on tests like COMPASS to indicate whether they are on track to being college ready.

Leadership. Success for a new initiative is often tied to its adoption by a highly regarded teacher or administrator.

Trust and collaboration. Community colleges are well positioned to take leadership in P-16 initiatives. Sharing grant resources widely brings more commitment from the partners involved, leading to better longer-term outcomes. Development of trust and collaboration is essential to a strong initiative.

More information about Lehigh Carbon Community College and the CCTI Initiative can be found at http://www.league.org/league/projects/ccti/projects/summary.cfm?key=LCCC.

■ ...it would be helpful to have norms for high school students on tests like COMPASS to indicate whether they are on track to being college ready.

Sinclair Community College

Elisabeth Barnett and Debra D. Bragg

OCCUPATIONAL AREA:	Science, Technology, Engineering, and Mathematics
CAREER PATHWAY:	Mechanical Engineering Technology
CCTI PROJECT DIRECTORS:	Ron Kindell, Project Director
	Meg Draeger, Project Manager
	Dave McDaniel, Project Manager
PROJECT PARTNERS:	Sinclair Community College
	Miami Valley Tech Prep Consortium
SCHOOL PARTNERS:	Centerville High School
	Dayton Public Schools
	Fairmont High School
	Miami Valley Career Technology Center
	Walter E. Stebbins High School
CORPORATE PARTNERS:	Dayton Area Chamber of Commerce
	Delphi Corporation
	Faraday Incorporated
GOVERNMENT PARTNERS:	Ohio Department of Education
	Ohio Board of Regents

■ **In sum, the CCTI project has provided a research and development opportunity that has transformed an existing partnership of this community college and its secondary and business partners to higher levels of effectiveness.**

Ronald Kindell, Director, Miami Valley Tech Prep Consortium, Sinclair Community College

The Project Partners

The CCTI project at Sinclair Community College builds upon a historically effective and well-developed Tech Prep program with a particularly strong engineering pathway. In 5 of the 58 schools that participate in the Miami Valley Tech Prep Consortium (MVTPC), additional dimensions associated with the national CCTI initiative have been strategically incorporated. Project leadership uses this group of schools as research and development sites for the consortium as a whole. Because of their history of success, the direction of Sinclair College and the MVTPC are closely observed by those in state government and other leaders in career and technical education around the state and nation. Thus, the CCTI project has become a true testing ground for the enhancement of career and technical education pathways statewide and beyond.

While the MVTPC offers 2+2 career pathways (junior and senior years of high school and two years of college) in 10 career clusters, the engineering cluster was chosen to be the focus of the CCTI initiative. The original approach to building a 4+2 pathway (four years of high school and two years of college) for the CCTI project involved adding 9th and 10th grade courses to the existing 2+2 plan for Manufacturing Engineering Technology. However, after Ohio became a Project Lead the Way (PLTW) state in 2004, several of the CCTI schools adopted the PLTW secondary-level courses as the focus of their high school engineering curriculum. As a result, high schools involved in this CCTI project use somewhat different routes to advance students into engineering technology options at the college level.

This CCTI project has been especially thoughtful about the ways that several of the CCTI project goals are addressed. A pilot project in high school math improvement has yielded positive results for participating students, with almost all showing readiness for college-level math by the end of their junior year in high school. This project has also developed a distinctive integrated career exploration course for 9th graders that incorporates the state standards for reading and writing. Finally, the project's use of Contextual Integrated Academic Learning Teams (CIALTs) to guide school-level activities has been a particularly effective way to promote high-quality implementation. These teams are comprised of core academic and technical education teachers who focus on ways to improve student learning using integrated instruction and contextualized learning across the curriculum.

Sinclair Community College *(SCC)* is a single-campus, comprehensive community college located in downtown Dayton, Ohio, with a population of 24,000 students. With an early history of offering courses under the auspices of the Dayton YMCA, Sinclair College came into being in 1948. It was officially chartered in 1966, and is Ohio's oldest community college. Also the largest such institution in the state, it enjoys an outstanding reputation in technical education, and in engineering technologies in particular. Sinclair Community College is often mentioned among colleges undertaking innovative, nationally recognized programs (Bragg, 2003). President Stephen Johnson has been very supportive of the CCTI initiative and considers it of great value in advancing relationships with the K-12 education system.

■ A pilot project in high school math improvement has yielded positive results for participating students, with almost all showing readiness for college-level math by the end of their junior year in high school.

Within the college, the CCTI project is most closely associated with the Engineering and Industrial Technologies Division, the largest division of this type in Ohio, and the third largest in the nation. The division has more than 50 tenure-line or annually contracted faculty, with more than 100 labs stocked with over $25 million worth of state-of-the-art equipment. The division is also a cofounder of the Advanced Integrated Manufacturing (AIM) Center at SCC, established in 1993 in partnership with the University of Dayton, with funding from the National Science Foundation. The center provides customized professional education to educators and area manufacturers, and has taken leadership in the recent introduction of Project Lead the Way as a curriculum option for local high schools.

The **Miami Valley Tech Prep Consortium** *(MVTPC)* was first established in 1992 as a planning committee to respond to a state-level Request for Proposals related to the formation of Tech Prep consortia. After securing funding, the consortium developed two 2+2 pathways leading to Associate of Applied Science degrees. These were in industrial engineering technologies and electronic engineering technologies. Many other pathways have been added over time, with multiple options now available within 10 career clusters. Each pathway is developed with attention to pertinent state education and industry standards as well as to alignment with four-year college and university programs. The MVTPC is comprised of Sinclair Community College, 58 public school districts, 7 career technical education planning districts, and hundreds of business partners within a six-county area. Like Sinclair Community College, the MVTPC is nationally known for the variety and quality of its programs, and it has received many awards, including the 1996 USDOE/OVAE award for the top Tech Prep initiative in the country (Bragg, 2003).

Five area high schools are partners in the CCTI initiative, selected from among those participating in Tech Prep programs. Because of the project leadership's interest in using CCTI as a way to test out initiatives that address needs of the entire MVTPC, the five schools were selected to represent the different kinds of schools found in the region – urban and rural schools, comprehensive and career technical high schools – and a diversity of student populations. The schools involved in this initiative are **Centerville High School**, **Dayton Public Schools Career Academy**, **Fairmont High School**, **Miami Valley Career Technology Center**, and **Walter E. Stebbins High School**.

■ Because of the project leadership's interest in using CCTI as a way to test out initiatives that address needs of the entire MVTPC, the five schools were selected to represent the different kinds of schools found in the region – urban and rural schools, comprehensive and career technical high schools – and a diversity of student populations.

The **Dayton Area Chamber of Commerce** and other business partners are interested in improving the quality of the local workforce, but are also concerned with the condition of local education in general. Business leaders cite the 40 percent dropout rate by the high school freshman year in the Dayton Public Schools as a reason to become involved. One of their major contributions to career technical education in the area is the provision of teacher externships through the Teachers in Industry for Educational Support (TIES) program. Teachers spend three weeks during the summer in a local business or industry setting to improve their understanding of the industry and to hone their skills.

The CCTI project leadership at Sinclair Community College has worked hand in hand with representatives of the **Ohio Department of Education** and **Ohio Board of Regents** in developing the project. Building on existing strong relationships formed around the development of the state Tech Prep initiative, Sinclair has held ongoing discussions about how to most effectively use the CCTI project as a research and development opportunity. While the focus has been on local needs, there has also been a selection of strategies with potential for statewide replication, and a commitment to gathering the kind of data that can provide evidence of effectiveness.

Sinclair Community College submitted a proposal for CCTI funding in order to build upon its long-term successes with Tech Prep and to take the program to the next level. The intent was not to create a new initiative, but rather to develop new program components that could be integrated into the existing initiative. Relatively short-term grant funding was seen as most appropriately used to build upon and enhance existing educational offerings. In addition, President Johnson saw the project as a way to benchmark the work of the college against other leading institutions as a reflection of his belief in continuous organizational improvement.

After receiving CCTI funding, the project took a special approach to the pursuit of the five CCTI objectives. In addition to the overall project advisory committee, five teams were formed, one to address each of the five CCTI objectives. However, because it was found that the five objectives often overlapped, it was decided that one multifunctional team would be more effective to provide guidance to the initiative. In addition, committees are often formed to advance specific program activities. For example, the Secondary/Postsecondary Math Alignment Committee is taking leadership in the development of the high school math-improvement pilot project.

Recent cutbacks in CCTI funding have required rethinking of some of the initial goals and methods. Some of the committees have been streamlined. For example, the Contextual Integrated Academic Learning Teams' membership and plan of action have been pared back so that they focus specifically on the improvement of math. Some reductions have also been made in professional development activities. However, the project leadership's response to this situation is to strategically support those efforts with the greatest likelihood of contributing to the learning agenda.

The Model Career Pathway

The Mechanical Engineering Technology Career Pathway developed for the CCTI project is based on a model that the Tech Prep consortium has used for a number of years to indicate the courses included in 2+2 pathways. This follows the system used in the State of Ohio, in which the state's Technical Competency Profile for a specific career area is adapted to local needs and conditions with extensive input from secondary, postsecondary, and business partners. Some changes have also been made to meet the standards of the CCTI project and to reflect the evolution of the curriculum in recent years. The CCTI career pathway template has become the model for all pathways in the MVTPC, and work is under way to complete a similar format for each of the other career pathways. It has also been adopted by the state as the preferred template for Tech Prep pathways statewide.

Beginning in 2004-2005, high schools in the Miami Valley Tech Prep Consortium were offered the opportunity to begin using the Project Lead the Way pre-engineering secondary school curriculum. First used in New York State in 1997, it is now available in more than 1,000 schools in 45 states. The five-course series begins with courses in Principles of Engineering, Engineering Design, and Digital Electronics, with more specialized courses following. Of the five schools involved in the CCTI project, three have opted to offer Project Lead the Way courses in place of those shown in the pathway. Because Sinclair Community College's Advanced Integrated Manufacturing (AIM) Center is coordinating the introduction of Project Lead the Way, new relationships are being forged in relation to the CCTI project, with some roles and responsibilities changing.

A large number of other MVTPC high schools have opted to continue with the existing curriculum in engineering. In the case of Stebbins High School, Engineering Technology teacher Jim Prater prefers a curriculum that includes considerable interaction with the faculty from Sinclair Community College, and integrates extensive project-based learning and off-campus experiences. Many of the MVTPC schools have a considerable investment in modern labs that they believe would be underused if the PLTW curriculum were to be implemented. Some were concerned that PLTW would increase program costs and decrease the diversity of material covered under the regular curriculum. However, CCTI Project Director Ron Kindell emphasizes that PLTW and the existing engineering pathways are not inconsistent with each other. Both use contextual approaches to math and science instruction, and both offer opportunities to earn articulated and dual credit.

The CCTI pathway incorporates opportunities for students to accelerate their education in several ways. Proficiency credit is earned when students take a college-administered exam and earn at least a C grade. Exams are generally scheduled to coordinate with the coverage of the pertinent material in the high school. Credit earned in this way is transcripted with a grade. Because of recent legislation in the State of Ohio, these credits are covered by the Transfer Assurance Guide, making them transferable to any public postsecondary institution in the state. An advantage to the use of proficiency credit is that grades of less than C are never transcripted. Thus students who are not successful in passing the exams do not end up with a poor college record that may limit their options in the future.

■ **An advantage to the use of proficiency credit is that grades of less than C are never transcripted. Thus students who are not successful in passing the exams do not end up with a poor college record that may limit their options in the future.**

In addition, articulated credit of the type traditionally available under Tech Prep may be earned. Under this plan, the high school teacher certifies that a student has achieved a C grade or better and mastered a specific set of competencies in a course that covers college-level material. This credit is typically only transferable to the college that awards it. A decision has been made in the MVTPC to make proficiency credit available in all of the pathways over a three-year period, while phasing out articulated credit in most cases. Some lab-based courses will continue to use articulated credit.

Finally, college engineering professors teach college courses at some area high schools. In the case of Stebbins High School, a four-block schedule is used. This makes it possible to embed a college class, taught by a professor from Sinclair, within the regular Engineering Technology classes. It is then supplemented by other material taught by the regular high school teacher. Students receive credit for both the college and high school classes. Since the college portion of the class accounts for about 40 percent of total class time, students' grades in the college course count for 40 percent of the total in the high school grade awarded. Sinclair College has not historically involved high school teachers as instructors for college courses in the high schools, although this may change in the future.

Curriculum and Instruction

The CCTI project at Sinclair has taken very seriously the idea of preparing students to enter college without the need for remediation. This issue is being addressed separately in the math and English arenas through two small programs that are expected to grow as evidence of their effectiveness is gathered and shared.

A math pilot project for juniors has been developed at two high school sites, Stebbins and Fairmont. College and high school faculty met in teams at each school to think about strategies that would help students to prepare to place into college-level courses based on ACCUPLACER scores and to succeed in college-level math classes. College math faculty members provided information on the knowledge and skills needed for successful performance in college. Together they developed a set of strategies that included additional planning time for high school teachers, better alignment of the high school and college curriculum, and additional testing for students to help them determine where they needed to fill gaps in knowledge. The two projects were very successful, and all but one student at each school placed into college-level math.

The CCTI project is now working to replicate this approach across all five of the CCTI schools. Each school has created a math team and is collecting baseline data on students. The goal is to graduate the CCTI class of 2006 with no math remediation needed in college. An additional goal is to have all students in the program take four years of high school college-preparatory math, so that they enter college more fully prepared for subsequent classes.

The approach to improving skills in English is very different. The CCTI project is addressing this in the 9th grade by creating a course that integrates career exploration with English language skills development. The course, called MEtaMorph, is a web-based, individualized program that incorporates the Ohio standards for 9th grade reading and writing. The course was developed under the sponsorship of the MVTPC and the CCTI project, with funding from a special visioning grant offered by the State of Ohio to improve Tech Prep implementation. The career guidance aspect of this course is also considered critical. Project leaders strongly believe that students who are considering entry into career-technical education need help to figure out what career makes sense for them. The course also helps students build technology literacy through their use of the web-based materials. A mixed-methods, quasi-experimental research project was conducted to assess learning outcomes (Lindsey, 2005). Participating students were found to have increased career awareness when compared with nonparticipants, and teachers reported that students enjoyed completing the unit.

The CCTI project schools are also very committed to real-world and project-based learning. Stebbins High School Engineering Technology teacher Jim Prater described the kinds of projects his students undertake that require an advanced understanding of science, math, and engineering concepts. Students in his classes are charged with building a *trebouche*, a type of catapult capable of hurling objects long distances, for which they use knowledge and skills in math, physics, drawing, documentation, and precision machining. Because of their skills in project development of this kind, the Stebbins team won gold medals at the state and national levels in the SkillsUSA Championships, a showcase for outstanding career and technical education students from around the country. A silver medal was won by the team from Fairmont.

Bridges With Four-Year Programs

Sinclair Community College's engineering programs were already well aligned with the University of Dayton (UD) and several other four-year institutions. In some cases, students in engineering have been dually admitted to SCC and UD. Under this plan, students begin their postsecondary education at SCC and then transfer to UD for their junior and senior years. Both institutions track their progress and provide support to make sure that the transition from one to the other is smooth and seamless.

With recent legislation governing the introduction of a Transfer Assurance Guide system, the college's engineering courses will transfer to any public college or university in Ohio. In a memo dated June 2005, the Chancellor of the Ohio Board of Regents informed all public college and university presidents that the system was fully in place (Chu, 2005). It states, "Beginning in the autumn of 2005, students will be able to complete courses and be guaranteed transfer and articulation to degree requirements should they elect to transfer in the winter of 2006. The guiding principle is that transfer students will be treated as equitably as native students, with the same degree and program requirements" (p. 1).

Student Support

In addition to the MEtaMorph career exploration class and the math pilot project, the CCTI project provides several other types of student support. SCC offers numerous opportunities for high school students to visit the college and learn about educational and career options. During the 2004-2005 academic year, two junior orientation events were jointly planned and conducted by high school and college faculty. The full-day sessions were structured around a game-show format "Who Wants to Be a Millionaire," with hands-on experiences and demonstrations related to engineering technology built in. In addition, regular visits are made to middle schools by engineering teachers and students to talk about engineering pathways.

In response to pervasive high numbers of students requiring remediation, Sinclair Community College recently decided to put extra effort into helping high school students prepare for college. The college created Academic Resource Centers (ARC) in several area high schools to work with juniors and seniors to improve their skills in math, reading, and writing. The centers use the PLATO system to assess and provide a plan for each student, and then allow each to progress at his or her own speed through assigned units of instruction. One of the ARCs is in Stebbins High School, one of the five CCTI schools. As it is well aligned with CCTI goals, the project has supported this effort and will follow its progress. The ARC leadership has commented on the significant gains students have made, noting, "Some gains, especially in reading and English, have been as great as five or six grade levels in as few as 15 to 30 clock hours of concentrated study" (Dunn & Smith, 2005, p. 2).

Special Features

This CCTI project has a distinctive problem-solving approach. When there are issues to be addressed at the project or school level, committees are formed comprised of people who are essential to the solution. This approach to problem solving uses the brainpower of varied, highly experienced people and also encourages their buy-in. Two examples of this approach include the initial committees that were created to implement the project and the school-based Contextual Integrated Academic Learning Teams (CIALTs).

This project also has multiple activities that are unusual and that are described elsewhere in this document, including

- The math pilot project;
- The MEtaMorph career-awareness course;
- Highly developed project-based learning;
- Dual admissions (SCC and UD);
- College courses embedded within high school courses;
- Widespread use of proficiency credit; and
- Team-developed strategies to promote integrated instruction.

■ When there are issues to be addressed at the project or school level, committees are formed comprised of people who are essential to the solution. This approach to problem solving uses the brainpower of varied, highly experienced people and also encourages their buy-in.

The Implementation Strategies

The CCTI project emphasizes several implementation strategies to attain the five CCTI objectives. These strategies are outlined in the table on page 178.

Sinclair Community College CCTI Program

CCTI Objective	Key Strategies
Decreased need for remediation at postsecondary level competencies.	• Update the engineering technologies cluster curriculum. • Pilot-test math instructional improvement methods with participation of high school and college faculty. • Develop a curriculum unit (MEtaMorph) that blends career exploration and reading and writing.
Increased enrollment and persistence in postsecondary education	• Provide on-campus recruitment and orientation activities for high school students. • Use the Academic Resource Centers to help high school students with college readiness.
Increased academic and skill achievement at the secondary and postsecondary levels	• Use Contextualized Integrated Academic Leadership Teams to improve curriculum and instruction. • Offer ACCUPLACER testing to 11th graders with results used to help students to advance academically.
Increased attainment of postsecondary degrees, certificates, or other recognized credentials	• Expand technical and academic dual, proficiency, and articulated credit options. • Build upon current financial aid options (*e.g.*, Tech Prep scholarships).
Increased entry into employment or further education	• Expand co-op and other work-based learning opportunities. • Build upon close relationships between educators and the business community, including teacher externships in local businesses.

Most Effective Strategies

Among the specific implementation strategies, the CCTI team has identified five of which it is particularly proud.

Integrate, integrate, integrate. Project Director Ron Kindell believes that the best way to sustain gains made through the CCTI project is to integrate new initiatives into the existing Tech Prep program. This builds on the firm foundation of the well-established program, while bringing in new resources and ideas that allow for the development of better practices.

Pilot testing lays the groundwork for replication of specific initiatives. As a result of the successful trial of the MEtaMorph course, the program will be offered to all 58 high schools in the MVTPC. An accompanying guide has been developed to aid with its implementation.

The CCTI pathways were developed with involvement from state education agency representatives who are represented on the project's partnership team. Partially as a result, the pathway format is now recommended for use by all Tech Prep consortia in the State of Ohio.

The project made use of committees, based at the college, that were organized around each of the CCTI objectives during project planning to make sure that each would be adequately addressed.

Joint secondary-postsecondary professional development has led to improved communication, skill development, and opportunities for problem solving around specific student needs.

Least Effective Strategies

The project leadership is still working on ways to offer dual-credit options to help students accelerate their progress toward degree completion.

Students tested with ACCUPLACER who are identified as needing extra help may have limited ways to obtain assistance if they are not in a school with an Academic Resource Center.

Plans for the Future

New pathways. Based on the CCTI career pathway approach, two new pathways, Exercise Science/Sports and Recreational Health Care and Criminal Science Technologies, are being developed that include coursework through the bachelor's degree level. This was done in collaboration with high school and business partners as well as representatives of four-year colleges and universities, including the University of Dayton, Wright State University, and Miami University. In addition, all of the existing Tech Prep pathways are being reformatted using the CCTI template. The goal is to complete this task by the end of 2006.

Tech Prep. Project Director Ron Kindell was recently asked to be part of a state task force, sponsored by the Ohio Board of Regents and the State Department of Education, that will focus on the redesign of Tech Prep in Ohio around pathways. In addition, there will be discussions of other aspects of the CCTI project that may serve as models for the state. Kindell believes that there is likely to be interest in the role of postsecondary education as defined under CCTI, noting that Tech Prep has tended to be more oriented to secondary education in the past. This may include discussions of ways to improve college-level career and technical education based around the five CCTI objectives.

State graduation test. The CCTI project will be paying attention to the influence of the new Ohio State graduation test, taken by students in the 10th grade. The Miami Valley area includes the highest ranking school in terms of pass rates (99 percent of students passed the test), as well as the lowest ranking school (less than 20 percent of students passed). The spotlight on the results of these and other NCLB-related tests will draw the attention of the region's educational leadership to the impact of any education initiative on test scores. CCTI project leadership will be discussing implications for the need to further integrate career and technical education and traditional academic subjects.

Lessons Learned

The project partners have identified several lessons they have learned that may be useful to others implementing similar programs.

Rather than create new projects, it often makes sense to build upon existing ones with proven effectiveness. In this project, the existing Tech Prep, Engineering curriculum, and Academic Resource Centers were the foundation upon which additional CCTI-sponsored activities were developed.

As mentioned, new initiatives should be tested at a limited number of sites while evidence of effectiveness is gathered. When data indicate that outcomes associated with the initiative are positive, widespread replication is likely.

Approaching decision-making groups, such as the MVTPC board, with concrete evidence of success is the best way to get their support for expansion of a project or activity.

Joint high school-college professional development sessions provide opportunities for the formation of closer relationships.

Approaches to the teaching of reading differ at the high school and college levels. It can be hard to get faculty members to understand each other's perspectives, and hard for families to understand why students who do well in high school English would not place into college-level English.

References

Bragg, D. (2003), *Case Study Report: St. Louis Community College, College and Career Transition Initiative*. Phoenix: League for Innovation in the Community College.

Chu, R. G. W. (2005). Implementation of HB95 and Transfer Assurance Guides (TAG) [memo]. Retrieved July 22, 2005, from the Ohio Board of Regents website. http://www.regents.state.oh.us/hei/transferassurance/memos/genmemos.htm#06022005

Dunn, H., & Smith, S. (2005). Getting High School Students Academically Ready for College at Sinclair Community College. Retrieved July 22, 2005, from the League for Innovation website. http://www.league.org/publication/abstracts/learning/lelabs200506.html

Lindsey, J. L. (2005). *Research Report for the Ninth Grade Career Exploration Guarantee Project*. Dayton, OH: Wright State University.

More information about Sinclair Community College and the CCTI Initiative can be found at http://www.league.org/league/projects/ccti/projects/summary.cfm?key=scc.

St. Louis Community College

Elisabeth Barnett and Debra D. Bragg

OCCUPATIONAL AREA:	Science, Technology, Engineering, and Mathematics
CAREER PATHWAY:	Mechanical Engineering Technology
CCTI PROJECT DIRECTORS:	Ashok Agrawal and Steve Long
	Michelene Moeller, CCTI Manager
PROJECT PARTNERS:	St. Louis Community College at Florissant Valley
	Metropolitan Technical Vocational Cooperative
	St. Louis Regional Academy of Engineering Technology
	9 school districts with 18 high schools
	Area businesses

The Project Partners

St. Louis Community College's CCTI project in Missouri has used the Project Lead the Way (PLTW) curriculum as the basis for the development of a 4+2+2 pathway from high school to the community college to four-year institutions. Project Lead the Way is structured so that high school students take a sequence of five courses in engineering, beginning in 9th grade, along with rigorous academic courses. These can serve as the foundation for a number of engineering specializations, including this project's CCTI pathway in Mechanical Engineering Technology. One partnering school has also adopted the PLTW middle school curriculum.

The project has grown very rapidly, with 520 students from 18 high schools participating during the 2004-2005 academic year, a number expected to more than double. The enthusiasm for the project among educators and business people at both the local and state levels has contributed to its rapid development. It is likely that the CCTI approach will take career-technical education to a new level in the region, increasing the use of career pathways and dual credit as strategies to help students with the transition to college and into careers in emerging industries.

Our participation in CCTI is helping us improve and enhance our relationships with the secondary schools and businesses in our area. The best thing about this is that the main benefactors are the students.

Henry D. Shannon, Chancellor, St. Louis Community College

St. Louis Community College (SLCC) is a multicampus urban college, one of 13 community colleges in the State of Missouri. It is the largest community college in the state, and one of the largest in the nation, with 130,000 students enrolled and an estimated $2.3 billion impact on the local economy. The college serves an area of about 700 square miles, with a population of about 2 million people. The district was founded in 1962 as the Junior College District of St. Louis-St. Louis County, but the name was changed to St. Louis Community College in 1976. The Florissant Valley campus is one of three SLCC campuses, and it has established a reputation for excellence in engineering and technology. The recently completed Advanced Technology Manufacturing Center, outfitted with state-of-the-art labs and equipment, houses a number of education and training programs, including the one in Mechanical Engineering Technology (Bragg, 2003).

Area school districts and high schools are becoming partners in the CCTI initiative in rapidly increasing numbers. Currently, nine school districts and 18 high schools are participating. Two districts have taken the leadership on this initiative locally – Hazelwood and Riverview Gardens – and both have received the official Project Lead the Way certification to offer the program. During the 2004-2005 school year, the Hazelwood district had 131 students enrolled in the pathway, while Riverview Gardens had 99 enrolled. A total of 520 students took PLTW courses throughout the region. Interestingly, the two area vocational centers are not participants.

The **St. Louis Regional Academy of Engineering Technology** (AET) is the umbrella organization under which the CCTI project is implemented. This partnership was developed with leadership from the St. Louis Metropolitan Vocational Cooperative, soon to be phased out as its funding expires, and the St. Louis Area Tech Prep Consortium, with a long history of developing articulation agreements between area high schools and the college. The academy partners include businesses, high schools, higher education institutions, and supporting agencies.

The project's **Industry Council** is comprised primarily of members of the St. Louis County Economic Development Council. Some of the more active participants include GKN, Engineered Support Systems, Millinckrodt/Tyco, Boeing, Essex Industries, and the Mart Corporation. According to the project leadership, St. Louis has been ranked among the top 10 cities for emerging high-tech industry in medical, pharmaceutical, chemical, and factory automation areas, but it faces shortages of skilled workers. The members of the Industry Council see the CCTI project as a way to bring new, highly qualified employees into their firms, and they have been proactive and committed partners.

The national **Project Lead the Way** organization (http://www.pltw.org/aindex.htm) has been an active partner with the initiative. Its curriculum model was first introduced into 12 New York schools in 1997, and participation has since grown to include over 1,000 schools around the U.S. Schools interested in offering the curriculum sign a contract with PLTW by which they commit to offer the full series of courses, have their teachers trained to teach each individual course, obtain needed equipment, and follow the program's requirements and standards. After two years of implementation, they are eligible to apply for certification.

History of the Partnership

In 2000, the St. Louis Metropolitan Vocational Cooperative led local school districts in a planning process that resulted in the development of several career academies intended to serve regional clusters of schools. These were designed to focus on three major career areas: (1) information technology, (2) engineering technology, and (3) life sciences. Research was done on the PLTW model as a curriculum option for the engineering technology academy, and an agreement was signed to begin offering courses in a limited number of schools in the fall of 2003, under the auspices of the St. Louis Regional Academy of Engineering Technology.

The PLTW approach received an added boost when the Missouri Department of Education officially approved it for use around the state and the state supervisor of Industrial Technology became a member of the AET advisory committee. State representatives were pleased that the PLTW curriculum was well aligned with the Missouri Show Me standards as well as with the standards of the National Council of Teachers of Mathematics and the National Council of Teachers of Science.

When SLCC obtained grant funding from CCTI, it was decided to build upon the PLTW high school curriculum and develop a Mechanical Engineering Technology Pathway through the postsecondary level. College faculty were asked to analyze the course content of the five PLTW courses to see whether they were aligned with existing college courses. Faculty undertook a curriculum study and determined that all five courses were aligned with current courses, although they were offered in conjunction with several different college programs. The decision was made to offer articulated credit through SLCC to students who passed the courses with a grade of B or better. An alternative credit-granting mechanism was also available through PLTW. The organization has an agreement with the Rochester Institute of Technology to award immediately transcripted college credits to students who pass the course exam and pay $200 per course.

■ Schools are eager to participate, because they see the value to their students. They are also given extensive assistance in starting up the program, with access to high-quality curriculum and support from the college to overcome logistical difficulties.

The program has grown rapidly since its inception in 2003. Schools are eager to participate, because they see the value to their students. They are also given extensive assistance in starting up the program, with access to high-quality curriculum and support from the college to overcome logistical difficulties. The two-week teacher training sessions are paid for under the grant. The state is encouraging participation by providing additional grant funding, and industry representatives are eager to help. Schools also like connectivity between the high school and college pathways.

The involvement of business and industry is particularly strong with this CCTI project. Business, especially high-tech industry, is growing rapidly in the St. Louis area, and there is considerable concern about the availability of skilled workers in the future. The Industry Council associated with the project is comprised of 18 companies. They have three major functions: (1) They serve in an advisory capacity to the program, especially in terms of the alignment of the curriculum with their workforce development needs; (2) They serve as mentors to individual teachers, providing support for classroom activities as well as opportunities for teacher internships; and (3) They have a marketing and advocacy role that includes help with overcoming obstacles to program development. They continually look for new ways to support the project and hope to increase their involvement with students and parents in the future.

The CCTI partners, in their statement of purpose, say that they intend to work together to create or enhance

- Articulation, dual-enrollment, and dual-credit opportunities;
- Diagnostic and college placement assessment for academy participants;
- Data collection for program improvement;
- Support for students and parents in planning for postsecondary transition;
- Extra help in high school to eliminate the need for remediation at the postsecondary level;
- Joint faculty development to improve students' performance and transitions;
- Opportunities for faculty to align and integrate curriculum;
- Joint counselor and advisor orientation to the academy; and
- Business involvement through internships, senior capstone projects, and employment opportunities.

The Model Career Pathway

The CCTI Career Pathway integrates the Project Lead the Way courses with rigorous academic courses at the high school level. Project Lead the Way recommends a four-year sequence of math courses that is included in the CCTI pathway. The course sequence also reflects a commitment to have students enter college without the need for remediation. At the college level, the courses included in the pathway are those required to complete an Associate of Applied Science degree in Mechanical Engineering Technology and progress to further education at a four-year college, if desired.

The development of this pathway represents a new, more highly-developed approach to career and technical education in the region. While Tech Prep has been well established, it has tended to involve many individual course-to-course articulations (estimated at 300+) rather than well-sequenced pathways. The two area vocational centers have been seen as terminal programs for those who did not intend to go to college. Project leadership believe that CCTI differs from traditional career education in its balanced emphasis on career-technical and academic education leading to postsecondary degree completion. CCTI is widely seen as the model for the future direction of career and technical education in the region and the state.

The pathway continues to depend on articulated rather than dual credit. Students passing the PLTW courses with an A or B are eligible to receive college credit if they complete an additional six credits at SLCC. This system makes the college credit earned nontransferable to other postsecondary institutions unless the student has also obtained credit from the Rochester Institute of Technology. However, discussions are currently under way to offer the courses for dual credit, a change that will require some extra work. The State of Missouri mandates that dual credit courses have the same syllabi, texts, and tests as college courses. Therefore, for the established PLTW courses to count for dual credit, the college has to develop parallel courses, a change from the usual way of creating new courses.

This CCTI project is one of very few in the nation to have an established middle school component. PLTW has created a course for middle school students called Gateway to Technology. The four-unit course is activity oriented and introduces students to the ways that science and technology are used to solve everyday problems. The principal of the Riverview Gardens Middle School learned about it and worked with the CCTI leadership to begin offering it in 2004. This has been very successful and has served to channel many new students into the high school PLTW courses. Another middle school in the district began offering this course in the 2005-2006 academic year.

Curriculum and Instruction

While the curriculum of this CCTI program is built around the PTLW courses, attention is also paid to articulation with and preparation for postsecondary education. Students are expected to take a rigorous series of courses in academic subjects that will prepare them for college without remediation. However, because students sign up to participate one course at a time, they may not be aware of the full sequence of recommended courses under the plan.

In most cases, the high schools offer the first three courses in the PLTW series, while the college offers the second two. The requirements for lab and equipment of the second two courses generally make it cost effective to send students to the college rather than to provide these courses at the high school. In addition, fewer faculty require training under this plan. However, one high school is planning to offer the entire sequence.

Instructors must attend a PLTW-sponsored two-week training session for each course they intend to teach. These are held in the summer at a range of locations around the country. The sessions are designed to prepare teachers to use the PLTW curriculum and materials, and are also billed as helping teachers to improve their overall teaching skills. Training is generally paid for with CCTI funds, and some school districts provide teachers with a stipend during the training as well. Most of the St. Louis-area high school teachers who have signed up to teach PLTW courses are specialized in the fields of math, science, business, or industrial technology.

Teachers throughout the region have been very pleased with the PLTW curriculum and instructional methods. They have indicated an appreciation of the blend of hands-on and book-based learning and say that students learn well and are more motivated and focused. The increased student motivation is

■ **PLTW has created a course for middle school students called Gateway to Technology. The four-unit course is activity oriented and introduces students to the ways that science and technology are used to solve everyday problems.**

attributed to the small group work, the hands-on and project-based learning, the freedom to choose projects leading to a greater sense of ownership, and the involvement in problem solving. Students say that they find the courses challenging but fun. The CCTI project manager has also noted that they seem to be able to articulately discuss advanced topics with greater ease.

As mentioned, the college-level courses in the pathway are those required for an AAS degree in Mechanical Technical Engineering. The facilities available through the new Advanced Technology Manufacturing Center allow a wider range of topics and skills to be covered in these classes. The building includes a machine shop, a CNC center, a plastics-processing and testing lab, a nondestructive testing lab, a hydraulics and pneumatics lab, a casting and welding lab, and a global positioning systems lab, among others.

An additional curriculum development project has been undertaken under the auspices of CCTI: a bridging math course being developed to help students enter college without the need for remediation in college. The instructor from the college and the instructor from the high school have been working together on the curriculum.

PLTW's certification process serves as a valuable quality-control measure. Certification is normally done after two years of program implementation and every five years thereafter. The process consists of a submission of relevant documents, followed by a site visit from a reviewer or review team.

Bridges With Four-Year Programs

The Manufacturing Engineering Technology pathway and other engineering technology programs are articulated with four-year programs at Southeast Missouri State University and the University of Missouri at Rolla. Two bachelor of science programs, Industrial Technology and Industrial Education, are offered at the SLCC Florissant Valley campus under the auspices of Southeast Missouri State University. A Master's Degree in Industrial Technology is also offered under a similar agreement.

In addition, the Rochester Institute of Technology awards immediately transcripted college credits, transferable to most postsecondary institutions, to students completing PLTW courses, passing a national exam, and paying $200 per course.

Student Support

Each school develops its own policy on student eligibility to enroll in pathway courses. Selectivity varies by school, but generally, the students' interest in the subject matter and career direction is considered to be the most important factor. Some schools believe that ability in math is necessary for success. Students enroll in PTLW courses as part of their regular course-selection process. In general, they sign up for individual classes rather than the entire pathway, but know that it is an option to continue in the sequence of courses offered.

The program has not been considered an elite program and is serving racially and ethnically diverse students, reflecting the demographic composition of the region. As with many similar programs, more boys than girls are enrolling. However, the project is making efforts to help girls to become interested in careers in engineering by hosting a career day for girls, providing a miniseries of presentations from women in the field, and having female students from area high schools make presentations to the middle schools about PLTW.

ACCUPLACER is used for college placement testing in conjunction with this project to identify high school students who need support in math, reading, and writing to be ready for college. However, project leaders note that the test is not well aligned with state tests related to NCLB requirements. In addition, it is not yet systematically used for students in the CCTI pathway. Discussions are under way on how to assist students identified as needing help in being college ready when graduating from high school. However, in several schools, online tutoring programs are used for remediation. The Novanet program is offered at Riverview. This self-paced software seems to work well and may also be used to complete extra math courses needed for graduation. ALEKS software is used for similar purposes in the Hazelwood school district.

...the project is making efforts to help girls to become interested in careers in engineering by hosting a career day for girls, providing a miniseries of presentations from women in the field, and having female students from area high schools make presentations to the middle schools about PLTW.

Special Features

This CCTI project has a number of distinctive aspects. The level of involvement by the business community is truly outstanding. Business representatives mentor individual teachers, offering them a wide array of supports. They are available to do classroom presentations and to speak with families during parent nights. They offer industry internships to teachers so that they can learn more about the contexts in which their students are being prepared to work. They offer guidance on curriculum content. In addition, they are very committed to the success of the overall project, encouraging the development of data systems that allow project leaders to track the progress of students and the project as a whole.

Riverview's middle school component, Gateway to Technology, is introducing students to the CCTI pathway at an early age. In addition to providing a foundation of knowledge about technology and engineering, it helps students to enter high school with the information needed to evaluate whether the PLTW course sequence would be an appropriate choice. High school PLTW teachers have noted that those who have participated in the middle school curriculum are better prepared for the high school material.

The CCTI project leadership has forged a partnership with state education officials that will permit them to have an influence well beyond the St. Louis area. A statewide PLTW leadership team has been formed to promote the curriculum more widely, and there is also a commitment to the creation of secondary and postsecondary pathways in engineering. There is an open flow of communication and desire to learn from one another that promises to improve the quality of career and technical education statewide.

The Implementation Strategies

The CCTI project emphasizes the following set of implementation strategies to attain the five CCTI objectives.

St. Louis CCTI Program

CCTI Objective	Key Strategies
Decreased need for remediation at postsecondary level	• Use of ACCUPLACER for student testing in 11th grade • Remediation using computer-based, self-paced learning programs • Creation of a bridge math course
Increased enrollment and persistence in postsecondary education	• A career pathway that promotes an easy transition from high school to college • Widespread marketing of the program, including to nontraditional students (gender, minority)
Increased academic and skill achievement at the secondary and postsecondary levels	• Training of teachers on integrated instructional strategies • Sessions with parents on monitoring student progress • Seeking out resources within the schools to help struggling students
Increased attainment of postsecondary degrees, certificates, or other recognized credentials	• Postsecondary certificate programs that build toward the AAS degree • College courses that parallel PLTW courses to enable the awarding of dual credit
Increased entry into employment or further education	• An increased number of participating schools and students • Development of mentoring relationships with industry partners

Most Effective Strategies

Among the specific implementation strategies, the CCTI project has identified four of which it is particularly proud.

***Each participating school district has a designated CCTI coordinator, usually a career-technical education teacher or administrator*.** The presence of this district-based person improves communication within and among school districts, as well as with the college, and contributes to quality implementation of the project.

***The role of the industry council is especially important*.** It provides the project with credibility, drive, and political momentum as well as concrete benefits such as mentoring of teachers. The group meets monthly and also convenes twice a year with teachers and business mentors to share best practices.

***A team of math faculty from the college and a partner high school are participating with others from other parts of the country to create a senior year catch-up course in math*.** This is expected to be widely used by schools concerned about the preparedness of their students for college-level math.

***The industry council has conducted a gap analysis in which curriculum content has been compared to skills needed by workers in local industry*.** This information is being used to adjust curriculum accordingly.

Least Effective Strategies

***Project leadership remain dissatisfied with the college placement testing process in the high schools, and with the degree to which results are used to reduce the need for remediation in college*.** On the other hand, their initial efforts to test students have raised awareness in the high schools of deficits in the math curriculum. Many students still take math only through the 10th grade, while remediation rates remain high.

***Student recruitment remains challenging*.** It can be hard to communicate to an 8th or 9th grader why taking courses in engineering would be not only interesting but also worth adding to an already full schedule. In addition, high school graduation requirements can make it difficult for students to fit in additional courses.

Plans for the Future

There are plans to administratively merge Tech Prep and the CCTI project within one office, to be coordinated by the current CCTI project manager. Both initiatives are seen as having common goals. This is part of a larger strategy to build on Tech Prep's historic success with creating articulation agreements and CCTI's use of sequenced secondary and postsecondary pathways. With the uncertainty of future funding streams for both projects, this is expected to reduce costs and provide greater likelihood of sustainability.

There are plans to work toward the expansion of the middle school program, introducing the Gateway to Technology course in additional schools. The course seems to be an effective way to introduce students to the PLTW curriculum and the CCTI pathway in Mechanical Engineering Technology.

The industry council continues to seek ways to expand its involvement with the program. It plans to add job-shadowing opportunities for students and possibly begin mentoring individual students.

Lessons Learned

The project partners have identified several lessons they have learned that may be useful to others implementing similar programs.

It is important to be realistic about the scale and pacing of the project. While having so many schools and students wanting to participate is exciting, keeping up with the rate of growth while maintaining the quality that is desired has been difficult.

The public relations aspects of the project are important. Thought should be given to how best to reach parents to help them understand this educational pathway and its benefits. Prevailing views of career-technical education as leading to dead-end careers need to be vigorously countered.

Students respond well to the instructional methods used in PLTW. The use of such methods as project-based and hands-on learning helps students feel engaged. More engaged students typically learn better and are more likely to remain in school.

Visiting existing PLTW programs before starting one can be very helpful to understand the benefits and challenges associated with them.

Students seem to benefit from taking classes on the college campus and interacting with the older students. They gain confidence in their abilities and also may behave in a more mature manner.

More information about St. Louis Community College and the CCTI Initiative can be found at http://www.league.org/league/projects/ccti/projects/summary.cfm?key=slcc.

Health Science

- Ivy Tech Community College of Indiana (IN)
- Miami Dade College (FL)
- Maricopa Community Colleges (AZ)

Ivy Tech Community College of Indiana

Elisabeth Barnett

OCCUPATIONAL AREA:	Health Sciences
CAREER PATHWAY:	Central Service Technician/Surgical Technology
PROJECT DIRECTOR:	Jennifer Steinwedel
PROJECT PARTNERS:	Ivy Tech Community College of Indiana
	C4 Columbus Area Career Connection
	Columbus East High School and eight feeder schools
	Columbus Regional Hospital

■ **A key benefit of participation in CCTI has been the improved collaboration between the administration, staff and faculty, and our secondary partners. A prime example has been the development and implementation of Career Pathways in all nine career clusters within Columbus Area Career Connection, our regional CTE provider. We have already seen the project expand and enhance the students' attainment of their educational and career goals.**

Jennifer Steinwedel, CCTI Project Coordinator, Ivy Tech Community College of Indiana, Columbus

The Project Partners

The CCTI partnership at Ivy Tech Community College of Indiana created a new pathway that prepares high school students as central service technicians (CST). Graduates have the option of seamlessly progressing into the Surgical Technology program at the college. Discussions with local health care providers led to an awareness among educators of a strong need for people trained in CST, which involves sterilizing, preparing, and packaging all materials and instruments used throughout a hospital. In order to create this pathway, new courses were developed at Columbus East High School, where secondary-level health occupations education is offered for the region, and new internship opportunities were made available by Columbus Regional Hospital.

Building on the relationships formed in establishing the CST/Surgical Tech pathway, a new pathway in nursing was developed in 2004 that allows high school nursing students to progress directly into the Licensed Practical Nurse or Associate of Nursing programs at Ivy Tech. These programs, in turn, are articulated with four-year institutions offering bachelor's and master's degree options in nursing. Most of the coursework for this pathway was already established; the main task involved was the analysis of course content to identify gaps or overlaps in the curriculum as well as potential opportunities for dual credit.

This CCTI project has also focused on professional development of faculty. Three workshops have been offered in collaboration with the Center for Occupational Research and Development (CORD). In addition, a group of adjunct faculty from C4's Health Careers was trained to serve in an advisory capacity to new students. Finally, project leadership has produced two CDs, one with resources pertinent to the CST/Surgical Tech pathway, the other with information and resources needed by new faculty at Ivy Tech.

Ivy Tech Community College of Indiana was created by the Indiana General Assembly in 1963 as Indiana Vocational Technical College, and was given its current name in 2005 to reflect a broadening of its mission. With 23 campuses statewide, it is Indiana's second largest public education system. The college is an open-access, two-year postsecondary institution offering courses, degree programs, certification training and testing, and continuing education. During the 2002-2003 year, 96,438 students across the state were enrolled in a variety of degree and certification programs. Statewide enrollment percentages in the five major degree divisions were as follows:

Technology	23%
Business	22%
Health Sciences	10%
Public Services	8%
Visual Technologies	2%

Through legislative action, the college has broadened its focus as it has become the community college of the State of Indiana, while maintaining its traditional role in preparing students to directly enter the workforce.

In Columbus, Ivy Tech classes were first offered in 1969 in City Hall. The Columbus campus opened at its current location in 1983, and by 2003 had 2,100 students. The majority of students (37 percent) are enrolled in technical certificate programs, followed by 31 percent in Associate of Applied Science programs. Ivy Tech also offers customized training opportunities and continuing education in response to the specific needs of local businesses.

The **Columbus Area Career Connection**, also called C^4, was established in 1972 under the name Columbus Area Vocational Program. It currently provides career and technical education programs for 10 high schools in four counties in south central Indiana, bringing together community and educational resources to help students prepare for employment and lifelong learning. All programs are delivered from three sites: Columbus East High School, Columbus North High School, and McDowell Adult Education Center, with students bused in from the other schools. Programs are organized around nine career clusters.

Columbus East High School, established in 1971, is a public, comprehensive four-year high school that enrolled 1,372 students in Grades 9 through 12 during the 2003-2004 school year. With a history of willingness to engage in innovative practices, it has recently received grant funding to develop small learning communities. All C^4 Health Careers courses are taught at Columbus East., serving students from eight high schools who spend nearly half of their school day studying one of four health careers: nursing, central service technician (CST), dental assisting, and vet tech. Work-based learning opportunities are integrated into each of these strands.

Columbus Regional Hospital evolved from the Bartholomew County Hospital, first established in 1917. In 1983, it was among the first of 150 hospitals in the country to be classified by the federal Medicare program as a Regional Referral Center. It is also the first hospital in Indiana to receive accreditation through the Magnet Recognition Program, awarded to health care organizations that demonstrate sustained excellence in nursing care. The Licensed Practical Nursing program was originally a part of the Bartholomew County Hospital. Shortly after Ivy Tech opened its health occupations program in 1973, the program moved to the college, where it currently resides.

A diverse group of community leaders associated with Columbus' Community Education Coalition, led in this effort by Karen Nissen of the Columbus Center for Teaching and Learning, developed the grant proposal for CCTI. Columbus' Community Education Coalition, founded by business leaders in 1997, has devoted considerable energy to unifying the education community around providing comprehensive and high-quality learning opportunities with a particular concern with workforce development. The CCTI project was seen as well-aligned with the goal to develop a seamless, lifelong education system.

For the CCTI proposal, the decision was made to focus on health occupations as an area with a high need for trained workers; this was also an Ivy Tech Community College priority for growth. A new pathway should be created for central service technicians, who would be prepared primarily at the high school level and would then be able to transfer into the Surgical Technology Program at Ivy Tech.

As the partners went about creating the Central Service Technician program, lessons learned in the development of the high school Dental Assisting program were of great value. This program, established in 2000, is the only high school program in the country accredited by the American Dental Association, and it has been widely recognized for its quality. Students may earn up to 33 dual-credit hours for Ivy Tech while in high school, and complete the program ready to take the Dental Assistant National Board certification test. Students may also complete two general education courses at Ivy Tech, whereupon they will have fulfilled the requirements for the Dental Assistant Technical Certificate.

The first five students enrolled in the CRCST program, located at Columbus East High School, in the fall of 2003. Another 11 enrolled in the fall of 2004. To build upon this success and that of the existing strong nursing programs, another pathway was developed that would allow high school students in nursing to enter the Licensed Practical Nursing (LPN) program or the Associate of Science in Nursing (ASN) program at Ivy Tech. In the 2004-2005 school year, 101 high school students were enrolled in the first- and second-year nursing programs offered through C^4.

The Model Career Pathway

There are two official career pathways associated with the Ivy Tech CCTI project: one that links the Central Service Technician program at the high school with the Surgical Technology program at Ivy Tech, and another that formalizes and improves that pathway between the high school and college in nursing. Both pathways were created by a group comprised of CCTI Project Director Jennifer Steinwedel, the C[4] Team Leader Andrea Quick, the college's academic dean, the college department chairs, and the high school Health Careers faculty.

Regarding the CST/Surgical Technology pathway, the secondary curriculum was developed by four health careers instructors, based on an online curriculum created by the International Association of Healthcare Central Service Materiel Management (IAHCSMM), the accrediting body for this profession. All four teachers have become certified by IAHCSMM as instructors, and two attended IAHCSMM's annual conference in the fall of 2004. To make this program more widely available in the community, including to adult students, Ivy Tech Community College has recently obtained state approval to offer a technical certificate in this area. Interested students will receive the training required to become a certified CST and take two general education courses, psychology and English, in order to qualify for Ivy Tech's technical certificate. High school students enrolled in the Health Careers CST program will receive 29 dual-credit hours from Ivy Tech and, upon graduation, be eligible to complete the two general education courses needed to receive a technical certificate. Students will also be eligible to sit for IAHCSMM's certification exam to become a Certified Registered Central Service Technician.

To prepare to be CSTs, students enroll in the program for a minimum of one year. They spend two to three hours per day in two courses. In addition, in order to become certified, they must log 400 clinical hours, an unusually high number originally based on the assumption that most applicants would already be full-time workers in hospital central processing or supply units. These students take classes with other health careers students for the first eight weeks, after which they separate out into their own group.

■ High school students enrolled in the Health Careers CST program will receive 29 dual-credit hours from Ivy Tech and, upon graduation, be eligible to complete the two general education courses needed to receive a technical certificate.

In the new pathway for nursing, students from C[4]'s Health Careers programs in Certified Nursing Assistant (CNA) or general nursing may continue into nursing programs at Ivy Tech. At the college level, they may choose between the Licensed Practical Nurse (LPN) and Associate of Science in Nursing (ASN) programs. The LPN is a one-year program and admission into it is less competitive than for the two-year ASN program. However, LPN students are eligible to progress into the ASN program upon completion of the LPN certification.

To create this pathway, few changes in curriculum were required. However, an examination of existing courses found three in which dual credit could be offered. A course titled Introduction to Health Careers is available to both nursing and CST students at the high school level. Medical Terminology may be taken by any of the health careers students. Finally, a Medical Law and Ethics course is available to advanced high school nursing students for dual credit. Three college credits are awarded for each of these courses if successfully completed with a grade of B or better. As with many dual-credit agreements around the country, acceptance of these credits is only guaranteed at the institution offering them. It is still too early to know how widely they will be accepted for transfer at other institutions.

Curriculum and Instruction

In addition to the career-oriented coursework, the schools connected with C^4 are committed to providing a strong academic foundation. Students take their academic courses at their home high schools, and academic standards are also woven into the career technical classes. The CCTI pathway calls for four years of high school English, math, science, and social studies, and recommends four years of a foreign language in addition to the health careers courses. This courseload will allow students to earn an academic or technical honors diploma.

To complement the courses offered, work-based learning experiences are available – and required – at both the high school (via C^4) and college levels. Assignments are generally made based on the student's interests and the nearness of the hospital or other work site to the student's home school. In health occupations, second-semester juniors and seniors are typically at their worksites four days a week. These placements are generally not paid, but they often lead to jobs or scholarships. New training sites were recently added for the CST students at the South Central Surgery Center in nearby Franklin and at Major Hospital in Shelbyville.

Professional development has been a focus of this project in order to improve instructional practices related to the pathways. A series of three workshops was conducted by Sandi Harwell of the Center for Occupational Research and Development (CORD) focusing on

- CCTI and the creation of career pathways,
- Contextual teaching and learning, and
- The use and design of electronic portfolios.

■ To complement the courses offered, work-based learning experiences are available – and required – at both the high school (via C^4) and college levels.

The workshops were attended by both high school and college faculty and administrators. While specifically pertinent to CCTI, the topics were also linked with the changes that Ivy Tech is making to become the community college system for Indiana. CCTI project leadership was pleased with the attendance, and also with the informal follow-up meetings among high school and college faculty to talk about related ideas.

Bridges With Four-Year Programs

The small city of Columbus, with a population of about 39,000, is especially endowed with postsecondary institutions. In addition to Ivy Tech Community College, there are also campuses of Indiana University-Purdue University Columbus (IUPUC) and Purdue School of Technology (PST). All three have traditionally offered primarily two-year educational programs oriented to workforce development. However, there has recently been a movement toward greater division of labor, with Ivy Tech concentrating on two-year degrees while the other two institutions focus on bachelor's and master's degree programs. There has also been improvement in the articulation among their programs. While traditionally there was little assurance that credits earned at one institution would transfer to another, great progress has been made in developing agreements to permit this, including in health fields. Work has been done to extend the nursing pathway to IUPUC, where students can earn a BSN, and to IUPU-Indianapolis, where both the BSN and MSN degrees are available.

Alignment has also been improved by the recent opening of the Columbus Learning Center, a state-of-the-art education facility managed by an independent board of directors and shared by the three postsecondary institutions along with other locally-based education programs. The CCTI offices are now housed in this building's administrative offices, where CCTI staff are able to work more closely with the staff of all three colleges. As a result, the CCTI staff have begun to take leadership roles in the negotiation of secondary dual-credit and articulation agreements for Ivy Tech across a range of disciplines.

Student Support

To help students plan their coursework through high school and beyond, Educational Development Plans are done at the high school level. Ninth graders participate in a semester-long career orientation course, during which they work on study skills and also complete their plan. In addition, students produce foundational pieces for their portfolios. While this system predates CCTI, it fits well with its goals.

The CCTI project introduced the concept of early college placement testing for high school juniors and seniors. CCTI staff has administered paper-and-pencil ASSET college placement tests to students enrolled in C^4's health careers courses since the project began. The tests are taken during regular class time. Results are provided to both teachers and students after the tests have been scored. Students who need extra help are encouraged to use the SkillsTutor program, a self-paced, web-based tutorial program that the college purchased after extensive research on available options.

While significant numbers of college students are using SkillsTutor, it is much less frequently used by high school students. It is not required, and the benefits may seem remote. However, the college is changing its policy to require high school students to meet course prerequisites in order to receive dual credit. For Medical Terminology and Medical Law and Ethics courses, such prerequisites include English. As a result, there may be more high school students seeking tutoring assistance than in the past.

A grant recently awarded by Indiana's South Central/Southeastern Area Health Education Center (AHEC) has been used to improve academic advising in health occupations. These funds were used to train adjunct faculty to be advisors for new and undecided students, as well as for students not accepted into nursing programs who needed information on alternative careers in health fields. A total of 16 faculty members, including five C^4 faculty who are also adjunct faculty at Ivy Tech, were trained. This group was available to provide academic advising during student registration. An added benefit of this arrangement has been the exposure of the high school faculty to Ivy Tech's health science programs, as well as their increased insight into the amount of remediation needed by incoming students, a message that they are expected to bring back to the high school.

Special Features

The CCTI staff created a CD for high school and college administrators, faculty, and students involved with the project to provide them with information and resources related to the CST/Surgical Tech pathway. The college administration was impressed with the usefulness of this product and has asked the CCTI staff, in conjunction with others on campus, to develop an interactive CD for all college faculty, to be distributed at faculty orientation. This would replace the typical three-inch binder that has been distributed in the past, and would include information about the college and faculty responsibilities as well as useful links to a variety of web-based resources.

■ Rather than being considered an add-on project, it is leading the way in developing new initiatives in relationships with the K-12 educational community, expanding business linkages, and strengthening ties with other postsecondary institutions.

This experience exemplifies the way this CCTI project is becoming increasingly integrated into the overall college environment. Rather than being considered an add-on project, it is leading the way in developing new initiatives in relationships with the K-12 educational community, expanding business linkages, and strengthening ties with other postsecondary institutions. This may be explained in part because the initiative grew out of a local coalition of organizations; it is also thanks to the leadership abilities of the CCTI Project Director.

Teachers involved with each of the C^4 clusters set annual goals designed to improve their programs as well as student outcomes. This year, along with other goals specific to each career area, all have set a goal to create high-school-to-college pathways for specific careers within each cluster that include more opportunities for students to earn dual credit. Their decision to do this was inspired by their experience with the CCTI project, although it was also influenced by issues raised by the Perkins reauthorization and their involvement with a state Career Majors grant (Tech Prep funding). C^4 Team Leader Andrea Quick states that CCTI pathways were a model for the region, and have helped the high school programs think more in terms of preparation for specific careers.

The C^4 leadership is also interested in creating new pathways specifically linking high school programs with Ivy Tech, based on the ones created in health fields. The next ones to be undertaken are likely to be in engineering, computer graphics, or criminal justice.

The Implementation Strategies

The project uses a set of implementation strategies to attain the five CCTI objectives. These strategies are outlined in the table below.

CCTI Objective	Key Strategies
Decreased need for remediation at postsecondary level	• Administration of college placement testing with remediation available using SkillsTutor • High school curriculum that includes four years of math and English
Increased enrollment and persistence in postsecondary education	• Guidance provided by high school teachers and guidance counselors as well as by college counselors and faculty advisors • Interactive CD for students and faculty on the CST/Surgical Tech pathway
Increased academic and skill achievement at the secondary and postsecondary levels	• Professional development opportunities for high school and college faculty on instructional strategies • Alignment of curriculum with standards for entry into two-year and four-year postsecondary programs
Increased attainment of postsecondary degrees, certificates, or other recognized credentials	• Multiple opportunities to obtain credentials in health care fields, while pursuing further education and employment • Increase in the number of courses for which dual credit is offered
Increased entry into employment or further education	• Extensive work-based learning opportunities in area hospitals, clinics, doctors' offices, etc. • Increased information about career and educational options during high school

Most Effective Strategies

Among specific implementation strategies, the CCTI project has identified five of which it is particularly proud.

Team approach. This project has drawn on the skills and talents of many different people in the education community, rather than relying only on the Project Director. For example, the Ivy Tech Director of Career and Employment Services conducts career interest surveys, the Director of the Center for Teaching and Learning helps to coordinate professional development, Columbus Regional Hospital's Manager of Central Processing arranges student placements, and the recently retired Director of Central Processing serves as an adjunct at the high school, providing students with instruction in Central Service.

Educational Development Plans. The use of Educational Development Plans helps students to think about the ways that their high school coursework should be structured to help them attain their goals for further education and careers.

Connections to business and industry professionals. Students have the opportunity for in-depth work-based learning experiences in which they interact with professionals in their fields of interest. For example, students in CST are matched with, closely monitored, and evaluated by Certified Registered Central Service Technicians, who in turn benefit by exposure to young, enthusiastic students.

Professional development. Joint high school-college professional development opportunities have been offered and well attended. These experiences have led to increased knowledge of the topics discussed, the development of shared language related to some of the topics, and the formation of professional relationships that span the secondary-postsecondary boundary.

College readiness and remediation. Students are tested for college readiness in the 11th and 12th grades. Those needing extra help are encouraged to use the SkillsTutor computer-based program available at the college. The results of these tests are also raising awareness among high school faculty and administrators about areas in which the high school curriculum may not be well aligned with college expectations.

Least Effective Strategies

Electronic portfolios. The CCTI project has been interested in broadening the use of electronic portfolios by high school students. However, it was decided that the system seems overly complex and costly for use in local high schools at this time.

Skills Tutor. The use of SkillsTutor by high school students needing extra help in English, reading, or math has been limited. Since it is not required, it seldom seems like a priority to busy students.

Lessons Learned

The project partners have identified several lessons they have learned that may be useful to others implementing similar programs.

Use of teams. It is important to institute a core team and advisory team that offer variety as well as depth of knowledge. This strategy allows the project to be better informed about and connected with local, state, and national issues and events. It also broadens the base of people who are aware of the CCTI project. The project's core team meets monthly, while the advisory team meets quarterly. The Project Director also works with individuals and small groups in addressing particular needs.

Project Director role. It is very helpful to have a full-time CCTI Project Director who is viewed as institution neutral. Although she is associated with one institution, it is clear to all concerned that her role is to develop a project that crosses institutional boundaries, making her a trusted collaborator.

Leverage related resources. The CCTI project staff has become involved with projects and committees that are not specifically part of CCTI, but are relevant to it. These are carefully selected to meet CCTI goals, including broadening the base of support for them.

Professional development. Attendance at professional development workshops is greatly influenced by college and high school leadership. People are much more likely to attend if it is an expectation that they do so, or if this behavior is rewarded.

Communication. Planning for effective, multilevel communication is extremely important. Project staff regularly reports on the project at varied meetings and makes presentations at important conferences. In addition, attractive materials have been developed that include significant information about CCTI and project a professional image.

More information about Ivy Tech State College and the CCTI Initiative can be found at http://www.league.org/league/projects/ccti/projects/summary.cfm?key=itsc.

■ The CCTI project staff has become involved with projects and committees that are not specifically part of CCTI, but are relevant to it. These are carefully selected to meet CCTI goals, including broadening the base of support for them.

Miami Dade College

Elisabeth Barnett

OCCUPATIONAL AREA: Health Occupations
CAREER PATHWAY: Nursing and Allied Health
PROJECT DIRECTOR: Pablo Martin
PROJECT PARTNERS: Miami Dade College-Medical Center Campus
Miami Dade College-Kendall Campus
Felix Varela High School
Baptist Hospital of Miami

The Project Partners

The CCTI partnership at Miami Dade College has developed a program that enables high school students to begin working toward college prerequisites for degrees in nursing and allied health and then move seamlessly into the subsequent course of study at the college. This program design is intended to help nursing and allied health programs at the college to enroll students directly out of high school, a plan that will keep them involved with health-related coursework and more likely to emerge with credentials in a timely manner. This is seen by the college as especially important to addressing the shortage of nurses in the Miami area, as well as to bringing a new generation of young, well-qualified people into the health care professions.

■ CCTI promises to help clear the pathway to possibility for students across the U.S. by showcasing best practices and catalyzing cutting-edge reforms that smooth, facilitate, and encourage transitions through education and into high-demand careers.

Gerardo de los Santos, President and CEO, League for Innovation in the Community College

The project involves students from the Health Science Technology Academy of Felix Varela High School, located in southern Dade County in Florida. Selected students join a learning community in which they engage in an intensive summer internship, take a series of eight to nine dual-credit courses, and participate in other activities to help them move toward careers in nursing or allied health. The students benefit from their membership in a high school organized around career academies in which rigorous academic courses are blended with career-technical courses and work-based learning experiences. In addition, they begin to form a connection with the Medical Center Campus at Miami Dade College, and are taught by college faculty from Kendall Campus who are experienced with teaching dual-credit courses to high school students.

Miami Dade College (MDC) first opened in September 1960 as a comprehensive community college serving Dade County, the poorest metropolitan county in the country. Since then, it has grown into a multicampus institution that awards more associate degrees than any other in the nation and also graduates the largest numbers of minority students. The college changed its name from

Miami-Dade Community College to Miami Dade College in August 2003, reflecting the addition of baccalaureate degree programs. **Chart A** shows the number of faculty and students connected with the college.

Chart A

MDC STUDENTS AND FACULTY (2000-2001)	
Total credit students, all campuses	71,616
Total noncredit students, all campuses	70,759
Total students served	145,097
Full-time faculty	686
Part-time faculty	2,502

The CCTI project was initiated by representatives of the Medical Center Campus, home of all nursing and allied health programs of the college, in cooperation with the faculty and student-support staff of **Kendall Campus**. The Nursing program is one of the largest in the country, with 500 graduates in 2004. **Chart B** shows the degree options offered by the **Medical Center Campus**.

Chart B

Programs Offered at Medical Center Campus	
Nursing	• Nursing - Associate Degree and other options • Midwifery - Associate of Science • Practical Nursing and Medical Assisting - Certificate programs
Allied Health	Associate of Science • Dental Hygiene • Physical Therapy Assistant • Diagnostic Medical Sonography • Physician Assistant • Emergency Medical Services • Radiation • Therapy Technology • Health Information Management • Radiography • Histotechnology • Respiratory Care Therapist • Medical Laboratory Technology • Veterinary Technology • Opticianry

Felix Varela High School is located in the southern part of Dade County. Its staff and students are proud of the fact that this was the first high school in the county founded in the 21st century. A total of 4,687 students were enrolled during the 2002-2003 year, making it the largest school in Dade County. The student body is very diverse, with about 80 percent speaking English as a second language. The school uses an academy structure, with all students selecting from among six academies, each of which has a number of pathways that may be followed leading to careers in new and emerging professions. According to the school's materials, the Health Sciences Technology pathway is "designed to prepare persons with the competencies required to assist qualified health professionals in providing diagnostic, therapeutic, preventative, restorative, and rehabilitative services to patients in health care facilities, in homes, and in the community."

Baptist Health South Florida is the largest nonprofit health care provider in the region. **Baptist Hospital of Miami** is one of a number of affiliated hospitals. Established in 1960, the hospital offers a full range of medical and technological services and has 551 beds. More than 30,000 people are hospitalized there annually, and about 86,000 receive care in the emergency center facilities. The hospital is actively seeking ways to address the shortage of health care personnel, especially nurses, through the provision of scholarships to its employees and other qualified candidates, and through initiatives such as CCTI. The hospital's active volunteer program helps with recruitment as well, and many of its volunteers are teenagers. Specific roles have been developed for teen volunteers, with a particular focus on familiarizing them with health career opportunities.

History of the Partnership

Representatives of the Medical Center Campus wrote the CCTI grant proposal in the spring of 2003 because of an interest in targeting high school students wishing to enter health careers to assist them in making a smooth and accelerated transition into nursing and allied health programs at the college. The plan was designed to allow students to complete their course prerequisites so they could enter nursing and allied health programs directly out of high school, avoiding past problems with students who became discouraged or diverted while completing the challenging prerequisite courses. This would occur before they even began attending classes at the Medical Center Campus, where extra support could be provided, and where they would begin to build relationships with faculty and other students involved in health care professions. The intent was to build on Florida's statewide initiative promoting college-level learning in high school that makes dual-credit course options widely available.

■ The intent was to build on Florida's statewide initiative promoting college-level learning in high school that makes dual-credit course options widely available.

A partnership committee was formed to develop this project that included representatives of the MDC, the school district, and several hospitals. This group thought carefully about how to structure the program, deciding early in the process that only highly academically qualified and motivated students would be able to successfully complete the challenging college-level courses while in high school. They formulated a career pathway, including courses and complementary learning activities, and they developed criteria for admission to the program. Program management was delegated to Miriam Reyes, an experienced nurse educator. Upon her departure in the fall of 2004, her assistant, Pablo Martin, became the project director.

Initial student recruitment efforts in the summer of 2003 taught the project leadership that it would be challenging to find the right students for the project. Of the students who initially expressed interest in enrolling, only two scored high enough on the college placement tests that would allow them to take dual-credit courses. A decision was made to begin identifying appropriate candidates early and to provide them with extra academic support, so that they would be able to qualify for participation.

The first cohort of 15 students entered the program in the fall of 2004. They were all members of the Health Sciences Technology Academy at Felix Varela High School, a highly qualified group of students who had met the criteria for entry into the program. These students have made considerable progress toward completing the prerequisites for entering a nursing or allied health program. Three students graduated at the end of the 2004-2005 academic year; two of them are attending MDC, and the other is enrolled in a nursing program at another college. A new cohort of students was recruited to participate in the program that began with a hospital internship during the summer of 2005.

The Model Career Pathway

The nursing career pathway is most fully developed at this site, while the one in allied health is being completed. The nursing pathway includes the courses that are needed to complete the requirements for the Health Sciences and Technology Academy at FVHS, as well as those required for the Associate of Science in Nursing degree at MDC. A student in this pathway would be able to complete the program in a total of six years, beginning in 9th grade.

An important feature of this plan is that it allows students to complete their studies at two locations rather than three, thus diminishing the chances that they become disconnected from the nursing program. College-level courses required as prerequisites for the nursing program are not available at the MDC Medical Center Campus. Thus, students who finish high school intending to enter nursing must begin their coursework at Kendall or another MDC Campus. It is easy to see how students who begin their studies for a health profession at another campus may end up in fields that are available in the location where they have already gained a sense of comfort.

The nursing pathway includes rigorous academic courses at the high school level, along with courses in career and technical education. The curriculum includes four years of English, three to four of math, and four of science, and encourages three years of a foreign language. This course of study meets or surpasses Florida's high school graduation standards and the minimum requirements for entrance into Florida State Universities, as well as those for Florida's Academic Merit Scholars Certificate. In addition, the college-level courses that must be completed before entering the nursing program may be considered rigorous academic courses. They include English Composition, Speech Communication, Intermediate Algebra, Chemistry, two levels of Anatomy and Physiology, Human Growth and Development, Critical Thinking and Ethics, and Psychology of Personal Effectiveness.

The pathway indicates the preferred timing for the administration of several important tests. The Postsecondary Articulation Software Services (PASS) diagnostic test, developed by MDC, helps students and teachers assess progress toward readiness for college coursework. It also serves as a practice test for the Computerized Placement Test (CPT), the college placement instrument used at MDC to determine readiness for credit-bearing classes. In addition, students may take the ACT or SAT exams.

Successful participation in this career pathway is highly dependent upon students' ability to enroll in and complete dual-credit courses. In Florida, dual-credit opportunities are well established, with no tuition or fees charged, and articulation agreements facilitate transfer of courses to a range of postsecondary institutions. Many courses eligible for dual credit are mandated by the state, and additional ones are available through agreements between MDC and the Miami-Dade County Public Schools. However, eligibility is restricted to those who pass the CPT and have an unweighted grade point average of 3.0, requirements that have posed a challenge for the CCTI project.

Curriculum and Instruction

Fox Valley High School is structured into six academies from which students choose, all intended to prepare them for both postsecondary education and the workforce. The academy themes were selected based on a district study that looked at where job opportunities were likely to be in the future, among other considerations. During the 2004-2005 year, all 10th through 12th grade students were enrolled in one of the following academies:

- Aerospace, Engineering, and Naval Science Technology;
- Business and Information Technology;
- Health Science Technology;
- Visual and Performing Arts;
- Design and Veterinary Technology; or
- Liberal Arts.

During the freshman year, all students enter the Freshman Academy, in which they take core academic courses, spend time improving their study skills, and are introduced to the range of career areas. In consultation with their parents, they select one academy in which to participate during 10th through 12th grades.

Students in the Health Science Technology Academy are eligible to participate in the CCTI project, and eligibility was broadened to include students from other academies during the 2005-2006 year. During the 2004-2005 academic year, 25 students enrolled in the program. Their experience began with a six-week summer internship at Baptist Hospital of Miami. The students spent at least 10 hours per week at the hospital and were assigned to different staff members, whom they shadowed and assisted. The students worked in a range of departments, including Labor and Delivery, Maternity, Pediatrics, Pharmacy, Social Work, and Patient Transportation, among others. Evaluations done at the end of the experience indicated that both students and hospital staff were very pleased and felt they had benefited. Of the 25 students who participated, 19 continued on as volunteers after the end of the internship.

Of those who participated in internships over the summer, 15 took college courses taught by college faculty at the Kendall Campus during the fall 2004 semester and at the high school during the spring 2005 semester. Original plans called for the students to attend all classes at Kendall Campus, but reductions in the CCTI grant made it impossible to provide daily transportation beyond the first semester. In addition, the courses had originally been envisioned as paired, with the instructors teaching collaboratively. Again, this proved to be unworkable, and the classes were offered independently. School leaders report that these classes were a highly valued addition to the curriculum.

Other enrichment experiences were also made available. Students had the opportunity to participate in related learning activities, such as blood drives and blood-pressure and vision screenings. They took field trips to the Medical Center Campus and other health facilities. They have also become involved in recruiting the next cohort of students by making presentations about the CCTI program in area middle schools.

Students had the opportunity to participate in related learning activities, such as blood drives and blood-pressure and vision screenings. They took field trips to the Medical Center Campus and other health facilities.

Bridges With Four-Year Programs

All of the FVHS academy programs have articulation agreements with either MDC or the American International University, with students typically earning an average of 8 to 15 transferable college credits during high school.

MDC Medical Center Campus has had many of its graduates continue on to earn bachelor's degrees at universities in Florida and elsewhere. They are helped in this regard by the Florida Statewide Articulation Agreement, which includes all public colleges and universities, and transfer of courses is also facilitated by the state's common course-numbering system.

Student Support

Student guidance and support is needed in this program for both potential enrollees and participants. Before entering, students need information about the program and its eligibility requirements. They also require help in determining whether it is a good fit for them personally, and in preparing an application for admission. Assistance may also be needed in preparing for and taking the PASS and CPT tests at the Kendall Campus. Once enrolled, some students need help to perform well in the challenging college courses that they take.

The project director has been directly involved with the school and the students throughout the program. He spent several days per week at the school, interacted with the CCTI students as a group and individually, and kept individual records on each student. He interacted frequently with staff and teachers at the school, especially with a teacher in the Health Sciences Technology academy, David Thomas, who has daily involvement with the CCTI students. He was available to counsel students on issues related to the program and became a resource to the larger school community on dual-credit opportunities at MDC.

Special Features

This project is working hard to find the right balance between access and rigor. The school is extremely diverse in terms of ethnicity, country of origin, family income, and academic achievement. The pathway, as it is structured, requires that students be very academically capable. A great deal of time and energy is needed to find students who will be able to succeed. This investment has paid off in that the students have been largely successful in their college courses and internships.

The placement of this program within a career academy appears to increase students' sense of membership in a group. This sense of membership can be an important factor in keeping students on track and in their likelihood of persisting through the program.

The intensive six-week internship reflects a strong level of commitment to this program from the principal business partner, Baptist Hospital of Miami. The Corporate Director of Education, Melitta Auclair, along with the management staff of the hospital's Volunteer Department, has made it a priority to find appropriate placements for students during their internship, and to structure the experience to maximize its value. Students were paid for their participation during the past summer, which heightened their commitment and made the experience more like a real job.

The placement of this program within a career academy appears to increase students' sense of membership in a group. This sense of membership can be an important factor in keeping students on track and in their likelihood of persisting through the program. In addition, placement within a career academy means that they have regular interaction, while in high school, with teachers who are involved with health professions and are able to acculturate them to the field.

The Implementation Strategies

The project uses a set of implementation strategies to attain the five CCTI objectives.

CCTI Objective	Key Strategies
Decreased need for remediation at postsecondary level	• Early student assessment with the PASS test • Computer-based tutoring at college
Increased enrollment and persistence in postsecondary education	• Participation in a career pathway that removes barriers to entry into postsecondary nursing and allied health programs • Use of small classes and learning communities to support engagement and persistence
Increased academic and skill achievement at the secondary and postsecondary levels	• Enrollment in a rigorous curriculum of academic and career technical courses • Involvement in an internship that provides hands-on experience as well as motivation to persist
Increased attainment of postsecondary degrees, certificates, or other recognized credentials	• Scholarship support available from the Baptist Hospital Scholars Program • Active recruitment of students able to undertake a challenging curriculum • Mentoring of students by high school and college staff and teachers
Increased entry into employment or further education	• High school curriculum alignment with postsecondary requirements and industry standards • Student internship providing early work experience and a chance to develop work-related skills

Most Effective Strategies

Among specific implementation strategies, the CCTI project has identified five of which they it is particularly proud.

The development of a pathway that addresses important barriers to the preparation of nurses and smoothes the transition from high school directly into nursing programs. Because college-level prerequisites for the nursing program are taken while in high school, students remain in a health-professions pathway rather than becoming diverted by needing to take courses at a different college campus.

A secondary school curriculum that emphasizes college preparedness beginning in 9th grade. FVHS works hard to offer students a rigorous, engaging curriculum through its career academies. The high school portion of the nursing pathway offered through the CCTI project is clearly aligned with a challenging college curriculum.

The use of two levels of testing, contributing to decreased need for remediation. The PASS test assesses student readiness for the College Placement Test as well as for progress toward readiness for college. The CPT is taken when the student is judged to be ready for it. This may also have both academic and psychological benefits, as students are more gradually prepared for the higher-stakes test.

The six-week internship at Baptist Hospital's multiple benefits. Students gain hands-on experience as well as a higher level of commitment to work in health care. They are individually mentored by experienced professionals. In addition, hospital representatives have commented on how much their staff has enjoyed the experience of working with excited young people, adding to their job satisfaction.

The presence of the CCTI project director as an on-site resource to the school as a highly valued implementation strategy. The director plays a role in mentoring students, assists teachers, and serves as an accessible source of information on MDC programs and services.

Least Effective Strategies

Difficulty of recruitment of students into this program. It is a challenging program that some students may not want to undertake. Of those students who wish to enroll, finding students who meet the eligibility requirements has been difficult. As a result, the CCTI project has widened the pool of students from which it recruits to those in other FVHS academies who may wish to enter the health professions.

The original testing plan. The original plan called for students to make regular use of computer-assisted tutoring at Kendall Campus in order to prepare to take the Computerized Placement Test. Because of funding cuts, this has not been possible. Students who are identified as needing assistance to become ready for college are less likely to receive tutoring or other support of this kind.

Plans for the Future

As the leadership of this project looks toward the future, there are several ways in which they hope to expand their activities.

- The program was originally intended to prepare students for careers in allied health as well as in nursing. A priority during the coming year will be to develop a career pathway in allied health.
- The program will be expanded to include another high school, John A. Ferguson High School, in the near future. Newly opened in the fall of 2003, this high school is also based on a career academy model and includes an academy in nursing and allied health. Additional pathways may be added, including imaging and medical technology.
- FVHS, in collaboration with MDC's Kendall Campus, offered the PASS test at the high school beginning in the spring of 2005. This will be administered to CCTI students as well as to other students interested in taking dual-credit courses.

- As the first students make the transition from the high school to the college portion of the pathway, the college is thinking about how to make sure that it is generally known that they are a part of the CCTI project. As with other CCTI sites, students who begin in CCTI pathways in high school are likely to be undifferentiated from the rest of the student population at the college. The college is thinking about ways to ensure that they continue to receive the support needed to complete the second portion of the pathway.

Lessons Learned

The project partners have identified several lessons they have learned that may be useful to others implementing similar programs.

Recruitment follow-up. When recruiting students and helping them through the admissions process, considerable monitoring and follow-up is needed. Students may express interest and then not take all of the necessary steps to apply for admission unless they receive guidance. The project director may need to spend a considerable amount of time to make sure that this occurs.

Partner roles and responsibilities. The success of the entire project depends on the success of each partner in carrying out their roles and responsibilities. Regular communication is needed to make sure that this is occurring. This project found that the Project Planning Committee was a very important forum for this communication, and that it was best to include multiple representatives from each partner on the committee. Student participation at some of the meetings has been helpful.

Dual-credit opportunities. This project can help the high school staff and students learn how to take advantage of dual-credit opportunities. Because of the presence of the project director at the school, students, counselors, teachers, and administrators are more likely to feel as though they can get their questions answered.

Student motivation. Project leaders have observed that students wanting to enter dual-credit courses may work harder to bring up their grades so that they become eligible to take the courses.

Relationships with business. The relationship with business partners must be carefully thought out. A project leader notes that it is important to think about what the project needs most before approaching a business partner. In her experience, business partners are more likely to share other resources, such as internship placements, when they are not asked for money. In the case of Baptist Hospital, the acute shortage of nurses in the area makes the hospital eager to support a program of this kind.

Articulation. Many programs that offer dual-credit courses struggle to make sure that the college credits students earn while in high school will be accepted by postsecondary institutions. Florida's common course-numbering system makes the transfer of credits to other Florida colleges and universities much easier. Other states should be encouraged to enact similar policies.

More information about Miami Dade College and the CCTI Initiative can be found at http://www.league.org/league/projects/ccti/projects/summary.cfm?key=mdcc.

■ ...business partners are more likely to share other resources, such as internship placements, when they are not asked for money.

Northern Virginia Community College

Elisabeth Barnett

OCCUPATIONAL AREA:	Health Occupations
CAREER PATHWAY:	Medical Health Technology in Respiratory Therapy
CCTI PROJECT DIRECTOR:	Charles Whitehead
NVCC MEDICAL EDUCATION CAMPUS WEBSITE:	http://www.nvcc.edu/medical/INDEX.htm
PROJECT PARTNERS:	Northern Virginia Community College Medical Education Campus Fairfax County Public Schools: West Potomac Academy Chantilly Academy Falls Church High School
CORPORATE PARTNERS:	Reston Hospital Inova Health System, Virginia Hospital Center

The Project Partners

The CCTI project at **Northern Virginia Community College** (NVCC) is working to better align the health education program at Fairfax County Public Schools and that of NVCC's **Medical Education Campus** (MEC). Traditionally, the secondary and postsecondary systems in the area have been fairly separate, but this is changing along with state and national trends, and aided by the CCTI project. Project partners have worked hard to find the best ways to bring the two systems together and create smooth student transitions from high school to college. The recently completed MEC, with full clinic and educational facilities, has made this process easier as high schools take note of the resources that are available to students.

■ Thanks to CCTI support, curriculum mapping and joint development of programs between high schools and the college have been accelerated.

Robert Templin, President, Northern Virginia Community College

The focus of the project has been on the alignment of the curriculum in nursing and several allied health areas, including Occupational and Physical Therapy Assistant, Respiratory Therapy, Fire and Emergency Medical Sciences, Dental Assisting, and Medical Health Technologies. In each area, representatives of the college and high school district have sought ways to reduce redundancy in coursework and award college credit to high school students where appropriate. In addition, this partnership is working to introduce high school students to the range of career options available in college health occupations programs, and to increase their readiness to enter college through the provision of college placement testing and tutoring. Finally, the project is helping students in the transition to college by assuring qualified students admission into programs for which waiting lists are often long; 50 percent of the seats in health occupations are prioritized for CCTI pathway students.

Northern Virginia Community College is the second largest multicampus community college in the U.S. and the most ethnically diverse one. Serving a student population of more than 60,000 credit students and more than 300,000 noncredit and continuing education students from 117 countries, it is committed to meeting the educational and training needs of people with differing abilities, education, experiences, and individual goals. NVCC is an open-enrollment institution providing educational opportunities in occupational-technical and transfer programs.

The college's mission is to "respond to the educational needs of its dynamic and diverse constituencies through an array of comprehensive programs and services that facilitate learning and workforce development in an environment of open access and through lifelong educational opportunities." It does this by offering programs at six campuses: Annandale, Alexandria, Loudoun, Manassas, Woodbridge, and MEC. The Medical Education Campus houses the college's Divisions of Nursing and Surgical Technologies and Allied Health as well as health education programs associated with two other institutions, George Mason University and the Virginia Commonwealth University.

The **Medical Education Campus** is the first specialized single-industry campus in the Virginia Community College System. It was designed to provide nursing and allied health academic pathways that serve seven levels of students ranging from those in high school through those undertaking graduate studies, including both full- and part-time enrollees. An important component of the campus is the Medical Mall, which contains primary care clinics, a Women's Center, a dental clinic, a pharmacy, a vision center, and a medical lab. The mall was originally developed in 1995 under a grant from The Pew Charitable Trusts, which encouraged a strong focus on community preventive care. Services are provided by students under the supervision of qualified faculty, with about 25,000 patient visits logged each year.

■ The Medical Education Campus ...was designed to provide nursing and allied health academic pathways that serve seven levels of students ranging from those in high school through those undertaking graduate studies, including both full- and part-time enrollees.

The **Fairfax County Public School System** serves a densely populated area that includes 25 high schools. Three of these have health occupations programs, and all three programs enroll students from any high school in the school system. In these programs, students spend about one-third of the school day at the academy in health-related classes and take their other courses at the home high school. The health and medical sciences programs at the three schools are overseen at the district level by Health and Medical Sciences Coordinator Anne-Marie Glynn.

Business partners for this initiative include three local hospitals. **Reston Hospital** was involved from the beginning of the CCTI project, and has shown great interest in working with the college to prepare students for local employment. Located near Washington Dulles International Airport, it is a full-service medical-surgical hospital with 127 beds, and has served the residents of western Fairfax and eastern Loudoun Counties since 1986. In addition, representatives of **Inova Health System** and **Virginia Hospital Center** have more recently become involved in the CCTI initiative. Inova Health System is comprised of full-service hospitals located in Alexandria, Leesburg, and Fairfax, and a children's hospital in Falls Church. Virginia Hospital Center is a 334-bed tertiary-care facility located in Arlington Center.

History of the Partnership

Partnerships among NVCC, local secondary school systems, and business and industry have existed for well over a decade in this region but were enhanced in the mid-1990s with the advent of Tech Prep. At that time, NVCC, as part of the Virginia Community College System, received funding to initiate a Tech Prep consortium. One of the first and most productive career education programs was in nursing and allied health. Efforts were focused on enhancing programs at both the secondary and postsecondary levels through articulation agreements. In addition, procedures were established to allow high school students to receive various types of college credit for participation in college-level learning experiences. Based on this history of cooperation, the college took leadership in responding to the request for proposals for CCTI.

However, when the CCTI initiative started, Project Director Charles Whitehead found that it was necessary to move fairly slowly. Because of some early negative experiences in creating dual-credit courses and a range of logistical problems related to transportation and scheduling, groundwork needed to be laid and relationships established before taking on major new activities. On the other hand, there was clearly interest at both the secondary and postsecondary levels in finding the best way to fully use the resources represented by the MEC. In addition, Robert Templin, NVCC's president, was committed to building partnerships with the K-12 education system. He strongly believes that the education community should think in terms of our students rather than separate secondary and postsecondary enrollees. Based on this foundation, the project is making good progress in improving secondary and postsecondary health occupations pathways.

The Model Career Pathway

The CCTI project at NVCC is working on the development of several different pathways related to health occupations but has chosen the Medical Health Technologies in Respiratory Therapy Pathway as its primary focus under the grant. However, eight pathways connecting high school and college health programs have been laid out that build on five of the health-occupations options currently available in Fairfax County public schools. A number of them provide opportunities for students to earn college credit while in high school.

■ ...eight pathways connecting high school and college health programs have been laid out that build on five of the health-occupations options currently available in Fairfax County public schools. A number of them provide opportunities for students to earn college credit while in high school.

To develop these pathways, the CCTI Project Director typically involves a range of stakeholders including college and high school faculty, the Fairfax County Public Schools Coordinator of Health and Medical Sciences, the regional Tech Prep coordinator, and the college's student services dean. Using the state-established competencies for each career as a foundation, the group looks at the relevant high school and college curricula to identify areas in which they overlap. In areas where content at the high school and college level is repeated or where national exams may be used to substantiate learning, high school students may be awarded college credit.

Career pathway (based on college programs)	Builds on (from high school curriculum)	College credits that may be earned in high school
Respiratory Therapy	Medical Health Technologies II (MHT)	1 credit for college-level Medical Terminology Course embedded in MHT course (articulated credit)
Medical Health Technology	Medical Health Technologies II	
Medical Laboratory	Medical Health Technologies II	
Radiology	Medical Health Technologies II	
Nursing	Practical Nursing	12-15 credits upon passing the LPN licensure exam (articulated credit)
Emergency Medical Technician (EMT)	Fire/Emergency Medical Sciences	Students who pass state certification for EMT-B earn 6 credits (dual credit)
Physical Therapy Assistant	Occupational and Physical Therapy	5 credits awarded for high school course in Musculo-skeletal Structure (articulated credit)
Dental Hygiene	Dental Assisting	

This CCTI project uses both dual credit, by which the student earns immediately transcripted high school and college credit, and articulated credit, by which the student must complete the next course at the college before college credit is awarded. Each has advantages. The dual credit is portable to other postsecondary institutions but costs students $70 to $80 per credit; the articulated credit is provided at no cost to the student. In some courses or programs, such as EMT, the college requires that students be at least 18 to enroll, which limits some opportunities for dual credit. The college also permits high school students to enroll in classes on campus or via distance learning, but these options have not yet been incorporated into the CCTI pathways.

Not every pathway is offered at every high school. All three schools offer Medical Health Technologies I and II. In addition, Falls Church offers Practical Nursing and Fire and Emergency Medical Sciences. West Potomac has Occupational-Physical Therapy and Dental Assisting. Chantilly also offers Dental Assisting. As indicated, Medical Health Technologies serves as the foundation for four CCTI career pathways.

Curriculum and Instruction

The school district is currently in the process of updating its curriculum to offer more pathway-specific course offerings for juniors and seniors. Under the new plan, all health-occupations students will begin with a general course, such as Medical Health Technologies I, in the sophomore or junior year. Following this, they can take more narrowly defined courses related to specific career areas in the following years. This change is being made partially in response to state-level updates in curriculum guidelines, which are also encouraging more secondary-postsecondary cooperation. There is also work under way to align courses more closely with national certification standards.

To support the high school curriculum, as well as to introduce students to opportunities available at NVCC, the CCTI project director has set up a number of student tours at the Medical Education Campus. Some of these permit students to see the campus as a whole, while others have a specific purpose. For example, students from the Falls Church Fire and Emergency Medical Sciences course attended sessions in the Gross Anatomy labs at the college, a very valuable experience.

In addition, high school students visiting the college are often invited to take college placement tests to assess their progress toward college readiness in math, English, and reading. Those who need extra assistance may attend the college's summer remediation program for students who need an extra boost before the fall semester begins. This course is designed for incoming freshmen, but it is also made available to others. This is an intensive classroom-based, two-week program that allows students to rapidly improve basic skills. While in the past this was provided free of charge, there is now a small fee attached.

An additional learning option is provided by area hospitals. All three hospitals involved with the CCTI project offer two-week summer camps in which student volunteers rotate through different departments at the hospital before coming for several days to the Medical Education Campus. At MEC, students rotate through different labs and learning experiences led by college faculty, designed to introduce them to a variety of health occupations. In the summer of 2005, about 100 students participated. Both the students and the hospitals were pleased with the experience.

In addition, the CCTI project has worked to provide learning opportunities for faculty. In the fall of 2004, a consultant from the Center for Occupational Research and Development (CORD) offered a much-appreciated workshop on integrated and contextual learning to high school and college faculty. Those who attended found it very helpful, and a number have begun using the recommended instructional methods. Because travel is difficult in the area and in-service training days are scarce, CCTI project leadership is working with CORD to establish an online training program for teachers, with a larger menu of options. Participating teachers will be able to earn continuing education units.

■ **All three hospitals involved with the CCTI project offer two-week summer camps in which student volunteers rotate through different departments at the hospital before coming for several days to the Medical Education Campus.**

Bridges With Four-Year Programs

The Medical Education Campus is a collaborative effort, with participation by George Mason University, Virginia Commonwealth University, and regional secondary school systems, as well as NVCC. In addition to the associate-degree options offered by NVCC, George Mason University offers both bachelor's and master's degrees for health care professionals, and Virginia Commonwealth University offers bachelor's, master's, doctoral, and postdoctoral degrees in health care fields. George Mason University works with its students onsite, while Virginia Commonwealth University offers web-based programs.

In addition, NVCC articulation agreements are in place in specific career pathways, permitting students who complete an associate's degree in nursing or allied health to transfer to a range of other colleges and universities, including Old Dominion University, Virginia Commonwealth University, and Virginia Tech.

Student Support

College placement testing for high school students, using the COMPASS test, has been an important aspect of this CCTI project. However, finding the best way to administer the test has been challenging. Teachers are protective of instructional time, and students are frequently tested for other purposes. Originally, testing was done using paper-and-pencil tests in the classroom at all three participating schools. More recently, a decision was made to move to an online format. Under the current plan, students who wish to be tested for college readiness go to MEC testing center. Results are available within five minutes, in the form of a report provided to students and to the Fairfax County Schools Coordinator of Health and Medical Science, who shares the report with the teachers. To encourage students to take advantage of this opportunity, the project director is looking into providing incentives such as gift certificates to those who test.

For students whose test results indicate that they are not on track to college readiness, options are somewhat limited. Counseling is available at the college, and the high school teachers at the academies try to help. Some teachers work to integrate math, reading, and writing into the health occupations curriculum. In addition, some students have taken advantage of the two-week summer class offered at the college for those wanting to improve their skills.

The CCTI project leadership is also very involved in marketing the project as well as the opportunities available at MEC in general. Activities have included talks at high schools, participation in career fairs, tours of MEC, and presentations at statewide meetings and conferences. Advertising has also been done at local malls.

Special Features

One of the major problems faced by students in nursing and allied health around the nation, as well as by employers eager for more trained staff, is the scarcity of slots available in college programs. This can be a major obstacle to the development of pathways that offer a smooth transition from high school to college. To address this issue, MEC Provost Charlene Connelly, in cooperation with President Templin, has committed to make 50 percent of the seats in all health programs available to CCTI students on a priority basis.

In addition, the Medical Education Campus is an extraordinary resource. A wide range of work-based learning opportunities is available through the on-campus Medical Mall. Students are able to participate in patient care in the primary care clinics, Women's Center, dental clinic, pharmacy, vision center, or medical labs. Furthermore, students who wish to continue their education beyond the associate's degree have access to two four-year universities that offer programs at their locations.

Finally, the summer camps at local hospitals and MEC have been very well attended and provide a valuable learning experience for students entering the health professions. Students participate on a volunteer basis, evidence that it is highly valued.

The Implementation Strategies

The CCTI project emphasizes the following set of implementation strategies to attain the five CCTI objectives.

Northern Virginia Community College CCTI Program

CCTI Objective	Key Strategies
Decreased need for remediation at postsecondary level	• Alignment of the high school and college curriculum in nursing and allied health • College placement testing of students with follow-up summer workshop available
Increased enrollment and persistence in postsecondary education	• Provision of priority enrollment opportunities for CCTI students in MEC health programs • Availability of articulated and dual credit for selected courses
Increased academic and skill achievement at the secondary and postsecondary levels	• Offer of professional development opportunities to faculty on contextual learning • Enhanced high school curriculum with more career-specific courses available
Increased attainment of postsecondary degrees, certificates, or other recognized credentials	• Moving of the high school curriculum toward preparing more students to earn national certifications • Articulation agreements with a range of four-year colleges and universities
Increased entry into employment or further education	• Hospital summer camps for high school students • Opportunities to apply skills in MECclinics

Most Effective Strategies

Among the specific implementation strategies, the CCTI project has identified five of which it is particularly proud.

Developing a system for the review of secondary and postsecondary courses as the basis for streamlining the curriculum and establishing articulation agreements. There have been notable improvements in the willingness of faculty at both the college and high school levels to participate in discussions of this kind.

Taking leadership in the development of a system for online college placement testing that increases access and improves record keeping. This system is being expanded to the other five campuses of NVCC as well as to off-site locations at high schools and community centers.

Hosting a professional development workshop on contextual teaching and learning, in cooperation with CORD.

Introducing the use of the HSSE and CCSSE surveys (measures of high school and community college student engagement) to the region. There is now considerable interest in administering these to additional groups of students at different campuses.

Creating summer internships that blend hands-on experiences in hospitals with classroom and lab experiences at MEC.

Least Effective Strategies

The use of pencil-and-paper college placement tests in the high schools proved to be frustrating. Teachers did not want to use instructional time for this purpose. In addition, the tests had to be hand graded, which was time consuming and caused delays in getting the results to students.

The Fairfax County Schools Medical Health Technologies course is proving to be not well aligned with programs offered through the Medical Education Campus. This course, along with the high school health curriculum in general, is currently under review.

Plans for the Future

Project Director Charles Whitehead believes it is important to institutionalize a number of the CCTI program activities within NVCC so that they are sustainable after the grant ends. Ideally, this will involve placing the testing functions and summer programs under the MEC Continuing Education Division, where there will be ongoing personnel and financial resources to support them.

In addition, discussions have been under way with the Arlington County Schools regarding their participation in the CCTI initiative. They currently have programs in Physical Therapy and Emergency Medical Technician that could be articulated with programs at MEC.

Finally, in addition to the curriculum revisions being undertaken, Fairfax County Public Schools is looking into the possibility of starting a new program in Pharmacy Tech.

Lessons Learned

The project partners have identified several lessons they have learned that may be useful to others implementing similar programs.

Scheduling the project. It can be challenging to develop an ideal schedule for the rollout of a project like CCTI. On the one hand, it is important to take adequate time to build relationships, research options, and plan. On the other, there is a need to start project activities promptly to show results and keep the interest of those involved.

Communication. Communications can be enhanced by working with stakeholders individually before bringing them together into group meetings. However, there can be difficulties if some individuals feel that they have not received timely information.

Innovation and experimentation. The CCTI project can serve as a testing ground for new ideas. Initiatives developed by the local or national project are observed by college leadership. In this case, online testing and data-gathering activities such as CCSSE are being replicated across the college's six campuses.

More information about Northern Virginia Community College can be found at http://www.league.org/league/projects/ccti/projects/summary.cfm?key=nvcc.

A President Reflects on CCTI

Because the Washington, DC, economy is red hot, worker shortages are emerging in many critical fields. For example, today Northern Virginia has a shortage of nearly 2,800 health care workers in 24 specialties. Of these, approximately 1,000 vacancies are RNs. Over the next 15 years, the region will be short over 16,000 skilled health care workers; 6,350 of these will be RNs, unless steps are taken to increase the supply of available workers. Northern Virginia Community College is the region's largest provider of highly skilled health care workers such as RNs, respiratory therapists, medical laboratory technologists, dental hygienists, diagnostic imaging technicians, and more than a dozen other health-related specialty fields.

In an effort to respond to the growing health care workforce crisis, NVCC has brought together a coalition of hospitals, colleges and universities, public school systems, the regional chamber of commerce, the regional technology council, and other business leaders to examine the extent and impact of the crisis and to develop a long-term strategy to solve worker shortages. The Northern Virginia HealthFORCE Alliance has been created and has developed a four-year, $23.5 million action plan to double the region's output of nursing graduates by 2009 and to increase by half the number of allied health workers being trained.

One of the key components of the HealthFORCE action plan is the creation of a pipeline strategy for new workers entering health fields. CCTI has supported NVCC's efforts to attack the health care crisis by working with middle and high schools in the region. A focused area of work has been creating greater awareness among students and parents of the significant number of career opportunities not requiring the baccalaureate that are available in health fields. Students are somewhat familiar with fields such as nursing but have little or no awareness of others, such as physical therapy assisting, emergency medical technician, or medical information technology. Now, partially with CCTI support, a communications, marketing, and outreach program is being established that coordinates the efforts of the health care industry and colleges and universities in educating middle and high school students, counselors, and parents regarding health careers and educational opportunities in Northern Virginia. Special attention is being given to outreach directed to schools that draw students from immigrant and low-income communities.

Another focal point has been the creation of joint efforts between schools and NVCC in curriculum planning and development. Thanks to CCTI support, curriculum mapping and joint development of programs between high schools and the college have been accelerated. Soon, high school students will be encouraged to complete substantial components of their lower-division general education and some skill requirements through dual enrollment, advanced placement, or international baccalaureate enrollment, reducing the time to the associate degree for them and providing significant financial savings for their families. The eventual goal is to establish health career programs in high schools that result in students graduating with a high school diploma, a marketable skill, and up to one year of college training, plus guaranteed admission into one of NVCC's nursing or allied health associate degree programs. Feasibility studies are now under way to determine if one or more magnet high schools, operated in a partnership with NVCC, should be established with an emphasis upon the life sciences and health careers with programs through the associate degree.

For sure, increasing the awareness of students about health careers and establishing collaborative efforts between schools and higher education institutions will not be enough by itself to solve Northern Virginia's health care worker shortage. But these efforts go a long way to ensuring that there will be a supply of qualified candidates who are interested in entering the front lines of tomorrow's health careers.

Robert Templin, President, Northern Virginia Community College

Appendices

COLLEGE: Anne Arundel Community College
HIGH SCHOOL(S): Annapolis, Arundel, Chesapeake, Glen Burnie, Meade, North Co., Northeast, Old Mill, Severna Pk

CLUSTER: Education and Training
PATHWAY: Teaching/Training
PROGRAM: Academy of Teaching Professions

	GRADE	ENGLISH	MATH	SCIENCE	SOCIAL STUDIES	REQUIRED COURSES RECOMMENDED ELECTIVE COURSES • OTHER ELECTIVE COURSES CAREER AND TECHNICAL EDUCATION COURSES			
ADULT LEARNER ENTRY POINTS — SECONDARY	9	English 9 (1)	Algebra I or Geometry (1)	Biology (1)	US Government (1)	Health (.5)	Physical Education (.5)	Keyboarding (.5)	Intro to Computers (.5)
	10	English 10 (1)	Geometry or Algebra II (1)	Chemistry or Earth Space Science (1)	AP European History or World Civ. (1)	Foreign Language (1)	Child Development I (1)	Bus. Pres (.5) Parenting (.5)	Intro to Teaching Prof. I (1)
	Accuplacer administered second semester, 10th grade to assess college readiness and address areas of weakness								
	11	AP English Language or English 11(1)	Algebra II or Precalculus (1)	AP Sci. elective Physics or Chem. or Physical Sci.(1)	AP US History or US History (1)	Foreign Language (1)	Child Development II (1)	SAT Prep (.5) Psychology (.5)	Intro to Teaching Prof. II (.5)
	12	AP English Literature or English 12 (1)	AP Calculus, Precalculus or Math Elective (1)	AP Science or Other Science Elective (1)	AP Psychology (1)	Prof. Career Internship (.5-1)	Found. of Ed. (3) [Concurrent]	Content area Courses if Secondary Ed	Content area Courses if Secondary Ed
	Administer college placement exams (reading, math, and writing) and other assessments to determine academic readiness and career skill preparedness; provide academic/career advising and additional preparation								
POSTSECONDARY	YEAR 1 1st Semester	■ ● Composition and Intro to Lit. I (3)	● Fundamental Concepts of Math I (4)	■ ● Fund. of Bio. or Envir. Sci. (4)	■ ● Intro to Psychology (3)	● Foundations of Education (3)			
	YEAR 1 2nd Semester	■ ● Composition and Intro to Lit. II (3)	● Fundamental Concepts of Math II (4)	● General Physical Science (4)	● World Geography (3)	● Growth and Development (3)			
	Passage of Praxis exam required for AAT								
	YEAR 2 1st Semester	● Fund. of Oral Comm. (3)	● Fundamental Concepts of Math III (4)	● The Solar System (4)		■ ● Education Psychology (3)	● Introduction to Special Education (3)		
	YEAR 2 2nd Semester				■ ● American History 1 or 2 (3)	● Foundations of Reading & Lang. Arts (3)	● Personal & Community Health (3)	■ ● American Government (3)	● Introduction to Fine Arts (3)

CCTI College and Career Transitions Initiative

Required Courses
Recommended Elective Courses
Career and Technical Education Courses
Mandatory Assessments, Advising, and Additional Preparation

Credit-Based Transition Program (e. g. Dual/Concurrent Enrollment, Articulated Course, 2+2+2)
(◆ = High School to Com. College)
(● = Com. College to 4-Year Institution)
(■ = Opportunity to test out)

COLLEGE: Corning Community College
HIGH SCHOOL(S): Campbell-Savona High School; Schuyler-Chemung-Tioga B.O.C.E.S., Watkins Glen High School

CLUSTER: Information Technology
PATHWAY: Network Technology
PROGRAM: Associate of Applied Science Degree

ADULT LEARNER ENTRY POINTS	GRADE	ENGLISH	MATH	SCIENCE	SOCIAL STUDIES	REQUIRED COURSES RECOMMENDED ELECTIVE COURSES • OTHER ELECTIVE COURSES CAREER AND TECHNICAL EDUCATION COURSES			
SECONDARY	9	English	Math	Science & Lab	Global Studies	Second Language	Physical Education/ Health	◆ Computer Keyboarding	
SECONDARY	10	English	Math	Science & Lab	Global Studies	Second Language	Physical Education	◆ Comp Network Technician or Networking I & II	Art/Music
	In 10th grade, assess for college readiness by administration of ACCUPLACER to all Tech Prep & CCTI students. Provide academic/career counseling. Provide Academic Intervention Services (AIS)as needed.								
SECONDARY	11	English	◆ Applied Math	Science & Lab	US History		Physical Education	◆ Comp Network Technician or Networking III	◆ ■ Basic Electricity
	In 11th grade, assess for college readiness by administration of ACCUPLACER to all Tech Prep & CCTI students. Provide academic/career counseling. Provide Academic Intervention Services (AIS) as needed.								
SECONDARY	12	◆ ● ACE English	◆ Applied Math	Science & Lab	Economics		Physical Education	◆ Comp Network Technician or Networking IV	Co-Op or Internship
	Upon successful completion of five (5) New York State Regents Exams and a minimum of 22 credits, student graduates with a Regents Diploma. Upon successful completion of the approved CTE courses, student receives a Regents Diploma with CTE Endorsement credential. Upon successful completion of all high school requirements and Tech Prep/CCTI portfolio, student receives a Certificate of Completion. Administration of ACCUPLACER to determine college level placement in math and writing skills.								
POSTSECONDARY	YEAR 1 1st Semester	◆ ● College Composition I	◆ Elements of Applied Math I	◆ Free Elective- Professionalism in the Workplace	◆ Free Elective- Foundations for Word Processing	◆ Computer Essentials	Wellness	◆ Network Fundamentals	◆ ■ Basic Electricity
POSTSECONDARY	YEAR 1 2nd Semester		◆ Elements of Applied Math II	Fiber Optics Lab Science			Wellness	◆ LAN-WAN Networking	Digital Computer Systems
POSTSECONDARY	YEAR 2 1st Semester	English			Social Sciences Elective	Data/Voice Communications	Wellness	◆ LAN Implement & Config.	Network Software
POSTSECONDARY	YEAR 2 2nd Semester	Technical Report Writing			Social Sciences Elective	Network Management	Network Troublshooting	◆ Network Project	

CCTI College and Career Transitions Initiative

Required Courses
Recommended Elective Courses
Career and Technical Education Courses
Mandatory Assessments, Advising, and Additional Preparation

Credit-Based Transition Program (e. g. Dual/Concurrent Enrollment, Articulated Course, 2+2+2)
(◆ = High School to Com. College)
(● = Com. College to 4-Year Institution)
(■ = Opportunity to test out)

COLLEGE: Fox Valley Technical College
HIGH SCHOOL(S): KSCADE Consortium

CLUSTER: Law, Public Safety and Security
PATHWAY: Law Enforcement
PROGRAM: Criminal Justice-Law Enforcement

ADULT LEARNER ENTRY POINTS	GRADE	ENGLISH	MATH	SCIENCE	SOCIAL STUDIES	REQUIRED COURSES · RECOMMENDED ELECTIVE COURSES • OTHER ELECTIVE COURSES · CAREER AND TECHNICAL EDUCATION COURSES			
SECONDARY	9	English I	Algebra I	Physical Science	History	Phy. Ed	Language	Elective	
SECONDARY	10	English II	Geometry	Biology	Government	Health	Language	Elective	
SECONDARY	11	English III	Algebra II	Chemistry	Geography	◆ Tech Prep (R): Oral/Interpersonal Communication	◆ Tech Prep (R): Intro to Microcomputers	◆ FVTC (R): Careers in Criminal Justice	
SECONDARY	12	English IV	Tech Prep (R): Business Math	Conceptual Physics	◆ Tech Prep (R): Intro to Psychology, Intro to Sociology	◆ Tech Prep (R): Written Communicaiton	◆ Tech Prep: MS Office Suite	◆ FVTC (R): Intro to Criminal Justice	
	College Placement Assessment - Accuplacer (Available to HS site onlne Jr/Sr year)								
POSTSECONDARY	**YEAR 1** 1st Semester	◆ ● ■ Gen Ed: Oral/Interpersonal Communication 10801196/3 cr. Prereq: None	■ ● Gen Ed: Contemporary Am. Soc. 10809197/3 cr. Prereq: None		◆ ● ■ Core Sup: Intro to Microcomputers 10107177/1 cr. Prereq: None	◆ ● ■ Core: Intro to Criminal Justice 10504121/3 cr. Prereq: None	● ■ Core: Juv. Law 10504116/3 cr. Prereq: Intro to Soc. 10809196 & Intro to Criminal Justice 10504121	●■ Core: Traffic Theory 10504113/ 3 cr. Prereq: Intro to Criminal Justice 10504121	
POSTSECONDARY	**YEAR 1** 2nd Semester	◆ ● ■ Gen Ed: Written Communication 10801195/3 cr. Prereq: None	■ ◆ Gen Ed: Intro to Sociology 10809196/3 cr. Prereq: None	● ■ Gen Ed: Eng. Comp. 10801175/3 cr. Prereq: Written Communication 10801195		● ■ Core: Comnty. Policing Strategies 10504129/3 cr. Prereq: Intro to Criminal Justice 10504121	● ■ Core: Prof. Police Com. 10504117/3 cr. Prereq: Oral/Interpersonal Com. 10801196	● ■ Core: Criminal Law 10504115/3 cr. Prereq: Intro to Criminal Justice 10504121	
POSTSECONDARY	**YEAR 2** 3rd Semester	● ■ Gen Ed: Psychology of Human Relations 10809199/3 cr. Prereq: None		● ■ Core Sup: Law Enf. Writing 10801195/2 cr. Prereq: English Composition 10801175	● ■ Core: Commercial Sec. 10504104/3 cr. Prereq: Intro to Criminal Justice 10504121	● ■ Core: Def. & Arrest Tactics 10504150/2 cr. Prereq: Conc.w/ Law Enf. Writing 10801195 & Prof. Pol. Com. 10504117	●■ Core: Criminal Inv. Theory 10504112/3 cr. Prereq: Prof. Police Com. 10504117	● ■ Core: Patrol Ops 10504114/3 cr. Prereq: Defense & Arrest Tactics 10504150, Traffic Theory 10504113, Ab. Psych. 10809130, Crim. Law 10504115, Law Enf. Writing 10801195	
POSTSECONDARY	**YEAR 2** 4th Semester	● ■ Core Sup: Abnormal Psych. 10809130/3 cr. Prereq: Psychology of Human Relations 10809199	● ■ Gen Ed: Intro to College Mathematics 10504129/3 cr. Prereq: None		● ■ Core: Forensics 10504133/3 cr. Prereq: Crim. Inv. 10504112, Crim. Law 10504115, Report Writing 10801195	● ■ Core: Constitutional Law 10504103/3 cr. Prereq: Criminal Law 10504115	● ■ Core Sup: Law Enf. Internship 10504119/2 cr. Prereq: Crim. Inv. Theory 10504112, Traf. Thry 10504113, Juv. Law 10504116	Recommended: Firearms 10504151/2 cr. And First Responder 10531103/1 cr.	

CCTI
College and Career Transitions Initiative

Required Courses	**Credit-Based Transition Program** (e. g. Dual/Concurrent Enrollment, Articulated Course, 2+2+2)
Recommended Elective Courses	(◆ = High School to Com. College)
Career and Technical Education Courses	(● = Com. College to 4-Year Institution)
Mandatory Assessments, Advising, and Additional Preparation	(■ = Opportunity to test out)

COLLEGE: Sinclair Community College-MVTP Consortium
IIGH SCHOOL(S): Centerville, Dayton Career Center, Kettering Fairmont, Stebbins, Miami Valley Career Technology Center

CLUSTER: ScienceTech, Engineering & Mathematics
PATHWAY: Engineering Technology
PROGRAM: Electronics Engineering Technology

ADULT LEARNER ENTRY POINTS	GRADE	ENGLISH	MATH	SCIENCE	SOCIAL STUDIES	REQUIRED COURSES RECOMMENDED ELECTIVE COURSES • OTHER ELECTIVE COURSES CAREER AND TECHNICAL EDUCATION COURSES			
SECONDARY	9	English I (1)	Integrated Algebra & Geometry or Algebra I (1)	Physical Science (1)	World History (1)	Health (.5) P E (.5)	Career Explor. integrated with English 9	Elective (1)	
SECONDARY	10	English II (1)	Geometry or Algebra II (1)	Biology (1)	American History (1)	Introduction to Engineering Design (1)	◆ Technology Word & Excel (.5) Art (.5)	Elective (1)	
SECONDARY	11	English III (1)	Algebra II or Adv. Algebra II & Trigonometry (1)	Conceptual Physics or Physics I (1)	American Government (.5) Soc.Stu. Elec. (.5)	◆ Tech Prep Engineering Tech (1)	◆ Tech Prep Engineering Tech (1)	P E (.5)	
	In 11th grade, assess for college readiness by administering the "ACCUPLACER TEST" (Reading, Math and Writing)								
SECONDARY	12	English IV (1)	Integrated College Math or Calculus (1)	Chemistry (1)	Elective (1)	◆ Tech Prep Engr Electrical Circuits (1)	◆ Tech Prep Engr PC Applications in Engineering (1)	Elective (1)	
	Mandatory College Placement Assessment (Reading, Math and Writing) and Acad. Advising + State O.G.T.Requirement								
POSTSECONDARY	YEAR 1 1st Quarter	● English Comp I ENG111 (3)	● Math131 Tech Math I (5)	Succeeding in Engineering EGR160 (1)		◆ Personal Comp. Appl. in Engr-MET198 (2)	◆ Basic Electronic Measurements EET114 (3)		
POSTSECONDARY	YEAR 1 2nd Quarter	● English Comp II ENG112 (3)	● Math132 Tech Math II (5)		● Social Studies Elective (3)	◆ Elec. Circuits Instruments I EET150 (4)	Electronics Schematics & LayoutsEET116(3)		
POSTSECONDARY	YEAR 1 3rd Quarter	● English Comp III ENG113 (3)	● Math 133 Tech Math III (5)	Technical Physics I - 131 (4)	● Social Studies Elective (3)	Electrical Circuits & Instruments II EET155 (4)	Programming for Electronics Tech EET259 (3)		
POSTSECONDARY	YEAR 2 1st Quarter	Interpersonal Communication COM206 (3)		Technical Physics II - 132 (4)	Electronics I EET201 (4)	Electrical Circuits & Instruments III EET205 (3)	Digital Logic & Circuits EET231 (4)		
POSTSECONDARY	YEAR 2 2nd Quarter		EET Elective (3)	Linear Integrated Circuits EET207 (4)	Electronics II EET202 (3)	Microprocessors Microncontrollers EET261 (4)	Digital Systems I EET251 (4)		
POSTSECONDARY	YEAR 2 3rd Quarter	General Education ● Elective (3)	EET Elective (3)		Electronics Capstone Project EET278 (4)	Microprocessor Applications EET262 (4)	Digital Systems II EET252 (4)		

CCTI College and Career Transitions Initiative

Legend	
Required Courses	Credit-Based Transition Program (e. g. Dual/Concurrent Enrollment, Articulated Course, 2+2+2)
Recommended Elective Courses	(◆ = High School to Com. College)
Career and Technical Education Courses	(● = Com. College to 4-Year Institution)
Mandatory Assessments, Advising, and Additional Preparation	(■ = Opportunity to test out)

COLLEGE: Ivy Tech Community College of Indiana
HIGH SCHOOL(S): Brown County, Columbus East, Columbus North, Crothersville, Hauser, N. Decatur, S. Decatur, Seymour
CLUSTER: Health Sciences Career Cluster
PATHWAY: Therapeutic and Support Services
PROGRAM: Assoc. of Applied Science Degree (Surgical Technology)

ADULT LEARNER ENTRY POINTS

	GRADE	ENGLISH	MATH	SCIENCE	SOCIAL STUDIES	REQUIRED COURSES RECOMMENDED ELECTIVE COURSES • OTHER ELECTIVE COURSES CAREER AND TECHNICAL EDUCATION COURSES			
SECONDARY	9	English (English 9) (2)	Math (Algebra) (2)	Science (Biology) (2)	Social Studies (World History) (2)	Foreign Language (2)	Fine Arts (2)	Career Orientation (2)	Health (Intro to Health Careers) (2)
SECONDARY	10	English (English 10) (2)	Math (Geometry) (2)	Science (Chemistry) (2)	Social Studies (US History) (2)	Foreign Language (2)	Computer App. I & II (2)	PE (1)	Speech (1) ◆ Medical Terminology (HS=1, College=3)
SECONDARY	11	English (English 11) (2)	Math (Algebra II) (2)	Science (Physics) (2)	Social Studies (AP Psych) (2)	Foreign Language (2)	Elective	◆ Health Careers (HS=2 College=3)	Health Careers (CST Program)(2)
In 11th grade, assess for college readiness by administering ASSET/COMPASS to all Health Careers Students; provide academic/career advising and apply appropriate enrichments									
SECONDARY	12	English (AP Comp/Lit) (2)	Math (Pre-Cal) (2)	Science (Medical Bio.) (2)	US Government(1) Economics (1)	Foreign Language (2)	Elective	Health Careers (CST Program)(2)	Health Careers (CST Program)(2)
Graduation Qualifying Examination (GQE) mandatory HS exit exam for Indiana. (GQE measures 9th grade competencies.) Upon completion of CST Health Careers Program, student is eligible to sit for CRCST exam and receive professional certification from IAHCSMM. Students are awarded a Central Service Technician Technical Certificate upon successful completion of English Composition & Intro to Psychology at postsecondary level. COMPASS/ ASSET administered to determine academic readiness and career skill preparedness; provide academic/career advising and additional preparations as needed or requested.									
POSTSECONDARY	YEAR 1 1st Semester	● ■ English Composition (3)	● ■ Intermediate Algebra (3)	■ Anatomy & Physiology I (3)	◆ Health Careers (3)	◆ ■ Medical Terminology (3)			
POSTSECONDARY	YEAR 1 2nd Semester	■ Intro to Interpers. Com. (3)		■ Anatomy & Physiology II (3)	● ■ Intro to Psychology (3)	Pharmacology (3)			
POSTSECONDARY	YEAR 1 3rd Semester			General Microbiology (3)					
Students are required to pass Health Occupation Aptitude Exam (HOAE). CPR certification required to continue into Year 2.									
POSTSECONDARY	YEAR 2 1st Semester (1st 8 wks)				Medical Law & Ethics (3)	Fundamentals of Surgical Technology (4)		Applications of Surgical Technology (2)	
POSTSECONDARY	YEAR 2 1st Semester (2nd 8 wks)					Surgical Procedures I (3)		Clinical Applications I (3)	
POSTSECONDARY	YEAR 2 2nd Semester					Surgical Procedures II (6)		Clinical Applications II (9)	
POSTSECONDARY	YEAR 2 3rd Semester					Surgical Procedures III (3) CST Certification Review (2)		Clinical Applications III (8)	
Upon Completion of Surgical Technology Program, students are eligible to sit for the National Certification Examination to become a Certified Surgical Technologist (CST).									

League for Innovation in the Community College .org

CCTI College and Career Transitions Initiative

Required Courses
Recommended Elective Courses
Career and Technical Education Courses
Mandatory Assessments, Advising, and Additional Preparation

Credit-Based Transition Program (e. g. Dual/Concurrent Enrollment, Articulated Course, 2+2+2)
(◆ = High School to Com. College)
(● = Com. College to 4-Year Institution)
(■ = Opportunity to test out)

Career Pathway Self-Assessment

Date: ____________ College Name: ____

Career pathways include different strategies to facilitate student transitions from secondary school to college and careers. Use this form to assess the level of implementation of strategies that can be associated with a career pathway. For each strategy, indicate the level of implementation of a career pathway by placing an X in the box using the following rating scale:

1. **Planning** – Goal setting, staff orientation, the formation of committees and teams, and the development of plans for the strategy
2. **Development** – The strategy is being designed and field-tested.
3. **Initial Implementation** – The strategy is beginning to be carried out.
4. **Advanced Implementation** – The strategy is actively carried out and regularly reviewed to ensure its smooth operation.
5. **Institutionalization** – The strategy is firmly planted in the partnership and demonstrates positive outcomes.
6. **Not Addressed (NA)** – indicates the characteristic does not exist in this partnership.

Key Strategies Associated with Implementation of a Career Pathway	PLANNING	DEVELOPMENT	INITIAL IMPLEMENTATION	ADVD. IMPLEMENTATION	INSTITUTIONALISM	NOT ADDRESSED (NA)
CURRICULUM						
1. The career pathway aligns secondary and postsecondary curriculum so that the sequential course work is clearly displayed and communicated.						
2. Secondary school curriculum that meets state academic standards and grade-level expectations						
3. Secondary school curriculum that meets high school testing and exit requirements						
4. Secondary school curriculum that prepares students for college, beginning in 9th grade						
5. Secondary school curriculum that meets college entry and placement requirements						
6. Opportunities for students to earn college credit (often called dual credit or dual enrollment) while still in high school						
7. Opportunities for students to earn articulated credit (often associated with deferred credit, credit by exam, and tech prep) when they enroll at the community college						

Key Strategies Associated with Implementation of a Career Pathway	PLANNING	DEVELOPMENT	INITIAL IMPLEMENTATION	ADVD. IMPLEMENTATION	INSTITUTIONALISM	NOT ADDRESSED (NA)
7. Secondary instruction in industry-recognized skills and knowledge in a specific career cluster						
8. Postsecondary instruction in industry-recognized skills and knowledge leading to specific career opportunities						
9. Collaboration among administrators, faculty, counselors, and other key staff to ensure cohesive curricular connections between secondary and postsecondary levels						
INSTRUCTIONAL APPROACHES						
11. Distance learning and computer-assisted learning applications at the secondary level						
12. Distance learning and computer-assisted learning applications at the postsecondary level						
13. Work-based learning options (*e.g.*, job shadowing, internships, co-op) at the secondary level						
14. Work-based learning options (*e.g.*, internships, clinical experiences, apprenticeships) at the postsecondary level						
15. Use of innovative instructional methods (*e.g.*, project-based learning, cooperative learning) at the secondary level						
16. Use of innovative instructional methods (*e.g.*, learning communities, service learning) at the postsecondary level						
17. Use of contextual and applied instructional methods at the secondary level						
18. Use of contextual and applied instructional methods at the postsecondary level						
SUPPORT AND GUIDANCE						
19. Pre-high school preparation program(s) to enhance student readiness for college						
20. College placement tests administered to high school students to determine academic readiness						
21. Individualized education and/or career plans (ICPs, IEPs)						
22. Academic advising at the secondary level						
23. Academic advising at the postsecondary level						
24. Career-related counseling services at the secondary level						
25. Career-related counseling services at the postsecondary level						
26. Counseling information and services for parents to assist them to fully understand and help their children make informed decisions about college and careers						

Key Strategies Associated with Implementation of a Career Pathway	PLANNING	DEVELOPMENT	INITIAL IMPLEMENTATION	ADVD. IMPLEMENTATION	INSTITUTIONALISM	NOT ADDRESSED (NA)
ARTICULATION AND PARTNERSHIPS						
27. Secondary-postsecondary articulation agreements formally aligning and sequencing curriculum in Grades 9-14 or beyond						
28. Alignment and articulation of career pathways with baccalaureate-degree programs						
29. Partnerships with businesses and/or labor in the chosen career cluster area						
30. Employer or labor sponsored initiatives (faculty externships and fellowships, employer-staff loans, student work-based learning)						
31. Employer assistance with curriculum development or student placement in employment						
32. Labor assistance with curriculum development or student placement in employment						
ACCESS						
33. Strategies to enhance access by minority, low income, and first-generation (underserved) students						
34. Strategies to enhance access by individuals preparing for nontraditional employment						
35. Student scholarships dedicated to college transition in the career pathway program						
36. Assistance for underserved (low income, minority, or first generation) career pathway students to obtain needs-based financial aid						
PROJECT MANAGEMENT AND EVALUATION						
37. Employment, business, and/or entrepreneurial opportunities made available for the career cluster at multiple exit points						
38. Systematic collection of information about essential strategies, programs, institutional effectiveness, and outcomes to help staff make informed decisions						
39. On-going dialogue maintained among secondary, postsecondary, and business partners						
40. Professional development opportunities for secondary and postsecondary faculty (concurrent training)						
41. Faculty, staff, administrators, and other key personnel actively leading and facilitating the continued growth and development of the career pathway						

The Career Pathway Self-Assessment was written by Debra Bragg, Terry O'Banion, and Elisabeth Barnett.

Acknowledgments

As is the case with most worthwhile projects and publications, many people have made significant contributions to the success of the College and Career Transitions Initiative (CCTI) and to this specific publication. As project director and editor of this publication I would like to acknowledge some of them:

- The CCTI Site Partnership Coordinators, their administration, partners, and staff. Without their good efforts, there would be no case studies to contribute to the literature on improving student transitions and college readiness.
- The CCTI Evaluation team consisting of Ken Kempner, Linda Montgomery, Terry O'Banion, Debra Bragg, and Elisabeth Barnett for their work on project evaluation of which the case studies in this publication are a part. Also the rest of the CCTI Leadership Team, Jon Alexiou, Sandi Harwell, and Scott Hess, for their advice and counsel.
- The U.S. Department of Education, Office of Vocational and Adult Education for its vision, leadership, and funding.
- The entire League for Innovation in the Community College staff who all have provided assistance on the CCTI project. Special thanks to Boo Browning and Cynthia Wilson for their publications expertise and Gerardo de los Santos for his support and guidance.
- The CCTI Project staff, Jean Petty and Addie Lou Thomas, for their continued assistance in managing and implementing this complex national project.
- Plato Learning, Inc., for their sponsorship of this publication.

Laurance J. Warford
Editor and CCTI Project Director

About the Authors

Laurance Warford is the Senior Workforce Consultant and Project Director of the College and Career Transitions Initiative for the League for Innovation in the Community College. He was previously a community college liason for the U.S. Department of Labor and served as Vice President at Lane Community College.

Scott Hess is Project Manager, College and Careers Transitions, U.S. Department of Education, Office of Vocational and Adult Education, Division of Academic and Technical Education.

Elisabeth Barnett is Senior Research Associate, NCREST, at Teachers College in New York.

Debra D. Bragg is Professor and Program Coordinator, Higher Education and Community College Leadership Department of Educational Organization and Leadership.

Terry O'Banion is Senior League Fellow and President Emeritus of the League for Innovation in the Community College.

About PLATO Learning, Inc.

For decades, PLATO Learning has been committed to improving student achievement for K-12 and adult learners at the postsecondary level with our computer-based curricula. Our partnership with the League for Innovation and the College and Career Transitions Initiative (CCTI) expands that commitment and provides an opportunity to study the student transition between secondary and postsecondary. PLATO Learning is proud to support the CCTI mission of strengthening the role of community and technical colleges and is dedicated to the task of easing student transitions to both college and future employment. Our products for both high school and postsecondary learning assist students in making this transition, and we are very pleased to be a part of this project.

PLATO Learning is especially proud to have its customers participating in the CCTI project as Site Partners. These institutions value the mission of CCTI and League for Innovation and have demonstrated this through their actions toward increasing student success. For example, Sinclair Community College worked to ease the transition from high school to college through its ARC program, which provides intervention assistance at local high schools to remediate math, English, and reading deficiencies before students enter the college. Sinclair Community College has seen tremendous results since their implementation of this program, which uses PLATO® Instructional Solutions to prescribe and instruct students through the self-paced courses. Successes such as this solidify PLATO Learning's commitment to helping all students achieve academic greatness and emphasize the importance of CCTI's mission.

For more than 40 years, PLATO Learning has been a leading provider of computer-based and e-learning instruction for kindergarten through adult learners, offering award-winning curricula in reading, writing, mathematics, science, social studies, and life and job skills, as well as innovative online assessment and accountability solutions and standards-based professional development services. Our mission, *Inspired Solutions for Teaching and Learning*, drives us to create technology that increases instructor teaching time while also providing engaging, motivating software for students.